DON'T TOY WITH ME, MISS NAGATORO

⑤

NANASHI

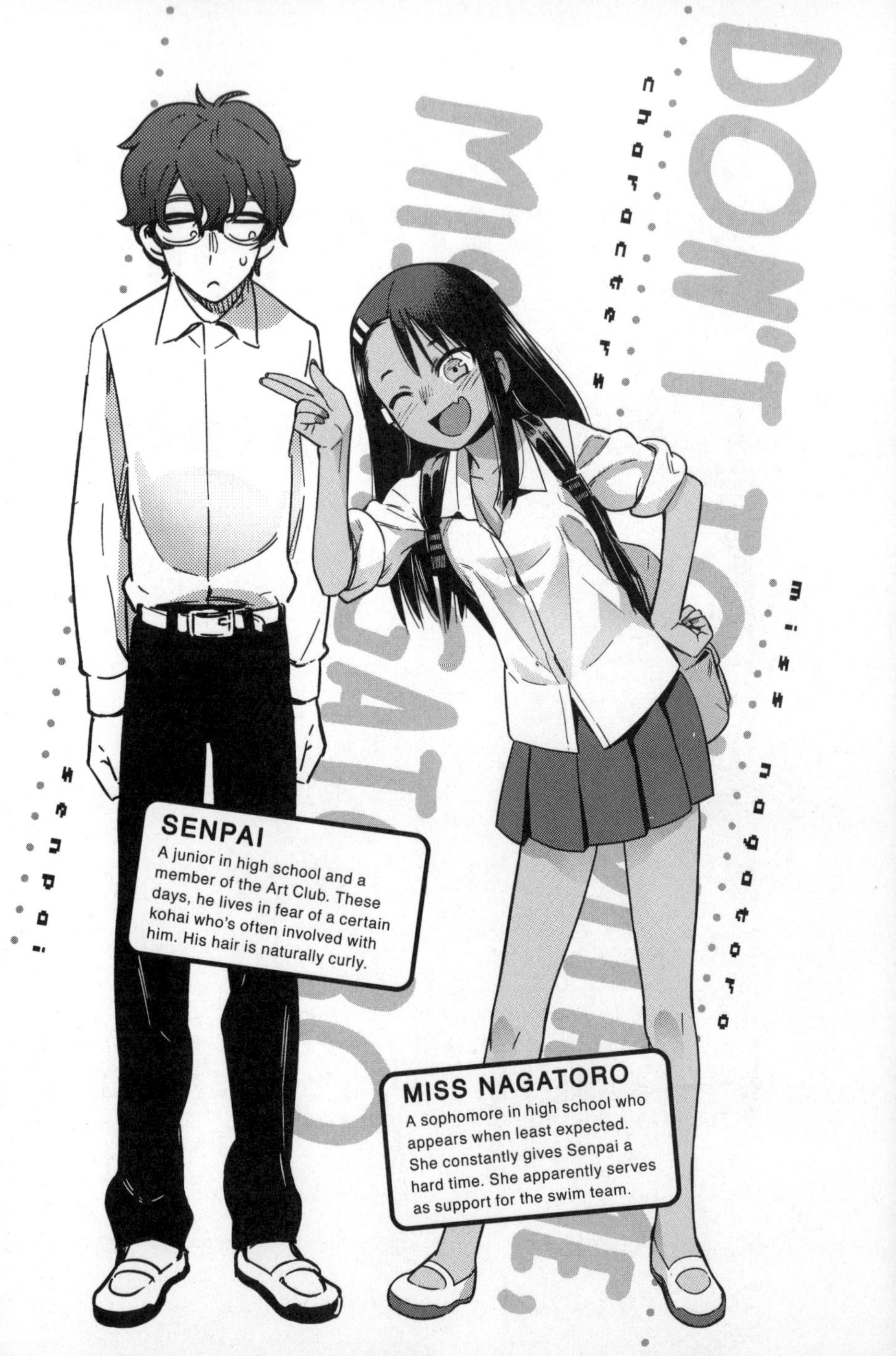
DON'T TOY WITH ME, MISS NAGATORO
SENPAI
A junior in high school and a member of the Art Club. These days, he lives in fear of a certain kohai who's often involved with him. His hair is naturally curly.
MISS NAGATORO
A sophomore in high school who appears when least expected. She constantly gives Senpai a hard time. She apparently serves as support for the swim team.

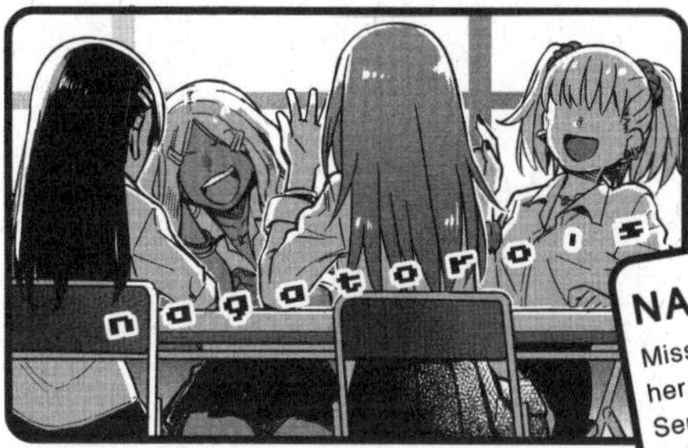
nagatoro's
friends

NAGATORO'S FRIENDS

Miss Nagatoro's pals who are often with her. All of them are one grade below Senpai. They've recently been spending a lot of time in the Art Club room.

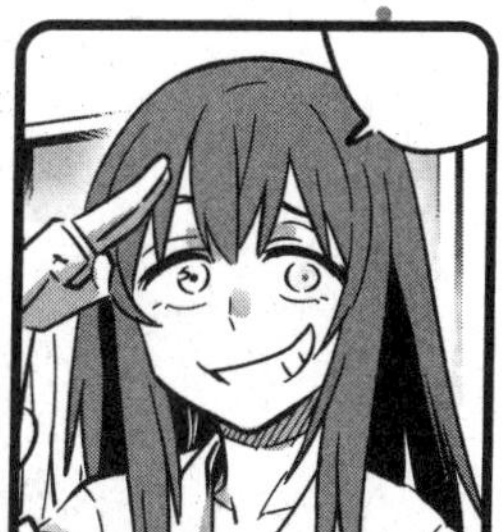
Gamo

GAMO

Has a somewhat harsh personality and semi-long hair. Enjoys tormenting people.

YOSSHII

Has pigtails and is a bit of an airhead. A dumb girl who loves Gamo.

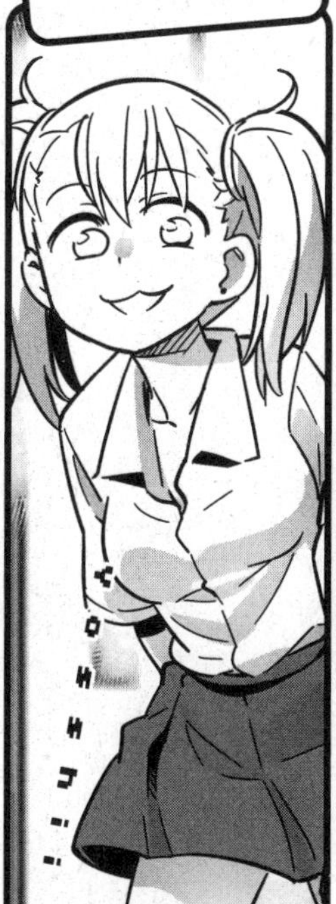
Yosshii!

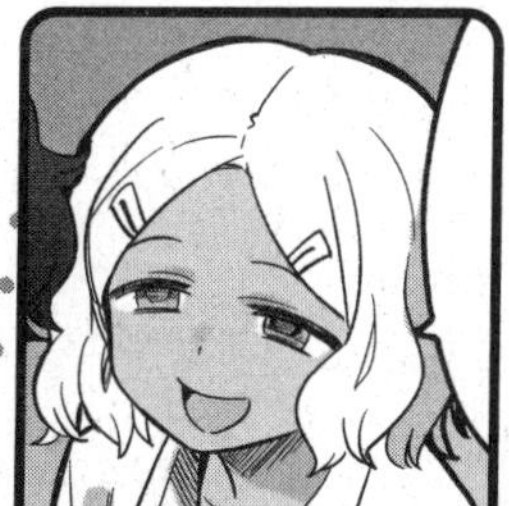
Sakura

SAKURA

Has tanned skin and soft, wavy hair. She's actually a little wicked and crafty.

CONTENTS

Chapter 31   You Have No Sense of Adventure, Senpai   5

Chapter 32   Senpai's a Closet Perv!!   21

Chapter 33   Senpai, What's in Your Bento Lunch?   41

Chapter 34   As If a Creep Like Senpai Could Go on a Proper Date!!   59

Side Story   It May Be More Fun Than You'd Expect, Ex-Senpai ♡   79

Chapter 35   We'd End Up Becoming Your Senpais, Right, Paisen?   89

Chapter 36   Senpai, You Made Me Do This....   99

Chapter 37   Senpai, You're Staring Off into Space   113

Chapter 38   Let's Go for It, Senpai!!   129

Bonus   Senpai, You've Gone Beet Red   147

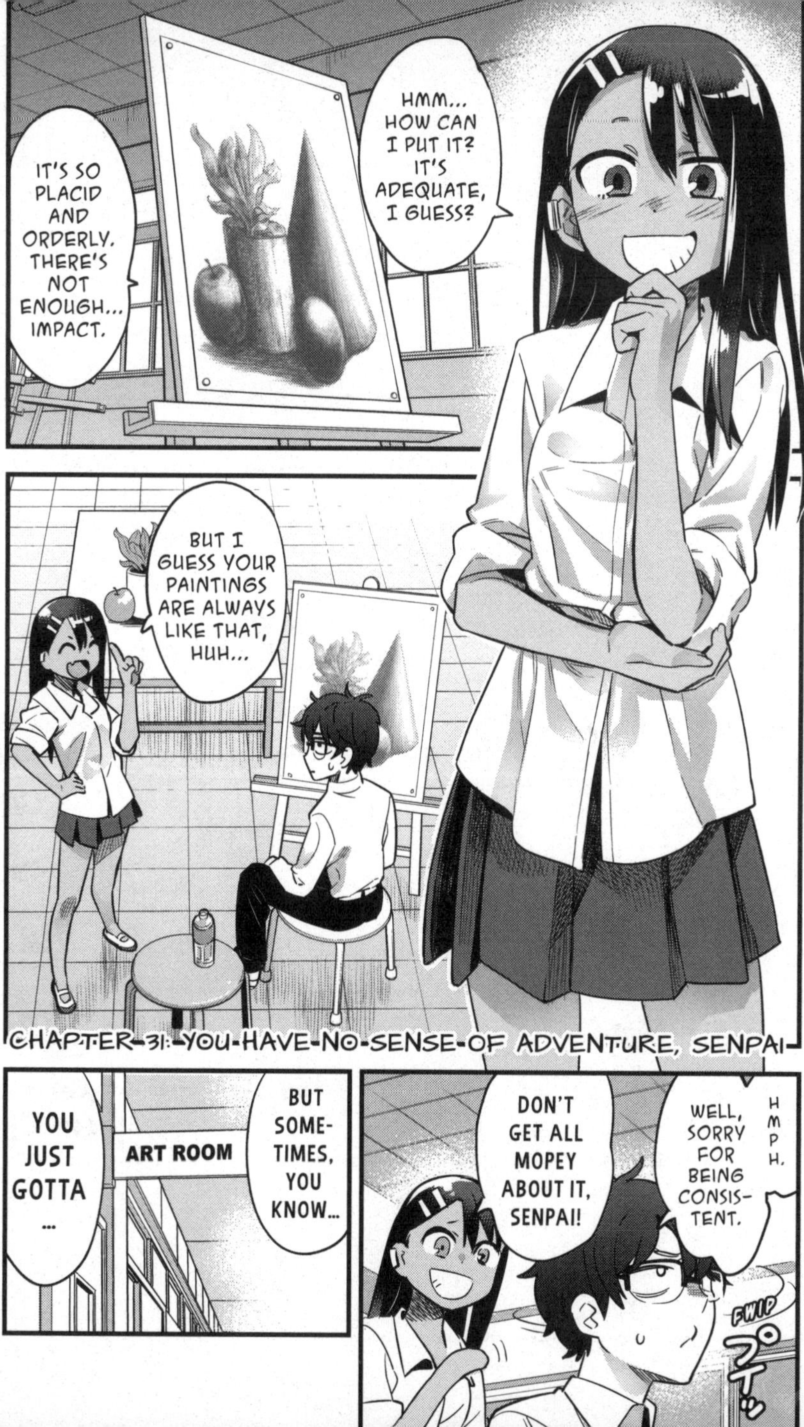
HMM... HOW CAN I PUT IT? IT'S ADEQUATE, I GUESS?
IT'S SO PLACID AND ORDERLY. THERE'S NOT ENOUGH... IMPACT.
BUT I GUESS YOUR PAINTINGS ARE ALWAYS LIKE THAT, HUH...
CHAPTER 31: YOU HAVE NO SENSE OF ADVENTURE, SENPAI
HMPH.
WELL, SORRY FOR BEING CONSISTENT.
DON'T GET ALL MOPEY ABOUT IT, SENPAI!
FWIP
ART ROOM
BUT SOMETIMES, YOU KNOW...
YOU JUST GOTTA ...

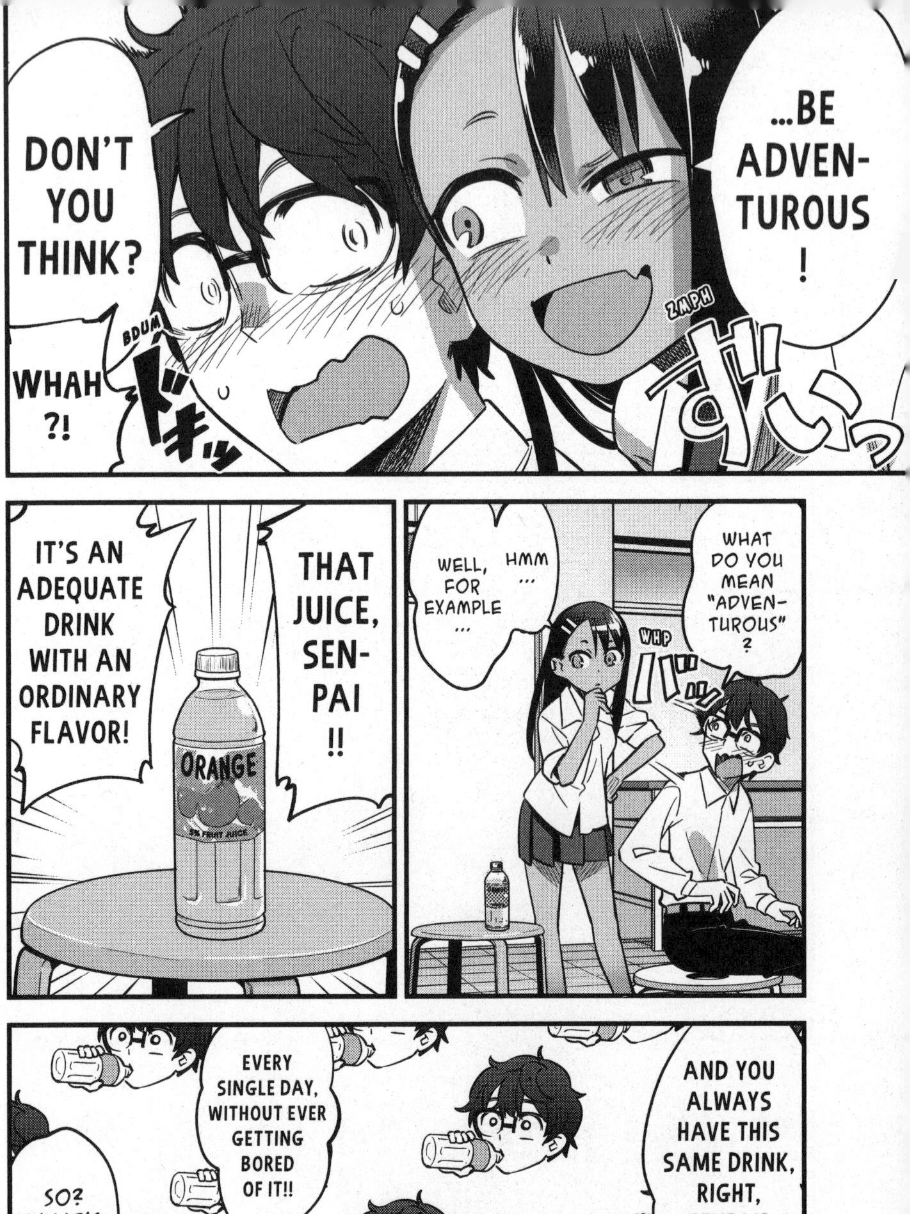
...BE ADVENTUROUS!
ZMPH
DON'T YOU THINK?
BDUM
WHAH?!
WHAT DO YOU MEAN "ADVENTUROUS"?
WHP
HMM...
WELL, FOR EXAMPLE...
THAT JUICE, SENPAI!!
IT'S AN ADEQUATE DRINK WITH AN ORDINARY FLAVOR!
ORANGE
AND YOU ALWAYS HAVE THIS SAME DRINK, RIGHT, SENPAI?
EVERY SINGLE DAY, WITHOUT EVER GETTING BORED OF IT!!
SO? WHAT'S WRONG WITH THAT?

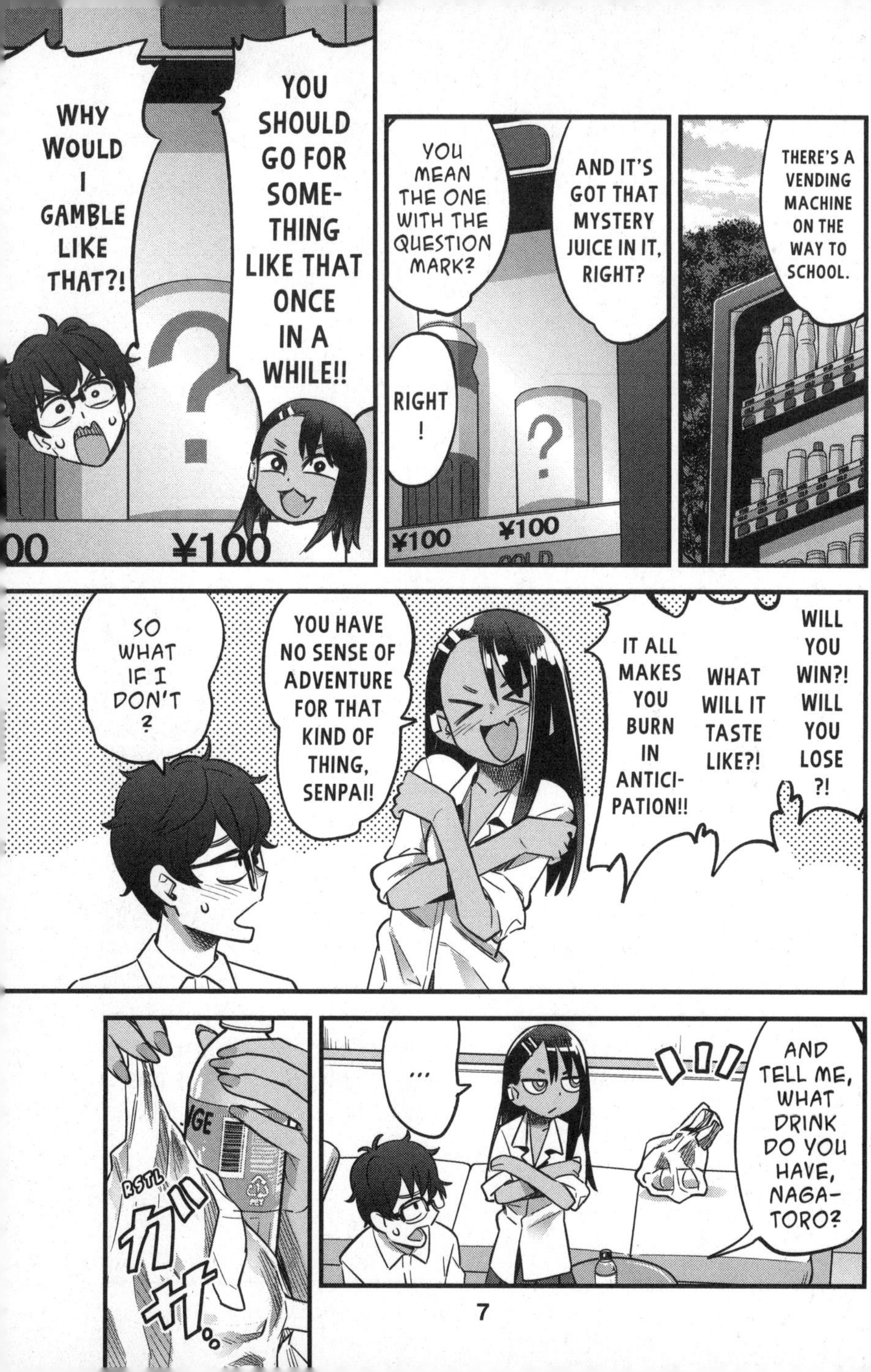
THERE'S A VENDING MACHINE ON THE WAY TO SCHOOL.
AND IT'S GOT THAT MYSTERY JUICE IN IT, RIGHT?
YOU MEAN THE ONE WITH THE QUESTION MARK?
RIGHT!
¥100
¥100
YOU SHOULD GO FOR SOME-THING LIKE THAT ONCE IN A WHILE!!
WHY WOULD I GAMBLE LIKE THAT?!
¥100
WILL YOU WIN?! WILL YOU LOSE?!
WHAT WILL IT TASTE LIKE?!
IT ALL MAKES YOU BURN IN ANTICI-PATION!!
YOU HAVE NO SENSE OF ADVENTURE FOR THAT KIND OF THING, SENPAI!
SO WHAT IF I DON'T?
AND TELL ME, WHAT DRINK DO YOU HAVE, NAGA-TORO?
...
RSTL
カサ

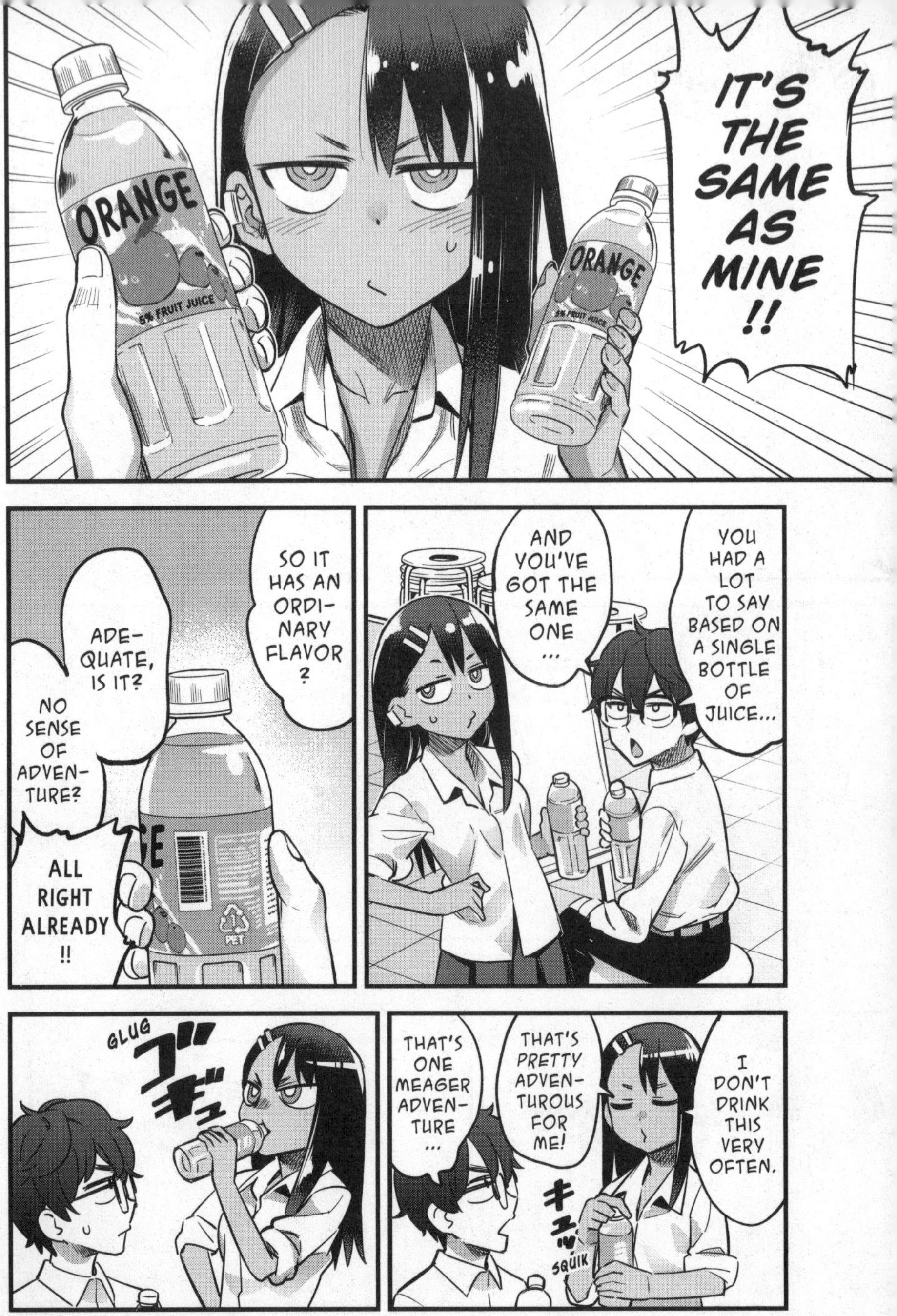
ORANGE
5% FRUIT JUICE
ORANGE
5% FRUIT JUICE
IT'S THE SAME AS MINE !!
YOU HAD A LOT TO SAY BASED ON A SINGLE BOTTLE OF JUICE...
AND YOU'VE GOT THE SAME ONE ...
SO IT HAS AN ORDINARY FLAVOR ?
ADEQUATE, IS IT?
NO SENSE OF ADVENTURE?
ALL RIGHT ALREADY !!
I DON'T DRINK THIS VERY OFTEN.
THAT'S PRETTY ADVENTUROUS FOR ME!
THAT'S ONE MEAGER ADVENTURE ...
キュッ
SQUIK
GLUG
ゴギュ

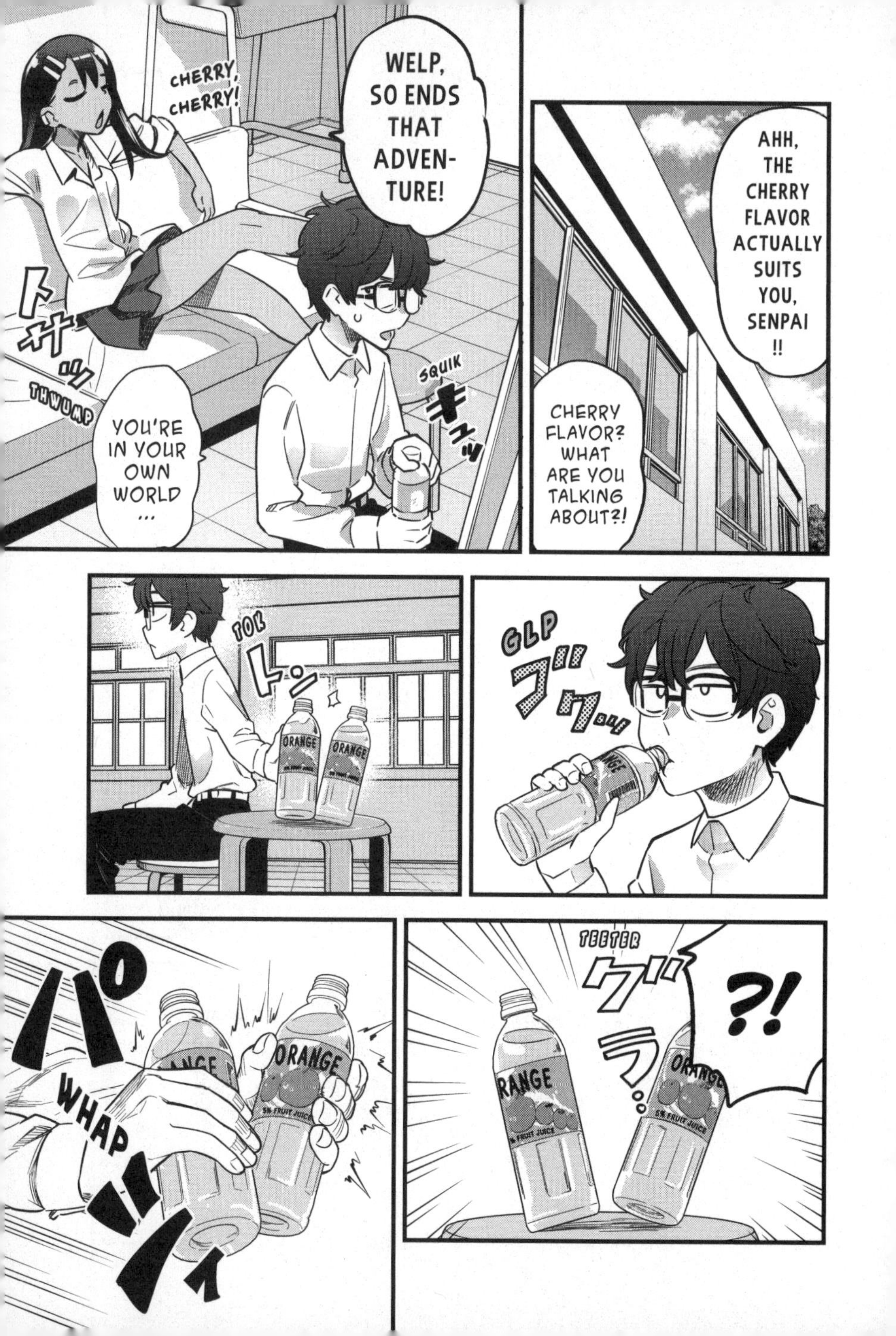
AHH, THE CHERRY FLAVOR ACTUALLY SUITS YOU, SENPAI !!
CHERRY FLAVOR? WHAT ARE YOU TALKING ABOUT?!
WELP, SO ENDS THAT ADVENTURE!
CHERRY, CHERRY!
SQUIK
THWUMP
YOU'RE IN YOUR OWN WORLD ...
GLP
TOK
ORANGE
ORANGE
TEETER
?!
ORANGE
5% FRUIT JUICE
WHAP
ORANGE
5% FRUIT JUICE

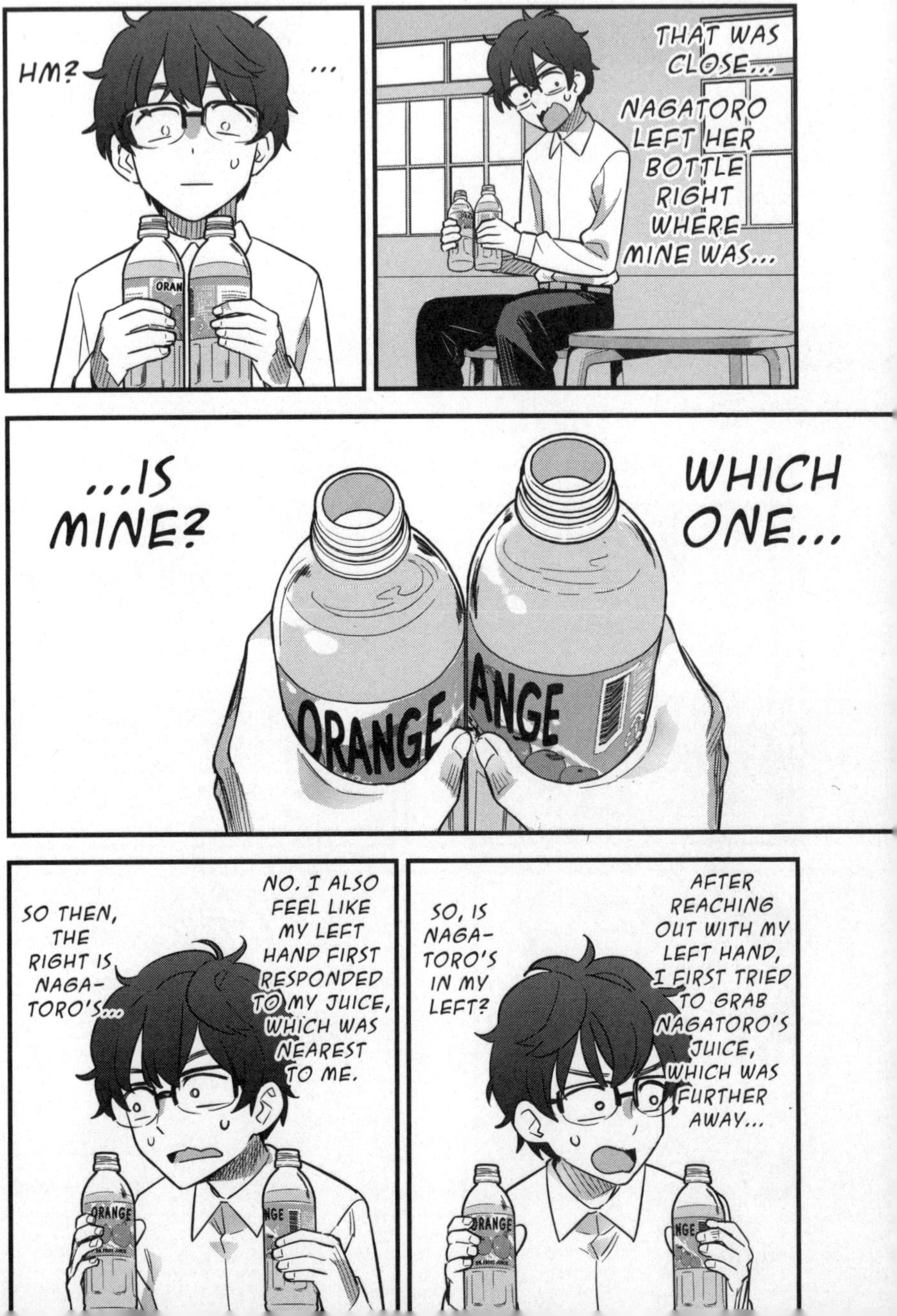
THAT WAS CLOSE...
NAGATORO LEFT HER BOTTLE RIGHT WHERE MINE WAS...
...
HM?
WHICH ONE...
ORANGE
ANGE
...IS MINE?
AFTER REACHING OUT WITH MY LEFT HAND, I FIRST TRIED TO GRAB NAGATORO'S JUICE, WHICH WAS FURTHER AWAY...
SO, IS NAGATORO'S IN MY LEFT?
NO. I ALSO FEEL LIKE MY LEFT HAND FIRST RESPONDED TO MY JUICE, WHICH WAS NEAREST TO ME.
SO THEN, THE RIGHT IS NAGATORO'S...

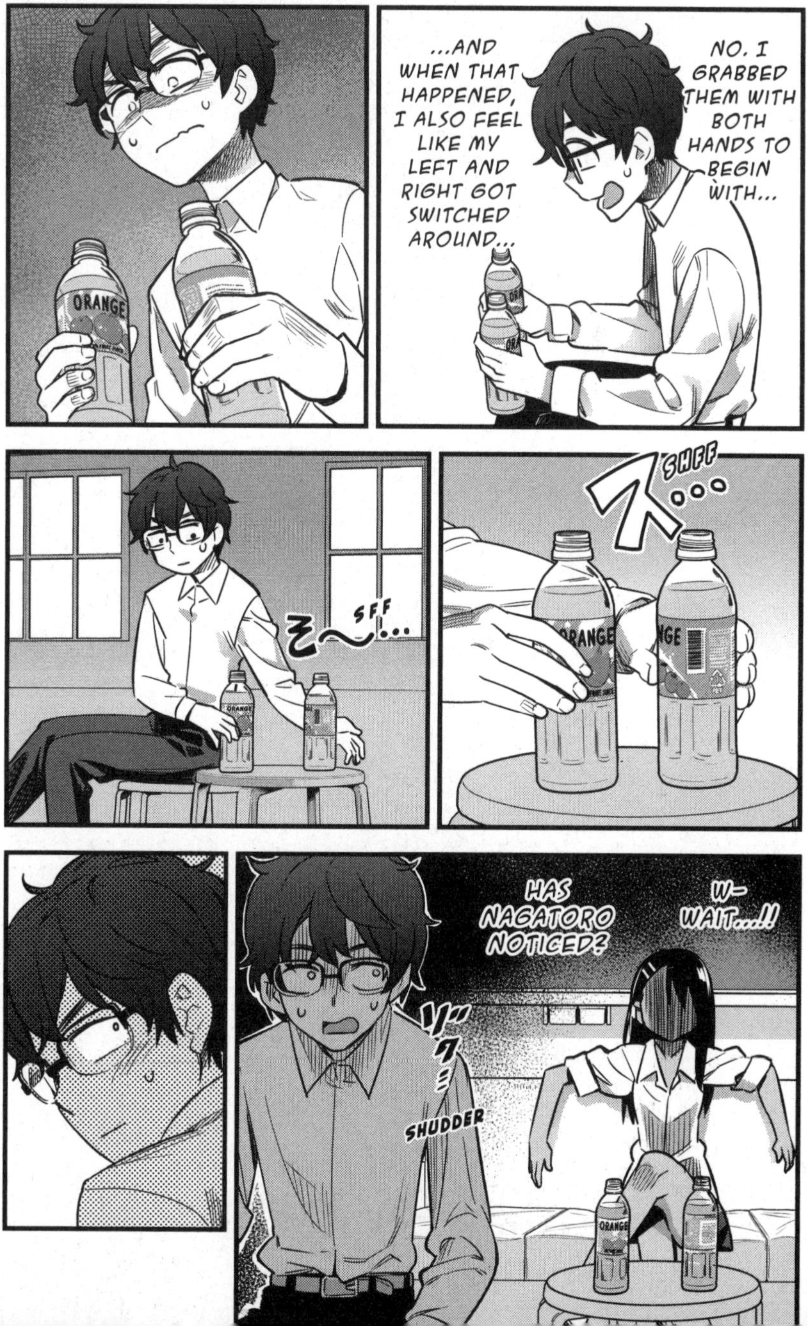
NO. I GRABBED THEM WITH BOTH HANDS TO BEGIN WITH...
...AND WHEN THAT HAPPENED, I ALSO FEEL LIKE MY LEFT AND RIGHT GOT SWITCHED AROUND...
ORANGE
SHFF...
ORANGE
そ～ SFF...
W- WAIT...!!
HAS NAGATORO NOTICED?
SHUDDER
ORANGE

W-WAS SHE WATCHING ?!

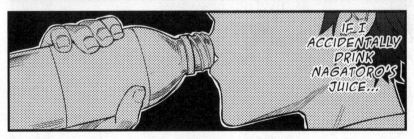

IF I ACCIDENTALLY DRINK NAGATORO'S JUICE...

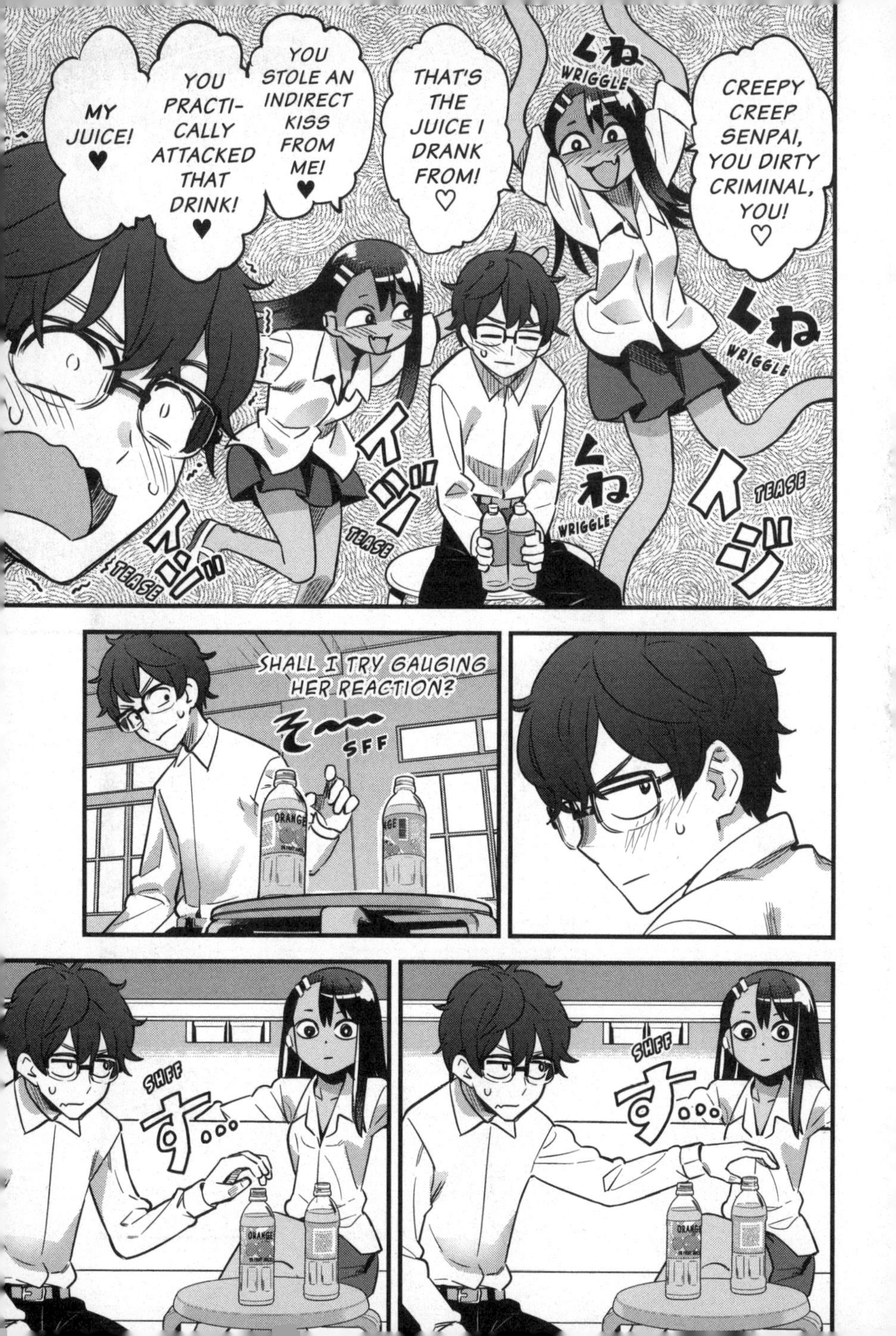
くね
WRIGGLE
CREEPY CREEP SENPAI, YOU DIRTY CRIMINAL, YOU! ♡
THAT'S THE JUICE I DRANK FROM! ♡
YOU STOLE AN INDIRECT KISS FROM ME! ♥
YOU PRACTI-CALLY ATTACKED THAT DRINK! ♥
MY JUICE! ♥
くね
WRIGGLE
イジ
TEASE
くね
WRIGGLE
イジ
TEASE
イジ
TEASE
SHALL I TRY GAUGING HER REACTION?
そ~
SFF
SHFF
す...
SHFF
す...

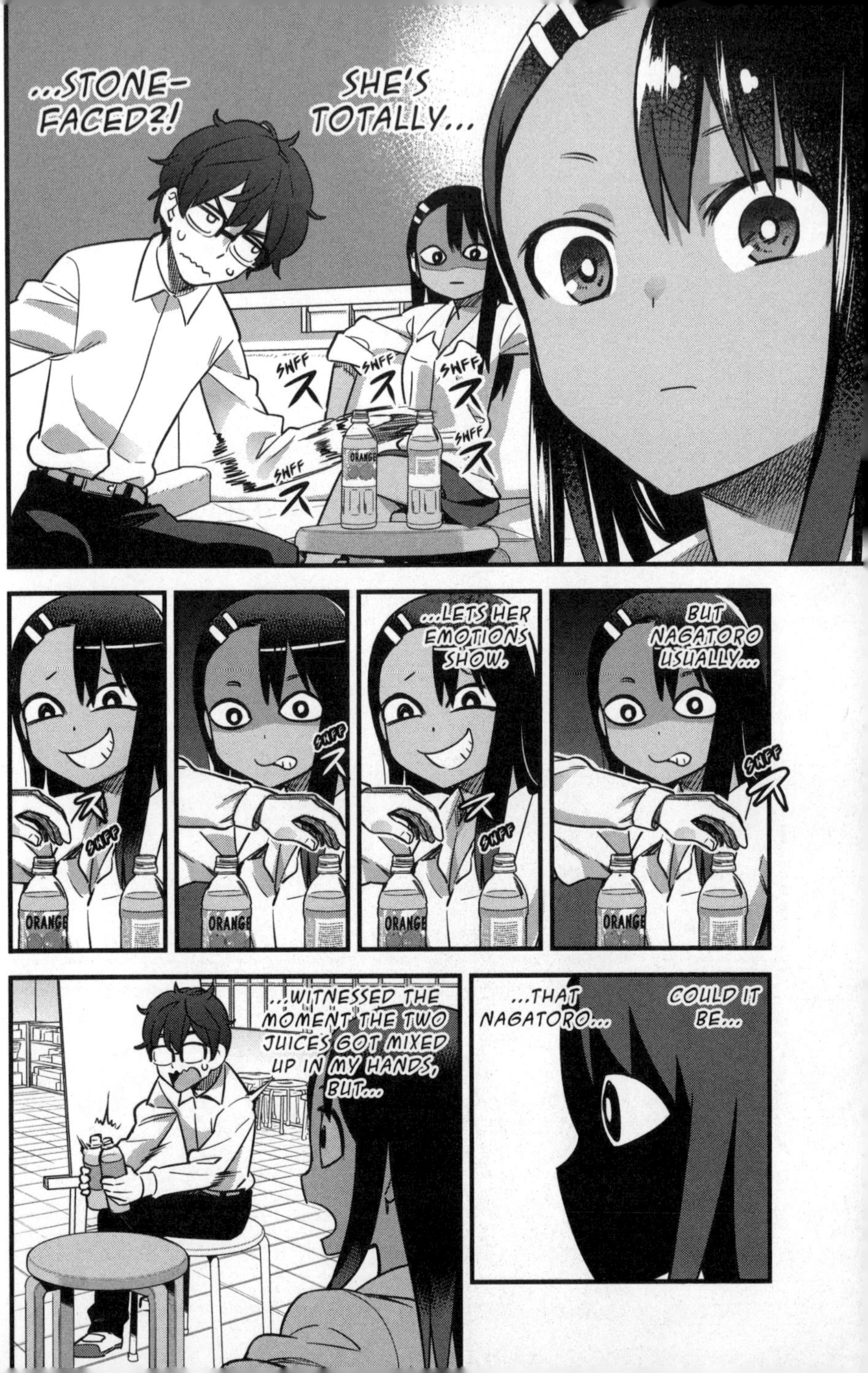
SHE'S TOTALLY...
...STONE-FACED?!
SWFF
SWFF
SWFF
SWFF
SWFF
ORANGE
BUT NAGATORO USUALLY...
SWFF
...LETS HER EMOTIONS SHOW.
SWFF
SWFF
SWFF
SWFF
ORANGE
COULD IT BE...
...THAT NAGATORO...
...WITNESSED THE MOMENT THE TWO JUICES GOT MIXED UP IN MY HANDS, BUT...

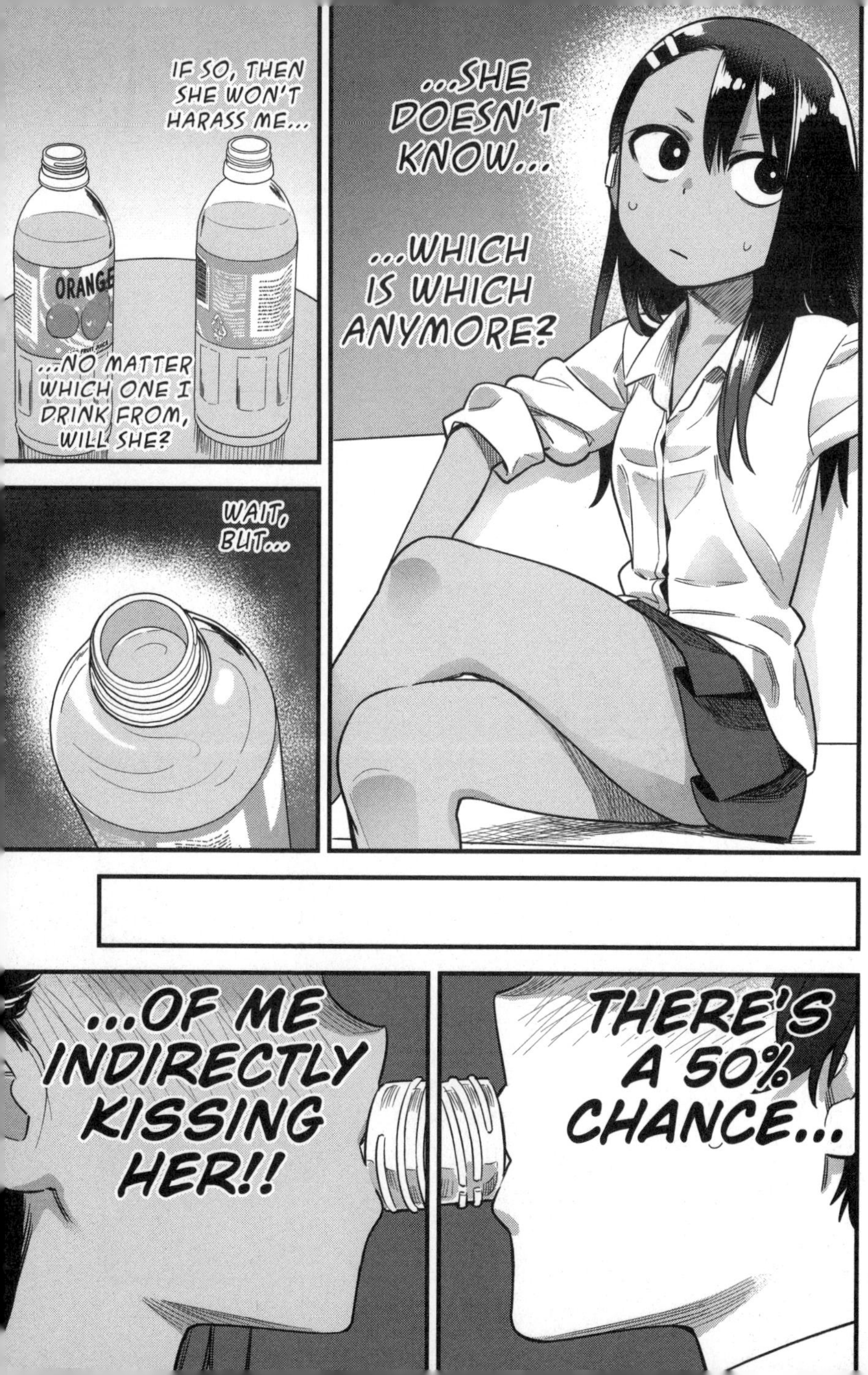
...SHE DOESN'T KNOW...
...WHICH IS WHICH ANYMORE?
IF SO, THEN SHE WON'T HARASS ME...
ORANGE
...NO MATTER WHICH ONE I DRINK FROM, WILL SHE?
WAIT, BUT...
THERE'S A 50% CHANCE...
...OF ME INDIRECTLY KISSING HER!!

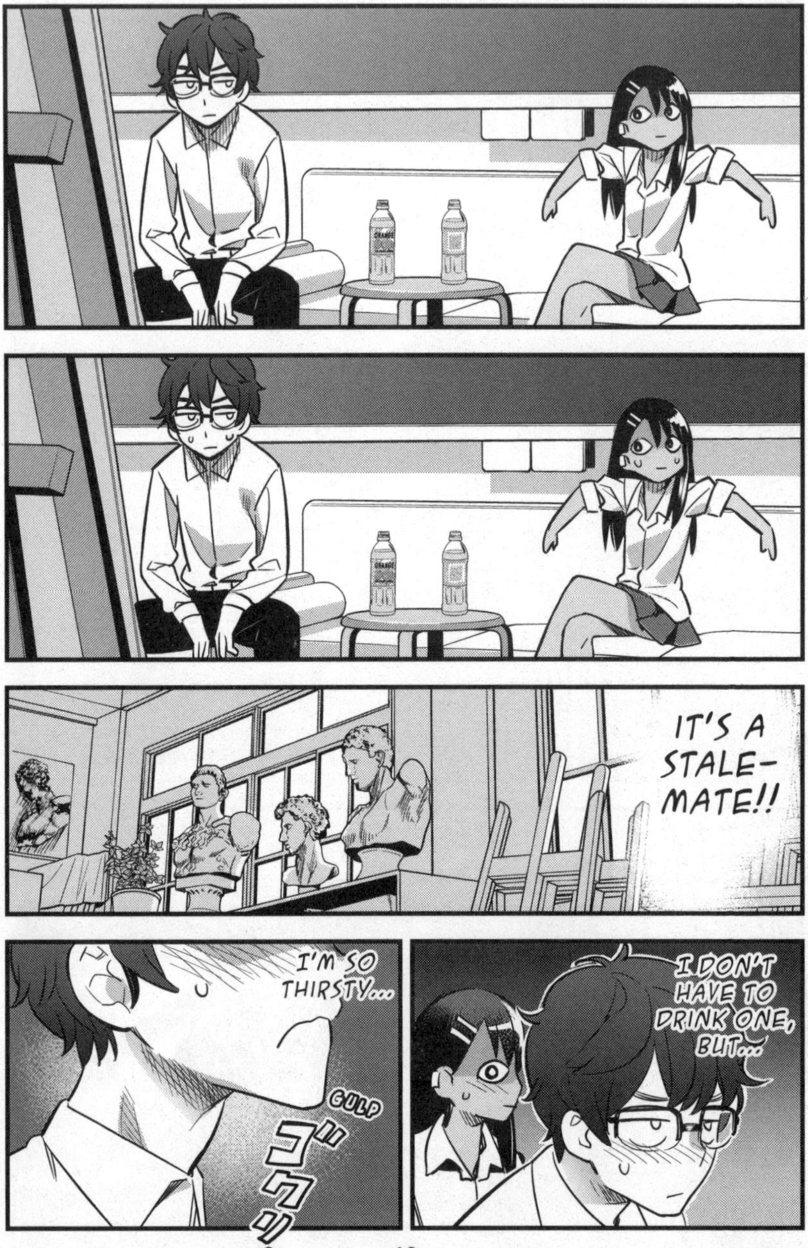
IT'S A STALE-MATE!!
I DON'T HAVE TO DRINK ONE, BUT...
I'M SO THIRSTY...
GULP

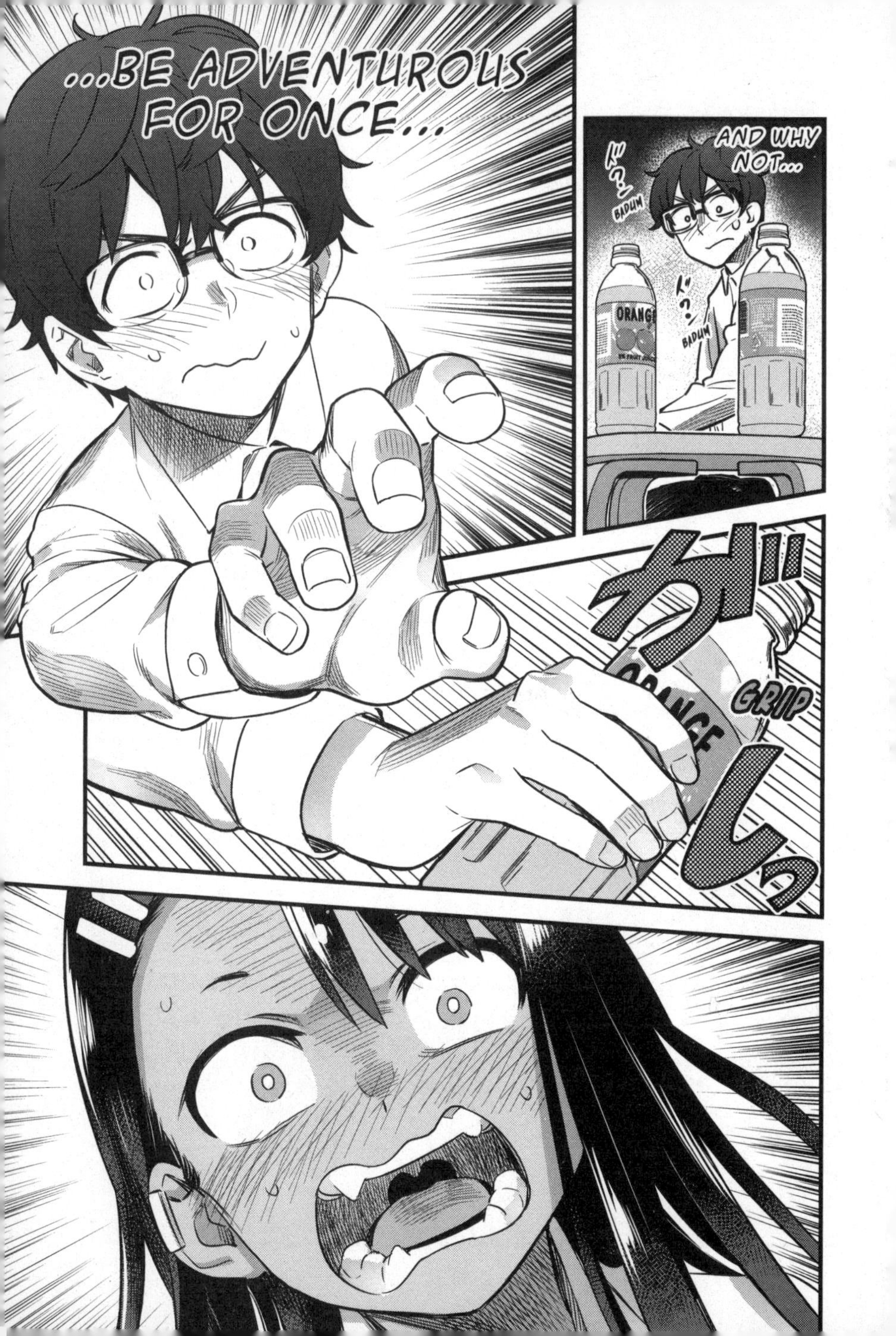

AND WHY NOT...
ドクン
BADUM
ドクン
BADUM
...BE ADVENTUROUS FOR ONCE...
ORANGE
がしっ
GRIP
ORANGE

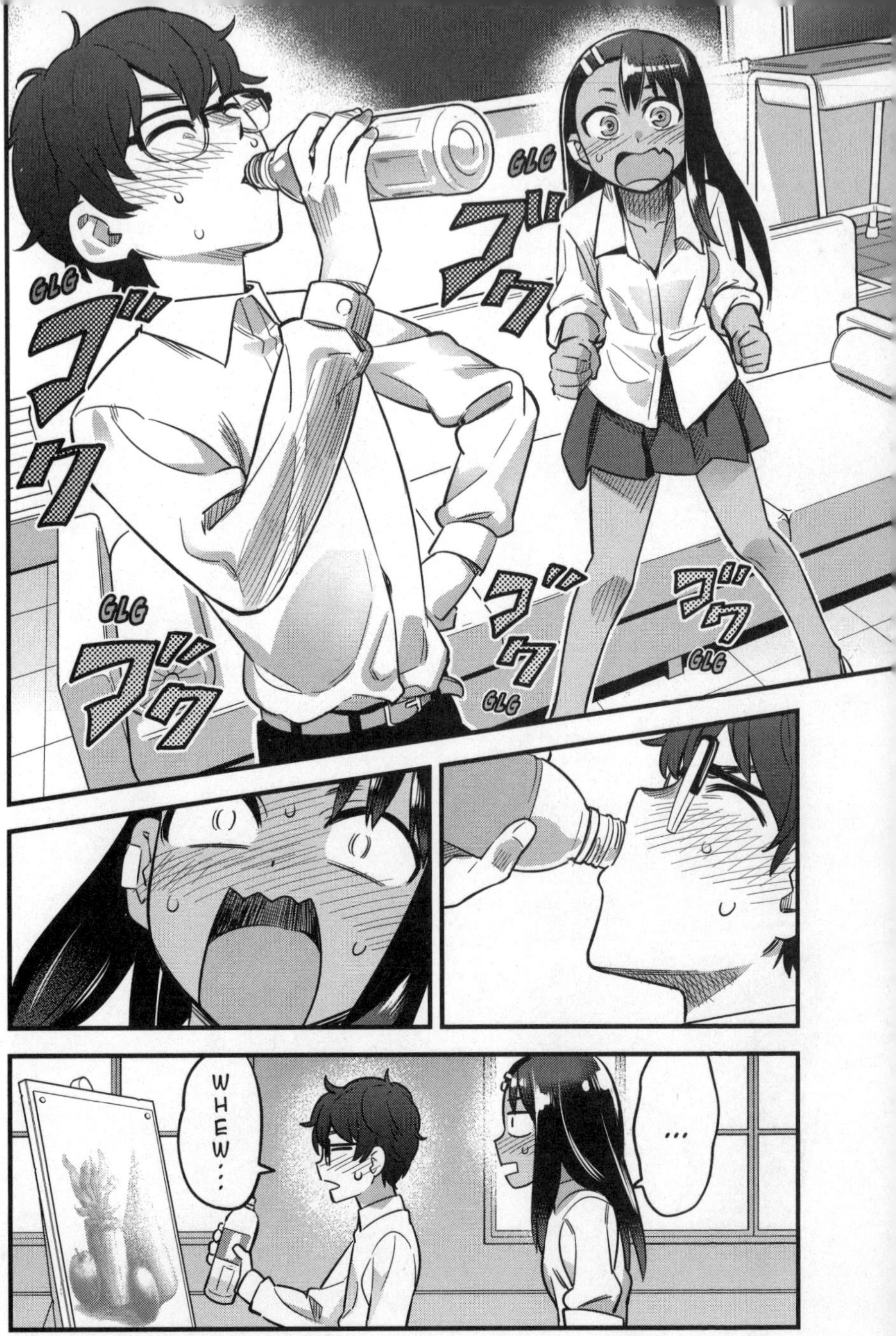

GLG
ゴク
ゴク
GLG
ゴク
GLG
GLG
ゴク
GLG
ゴク
...
WHEW...

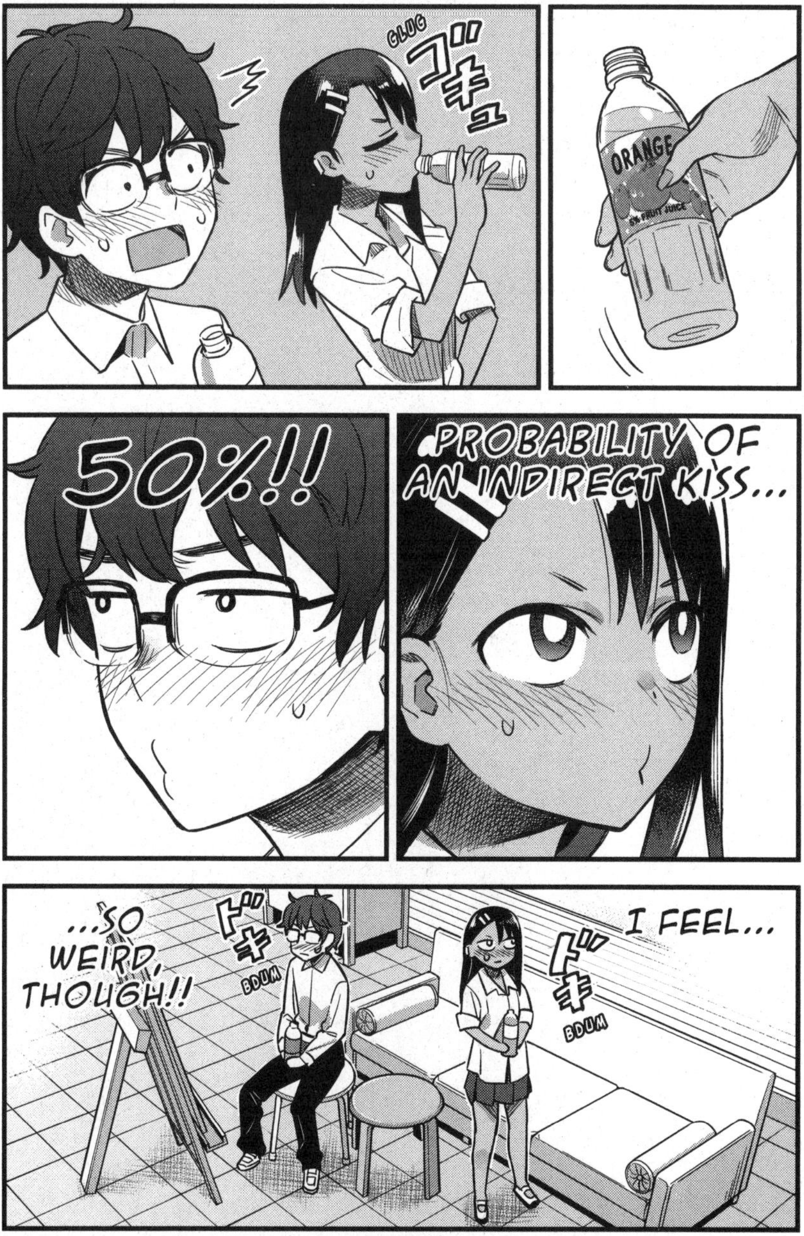
GLUG
ゴキュ
PROBABILITY OF AN INDIRECT KISS...
50%!!
I FEEL...
ドキ
BDUM
...SO WEIRD, THOUGH!!
ドキ
BDUM

END

DON'T
COPY ME,
OKAY?

CHAPTER 32:
SENPAI'S A CLOSET PERV!!

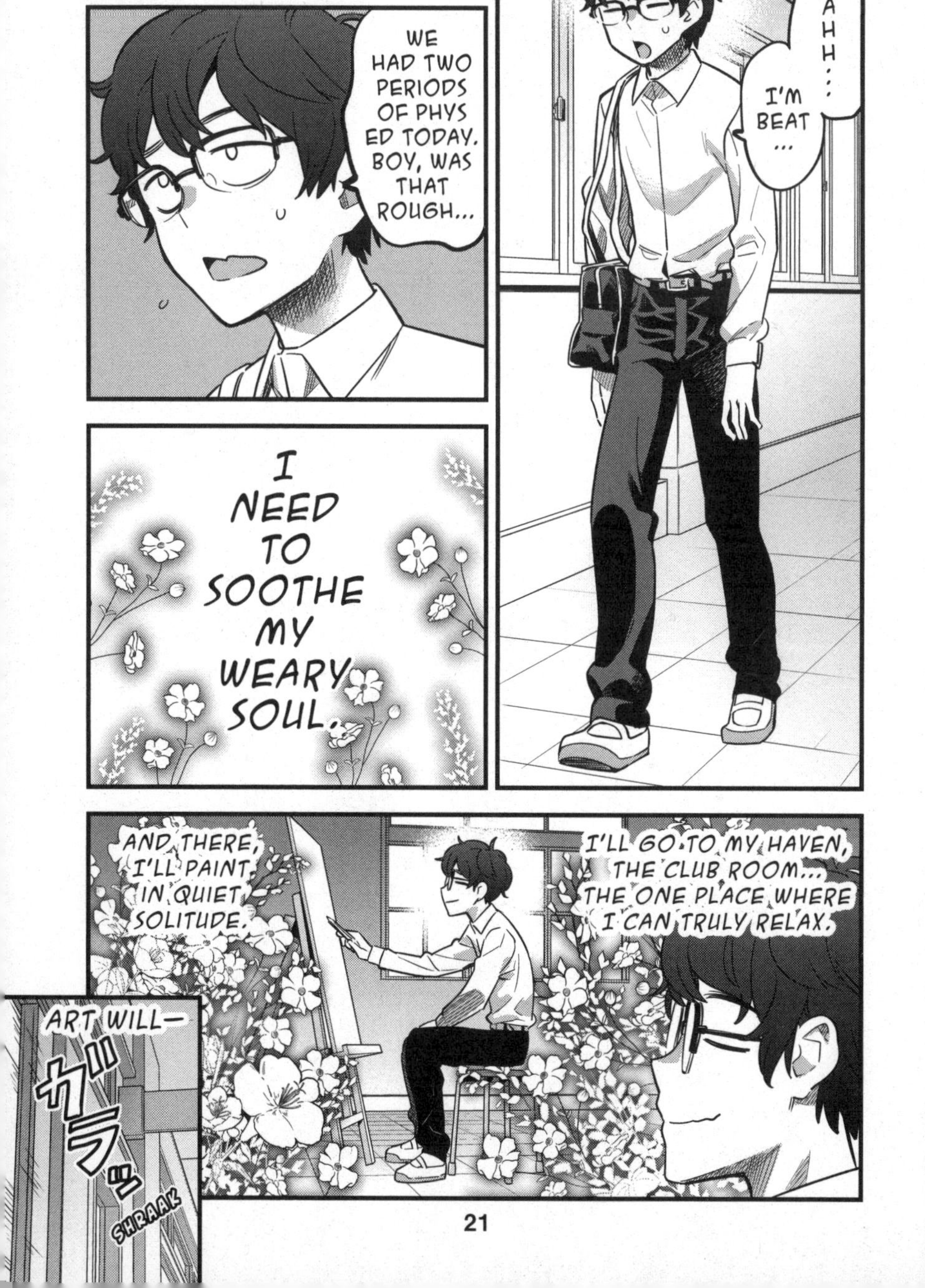
HAHH...
I'M BEAT...
WE HAD TWO PERIODS OF PHYS ED TODAY. BOY, WAS THAT ROUGH...
I NEED TO SOOTHE MY WEARY SOUL.
I'LL GO TO MY HAVEN, THE CLUB ROOM... THE ONE PLACE WHERE I CAN TRULY RELAX.
AND THERE, I'LL PAINT IN QUIET SOLITUDE.
ART WILL—
ガラッ
SHRAAK

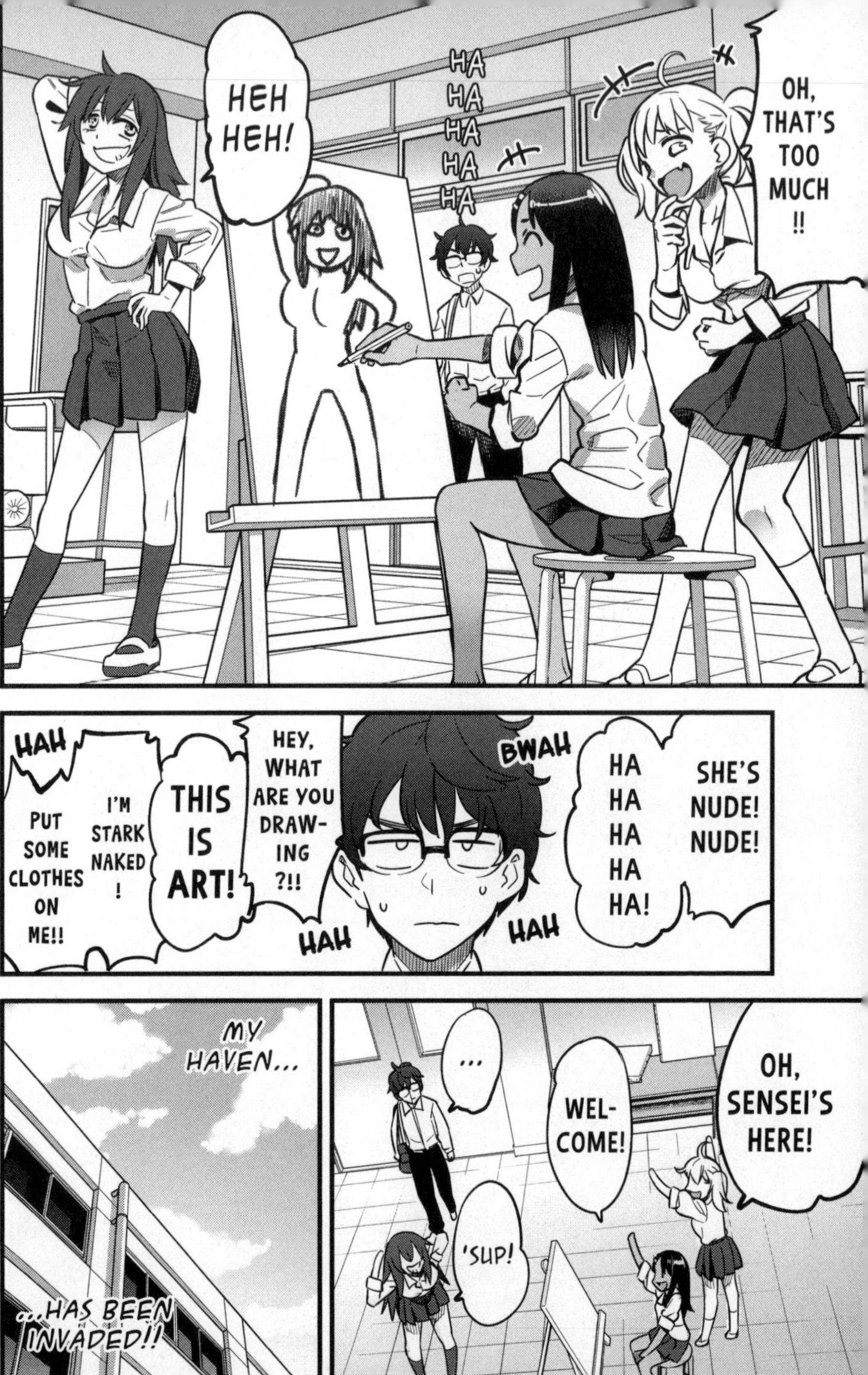
OH, THAT'S TOO MUCH!!
HA HA HA HA HA
HEH HEH!
SHE'S NUDE! NUDE!
HA HA HA HA HA!
BWAH
HAH
HEY, WHAT ARE YOU DRAW-ING?!!
THIS IS ART!
I'M STARK NAKED!
PUT SOME CLOTHES ON ME!!
HAH
HAH
OH, SENSEI'S HERE!
WEL-COME!
...
'SUP!
MY HAVEN...
...HAS BEEN INVADED!!

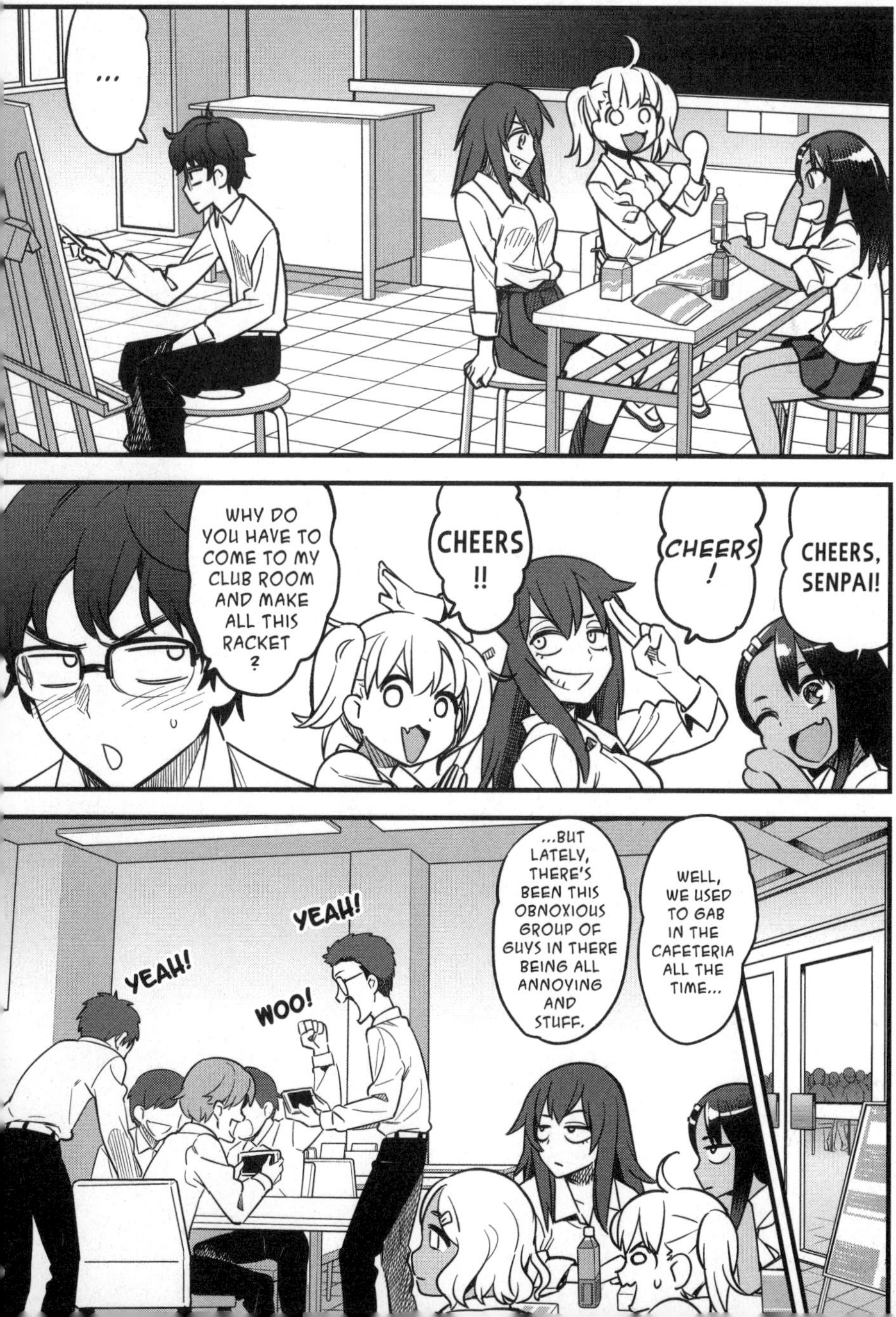
...
CHEERS, SENPAI!
CHEERS!
CHEERS!!
WHY DO YOU HAVE TO COME TO MY CLUB ROOM AND MAKE ALL THIS RACKET?
WELL, WE USED TO GAB IN THE CAFETERIA ALL THE TIME...
...BUT LATELY, THERE'S BEEN THIS OBNOXIOUS GROUP OF GUYS IN THERE BEING ALL ANNOYING AND STUFF.
YEAH!
YEAH!
WOO!

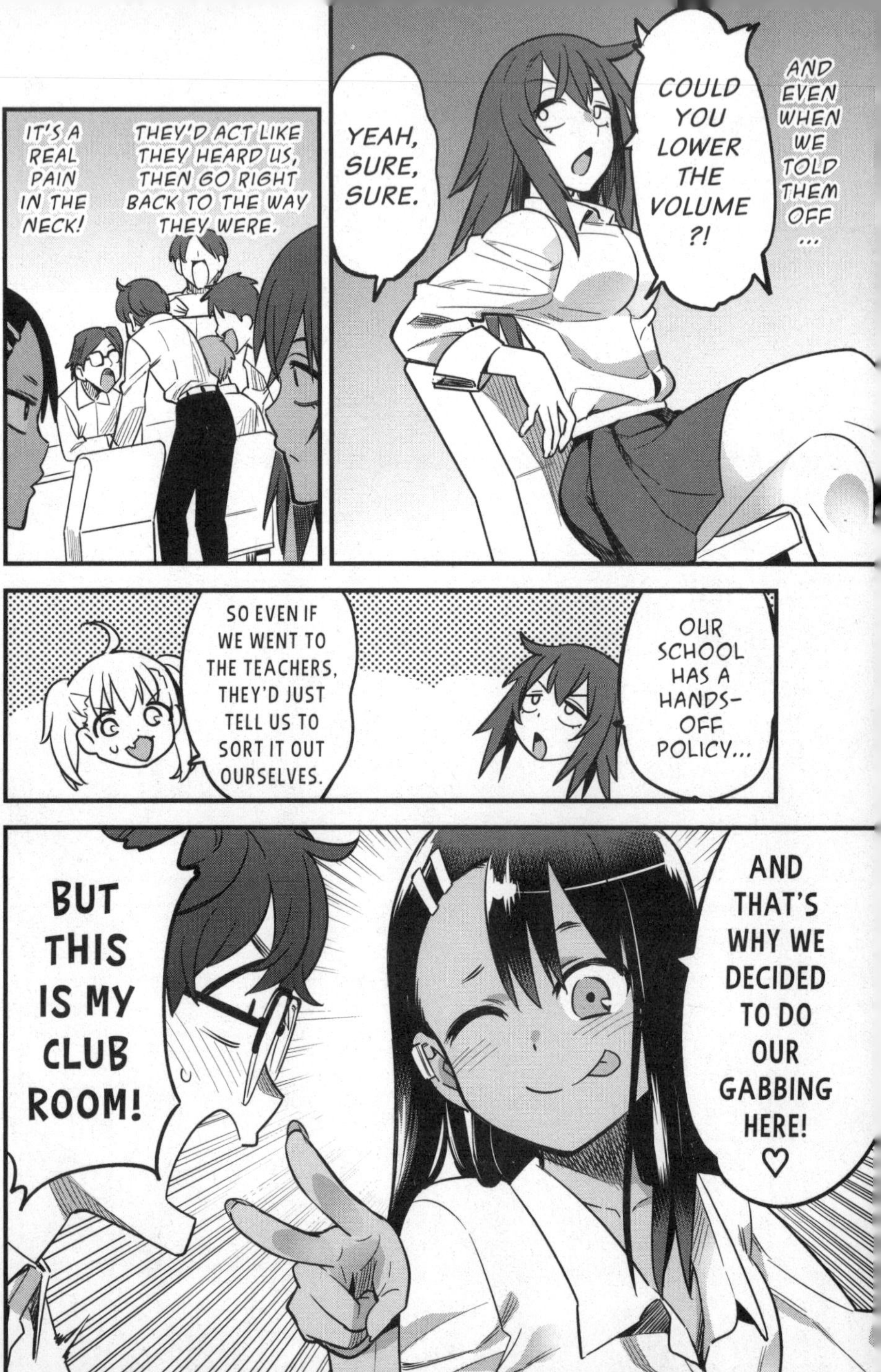
AND EVEN WHEN WE TOLD THEM OFF...
COULD YOU LOWER THE VOLUME?!
YEAH, SURE, SURE.
THEY'D ACT LIKE THEY HEARD US, THEN GO RIGHT BACK TO THE WAY THEY WERE.
IT'S A REAL PAIN IN THE NECK!
OUR SCHOOL HAS A HANDS-OFF POLICY...
SO EVEN IF WE WENT TO THE TEACHERS, THEY'D JUST TELL US TO SORT IT OUT OURSELVES.
AND THAT'S WHY WE DECIDED TO DO OUR GABBING HERE! ♡
BUT THIS IS MY CLUB ROOM!

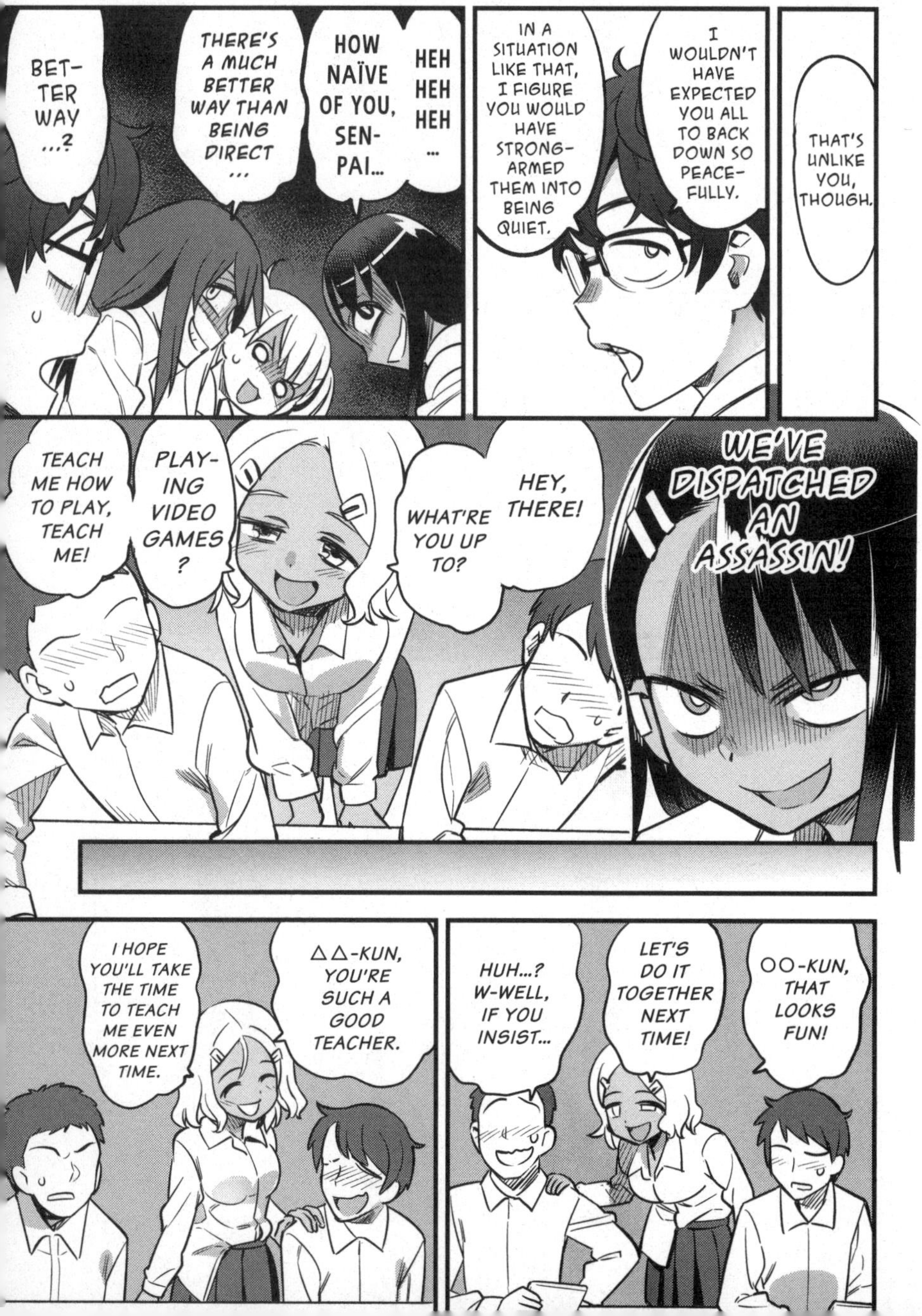
THAT'S UNLIKE YOU, THOUGH.
I WOULDN'T HAVE EXPECTED YOU ALL TO BACK DOWN SO PEACEFULLY.
IN A SITUATION LIKE THAT, I FIGURE YOU WOULD HAVE STRONG-ARMED THEM INTO BEING QUIET.
HEH HEH HEH ...
HOW NAÏVE OF YOU, SENPAI...
THERE'S A MUCH BETTER WAY THAN BEING DIRECT ...
BETTER WAY ...?
WE'VE DISPATCHED AN ASSASSIN!
HEY, THERE!
WHAT'RE YOU UP TO?
PLAYING VIDEO GAMES?
TEACH ME HOW TO PLAY, TEACH ME!
OO-KUN, THAT LOOKS FUN!
LET'S DO IT TOGETHER NEXT TIME!
HUH...? W-WELL, IF YOU INSIST...
△△-KUN, YOU'RE SUCH A GOOD TEACHER.
I HOPE YOU'LL TAKE THE TIME TO TEACH ME EVEN MORE NEXT TIME.

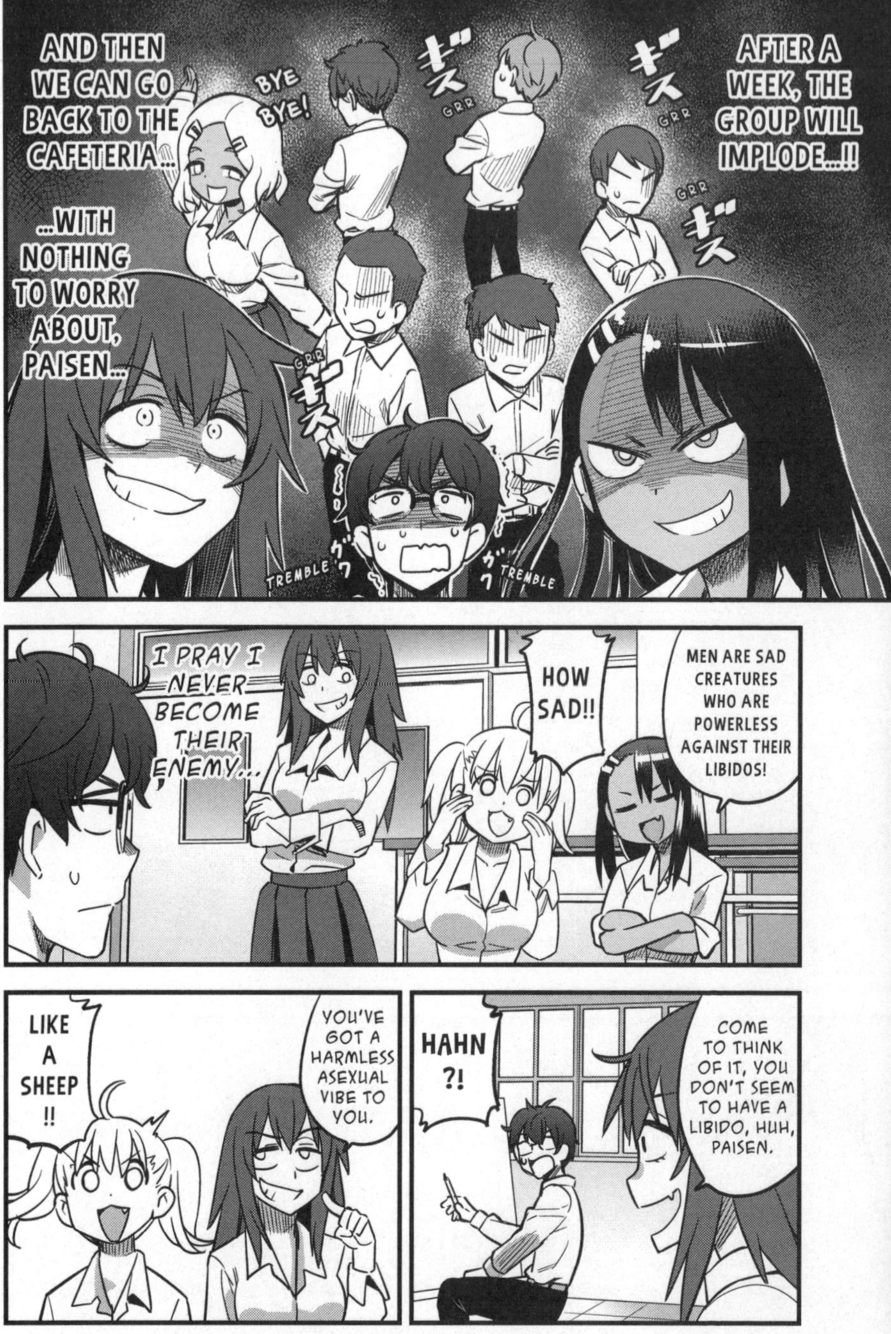
AFTER A WEEK, THE GROUP WILL IMPLODE...!!
GRR
GRR
GRR
AND THEN WE CAN GO BACK TO THE CAFETERIA...
BYE BYE!
...WITH NOTHING TO WORRY ABOUT, PAISEN...
GRR
TREMBLE
TREMBLE
MEN ARE SAD CREATURES WHO ARE POWERLESS AGAINST THEIR LIBIDOS!
HOW SAD!!
I PRAY I NEVER BECOME THEIR ENEMY...
COME TO THINK OF IT, YOU DON'T SEEM TO HAVE A LIBIDO, HUH, PAISEN.
HAHN ?!
YOU'VE GOT A HARMLESS ASEXUAL VIBE TO YOU.
LIKE A SHEEP !!

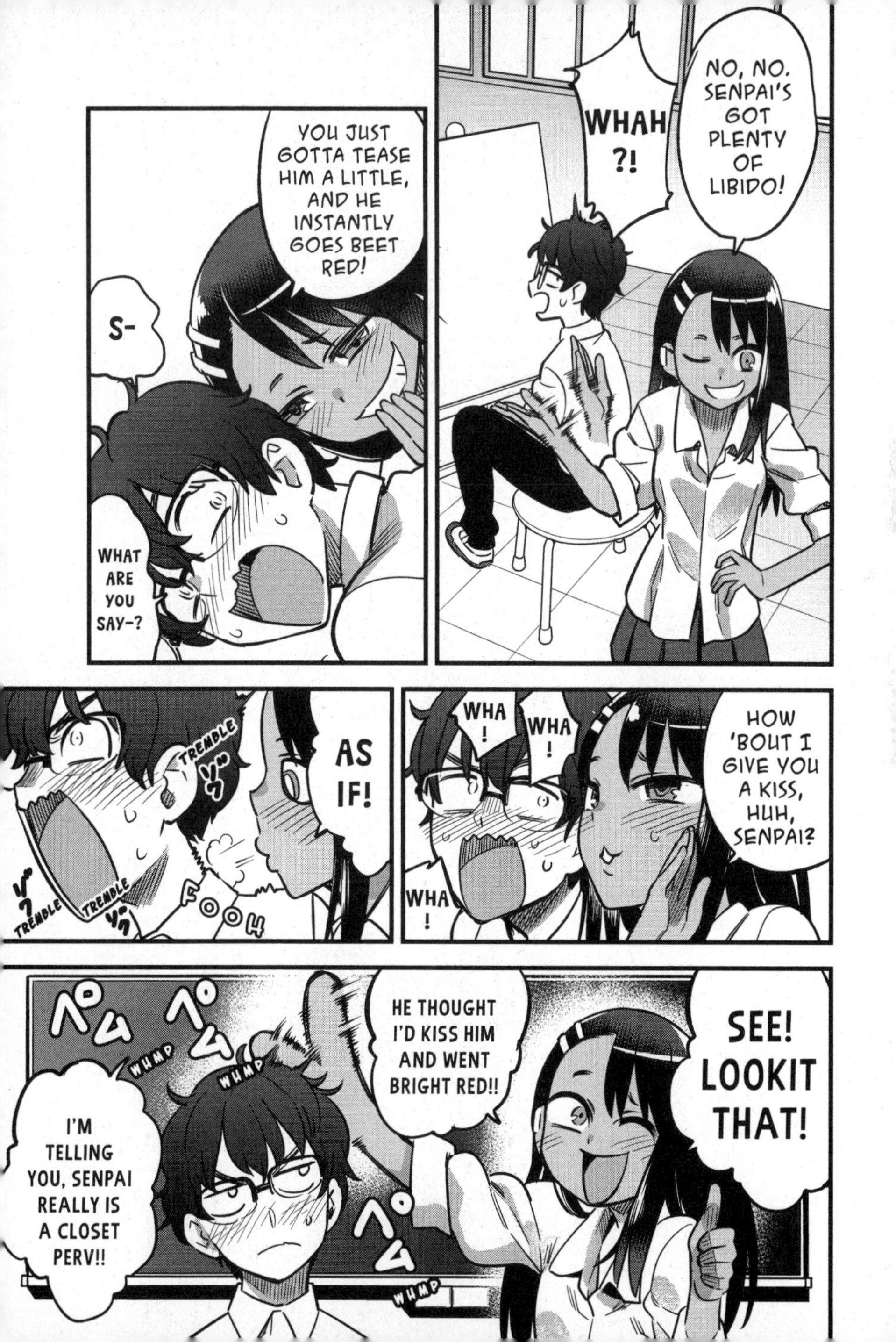
NO, NO. SENPAI'S GOT PLENTY OF LIBIDO!
WHAH ?!
YOU JUST GOTTA TEASE HIM A LITTLE, AND HE INSTANTLY GOES BEET RED!
S-
WHAT ARE YOU SAY-?
HOW 'BOUT I GIVE YOU A KISS, HUH, SENPAI?
WHA!
WHA!
WHA!
AS IF!
TREMBLE
TREMBLE
TREMBLE
FOOH
SEE! LOOKIT THAT!
HE THOUGHT I'D KISS HIM AND WENT BRIGHT RED!!
WHMP
WHMP
I'M TELLING YOU, SENPAI REALLY IS A CLOSET PERV!!
WHMP

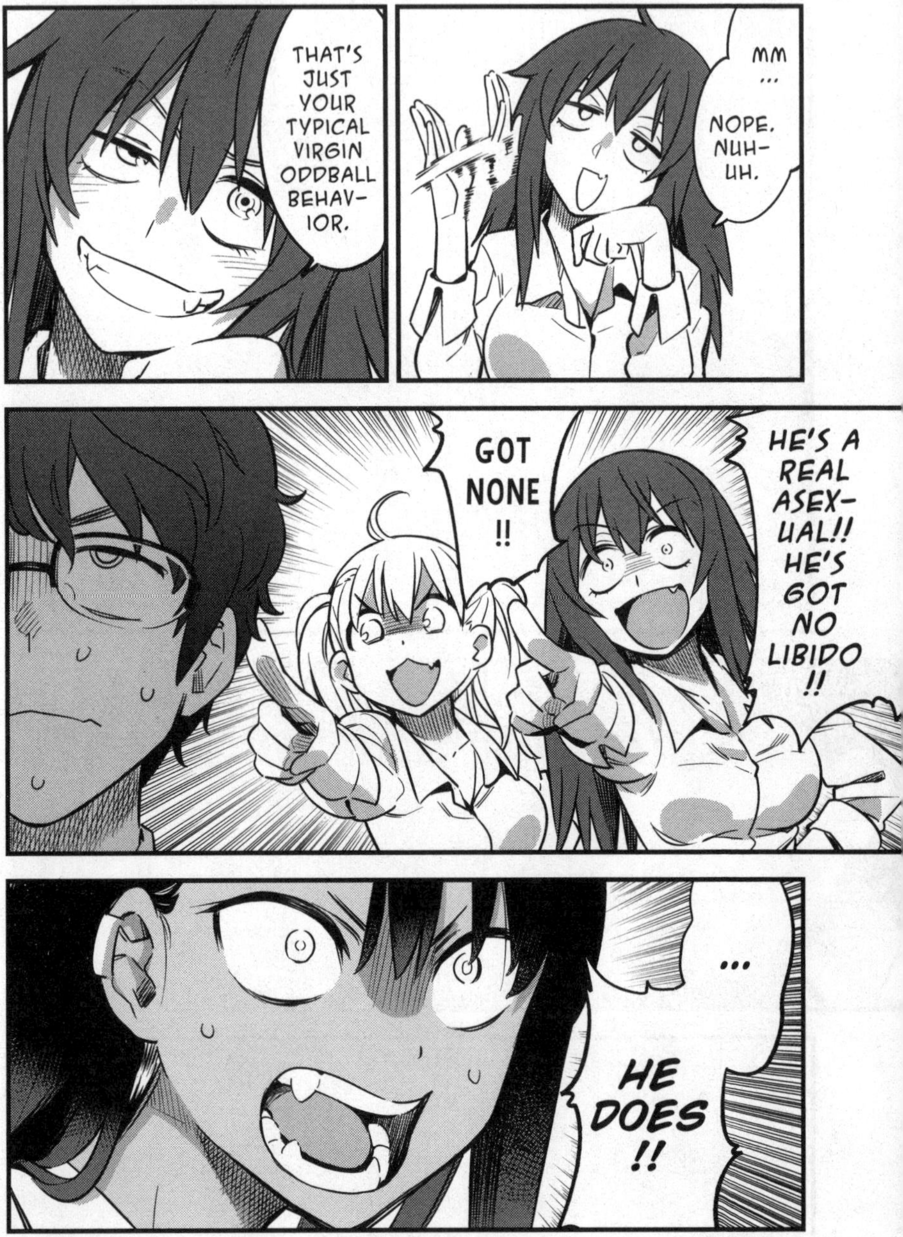
MM ... NOPE. NUH-UH.
THAT'S JUST YOUR TYPICAL VIRGIN ODDBALL BEHAVIOR.
HE'S A REAL ASEXUAL!! HE'S GOT NO LIBIDO!!
GOT NONE!!
...
HE DOES!!

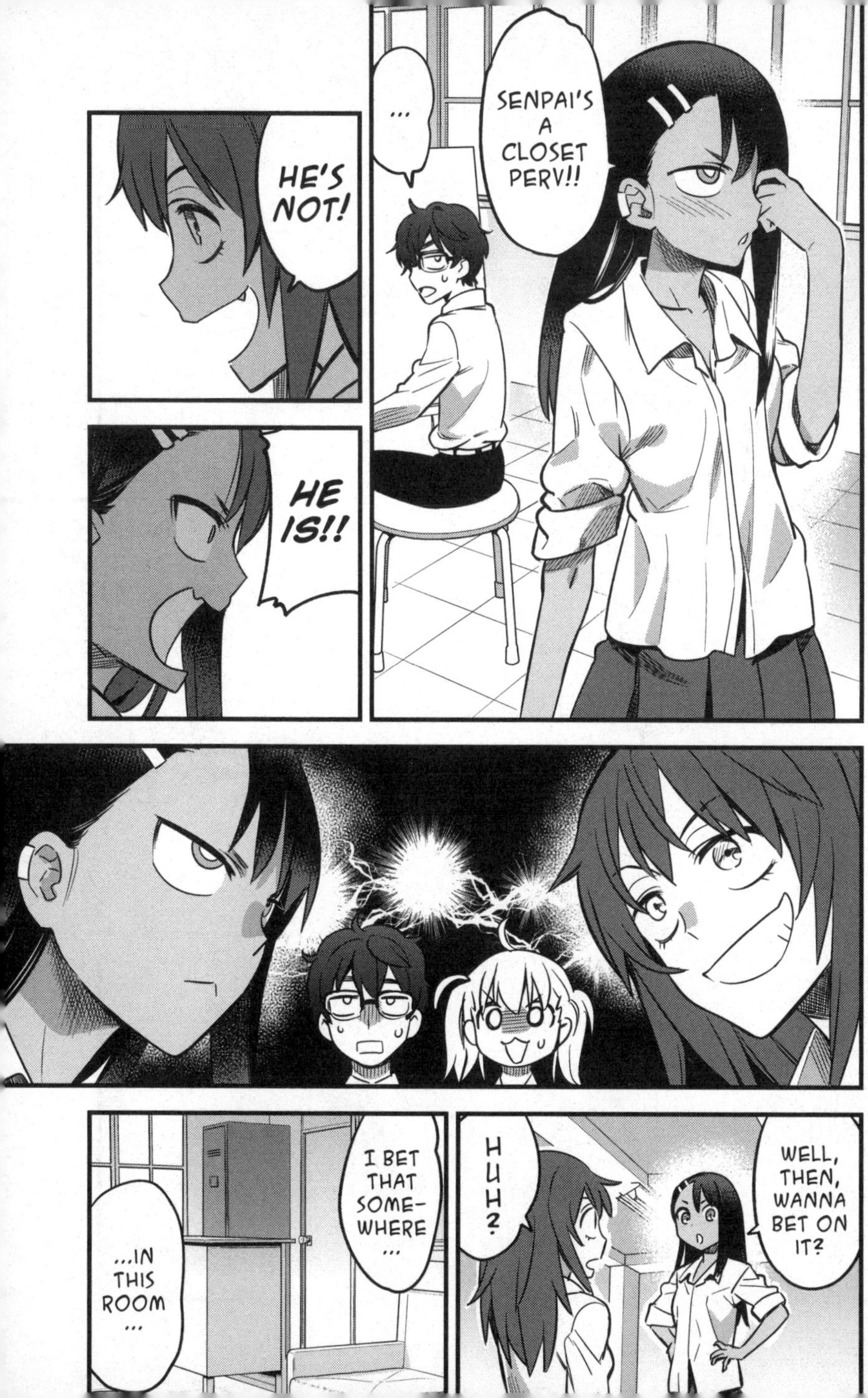
SENPAI'S A CLOSET PERV!!
...
HE'S NOT!
HE IS!!
WELL, THEN, WANNA BET ON IT?
HUH?
I BET THAT SOME-WHERE ...
...IN THIS ROOM ...

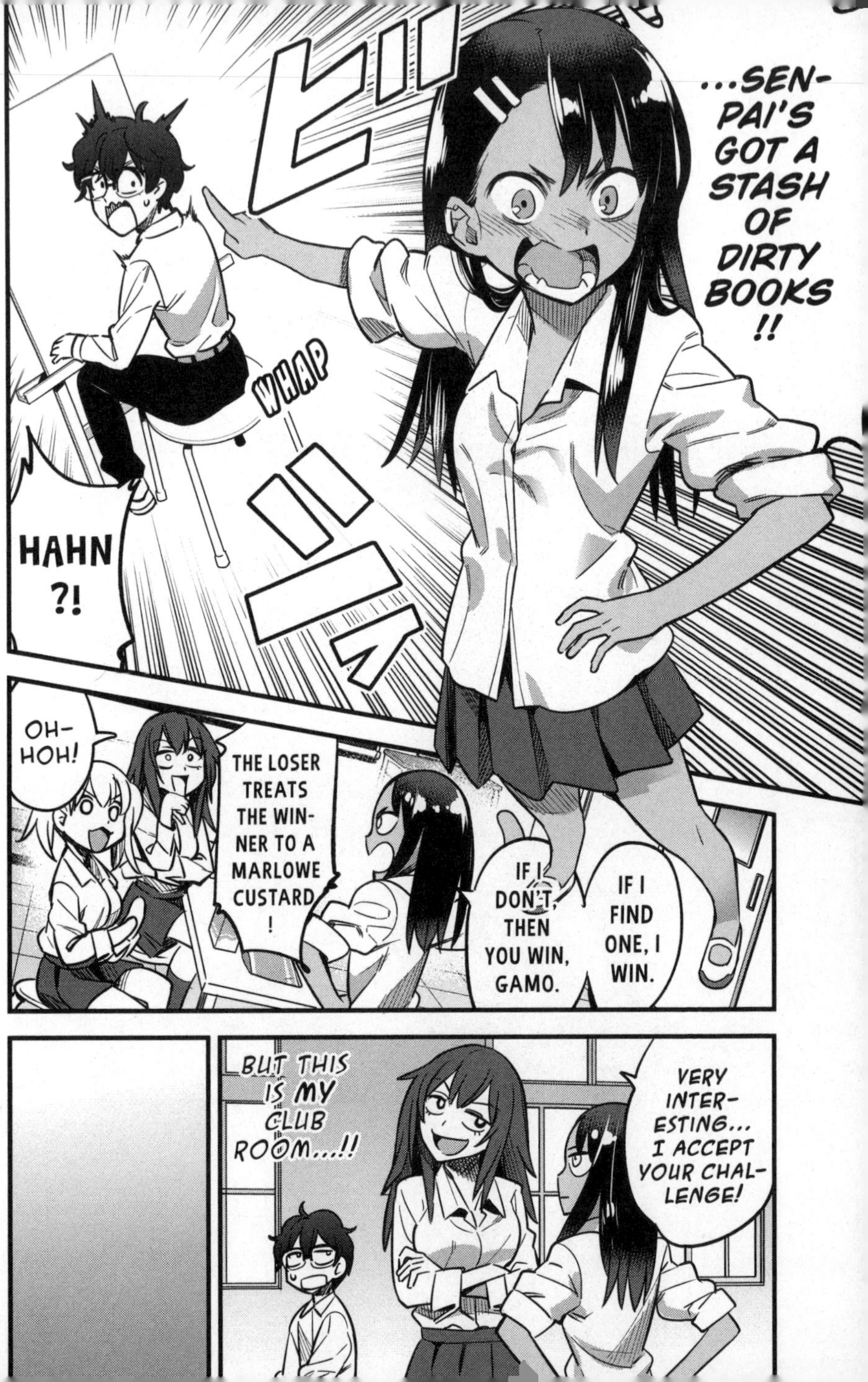
...SEN-PAI'S GOT A STASH OF DIRTY BOOKS !!
WHAP
HAHN ?!
IF I FIND ONE, I WIN.
IF I DON'T, THEN YOU WIN, GAMO.
THE LOSER TREATS THE WIN-NER TO A MARLOWE CUSTARD !
OH-HOH!
VERY INTER-ESTING... I ACCEPT YOUR CHAL-LENGE!
BUT THIS IS MY CLUB ROOM...!!

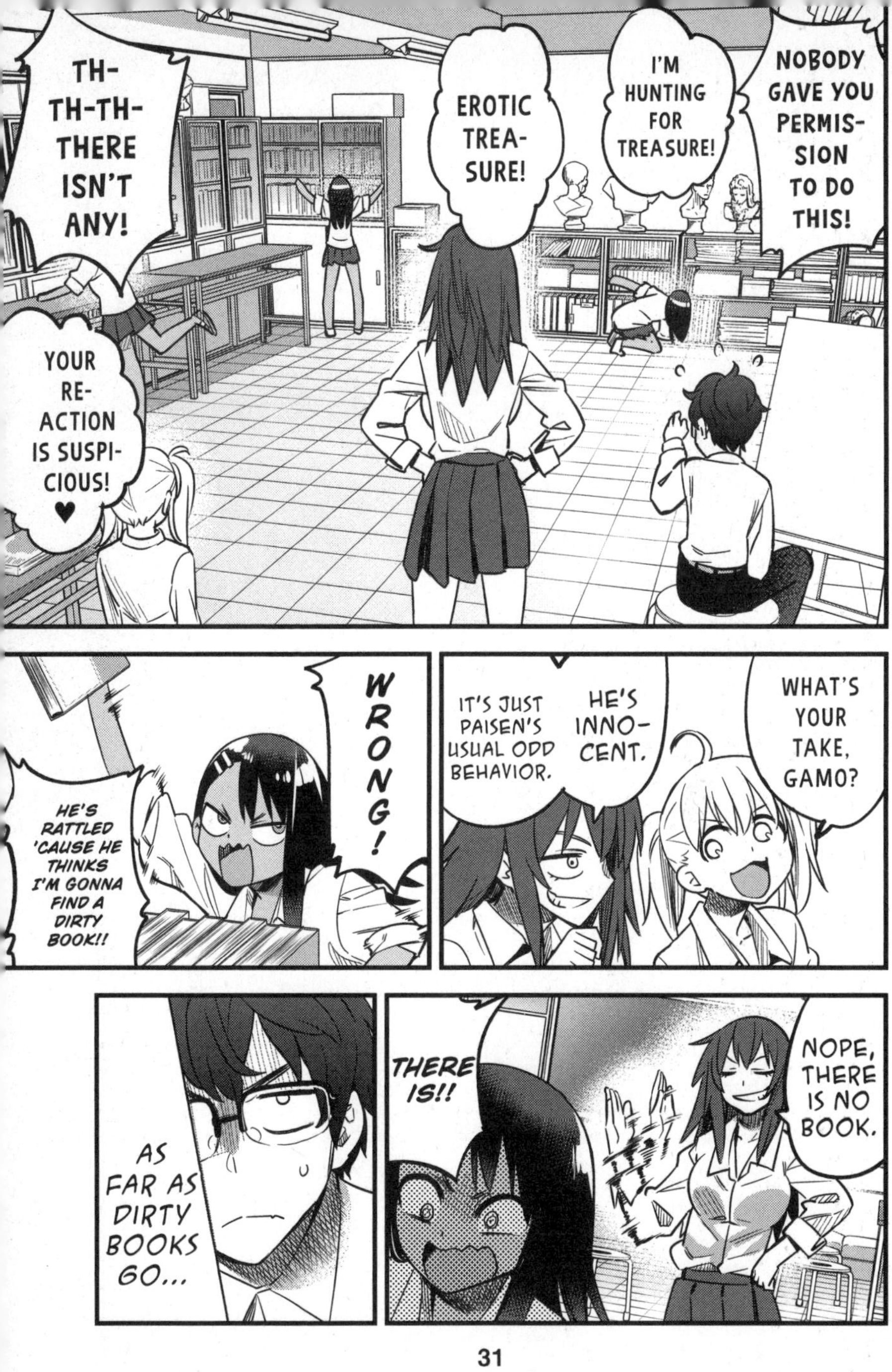
NOBODY GAVE YOU PERMISSION TO DO THIS!
I'M HUNTING FOR TREASURE!
EROTIC TREASURE!
TH-TH-TH-THERE ISN'T ANY!
YOUR REACTION IS SUSPICIOUS! ♥
WHAT'S YOUR TAKE, GAMO?
HE'S INNOCENT.
IT'S JUST PAISEN'S USUAL ODD BEHAVIOR.
WRONG!
HE'S RATTLED 'CAUSE HE THINKS I'M GONNA FIND A DIRTY BOOK!!
NOPE, THERE IS NO BOOK.
THERE IS!!
AS FAR AS DIRTY BOOKS GO...

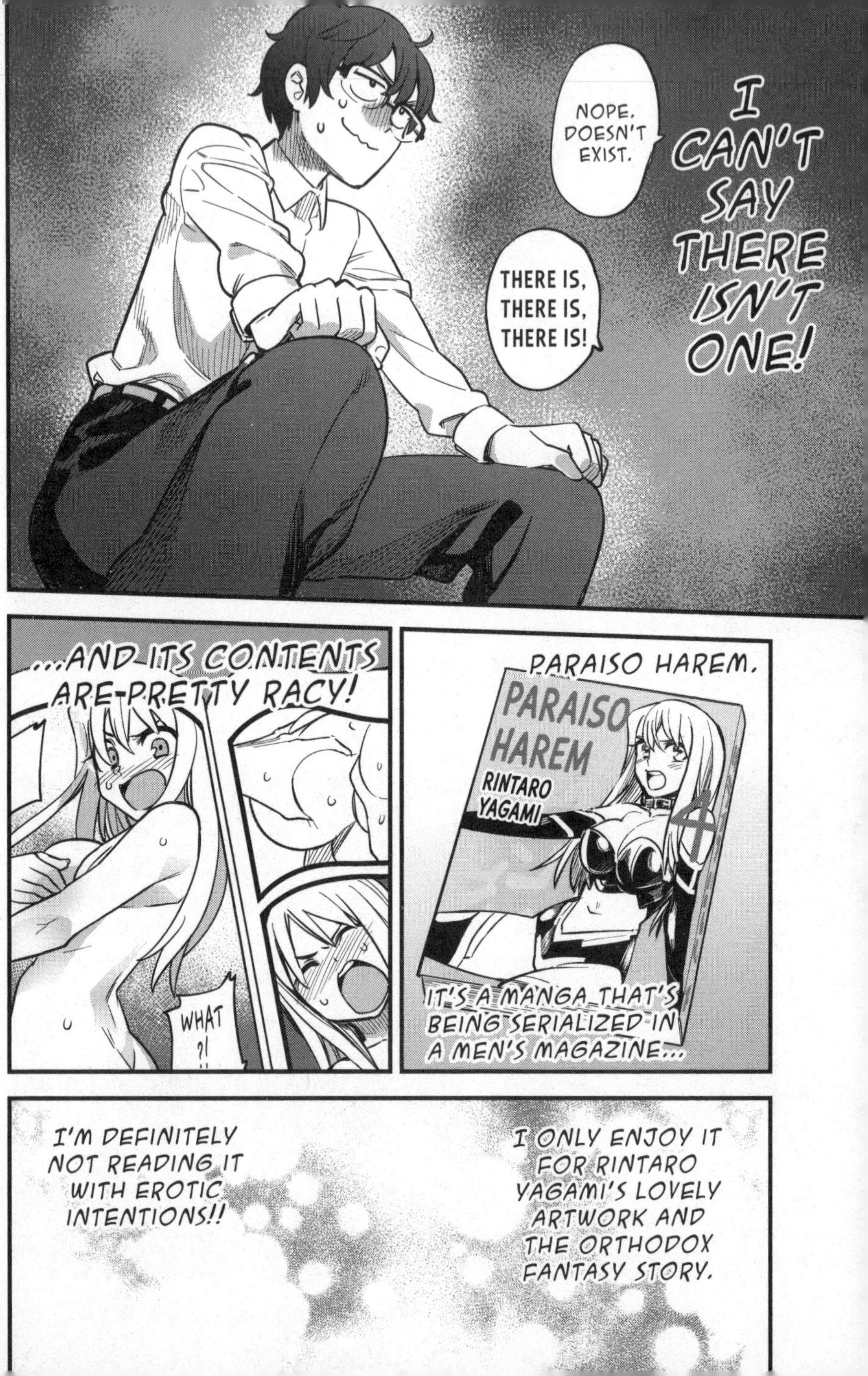
I CAN'T SAY THERE ISN'T ONE!
NOPE. DOESN'T EXIST.
THERE IS, THERE IS, THERE IS!
PARAISO HAREM.
PARAISO HAREM
RINTARO YAGAMI
IT'S A MANGA THAT'S BEING SERIALIZED IN A MEN'S MAGAZINE...
...AND ITS CONTENTS ARE PRETTY RACY!
WHAT ?!
I ONLY ENJOY IT FOR RINTARO YAGAMI'S LOVELY ARTWORK AND THE ORTHODOX FANTASY STORY.
I'M DEFINITELY NOT READING IT WITH EROTIC INTENTIONS!!

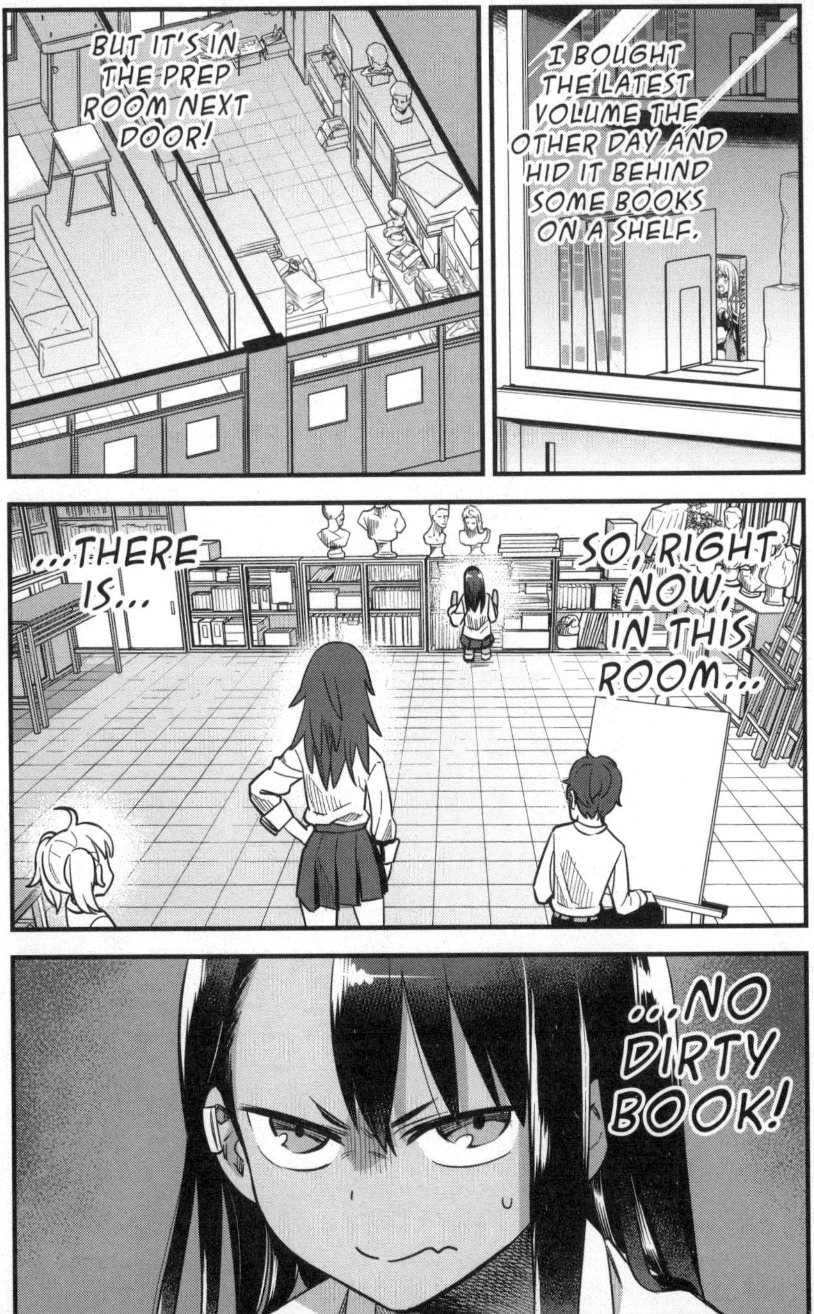
I BOUGHT THE LATEST VOLUME THE OTHER DAY AND HID IT BEHIND SOME BOOKS ON A SHELF.
BUT IT'S IN THE PREP ROOM NEXT DOOR!
SO, RIGHT NOW, IN THIS ROOM...
...THERE IS...
...NO DIRTY BOOK!

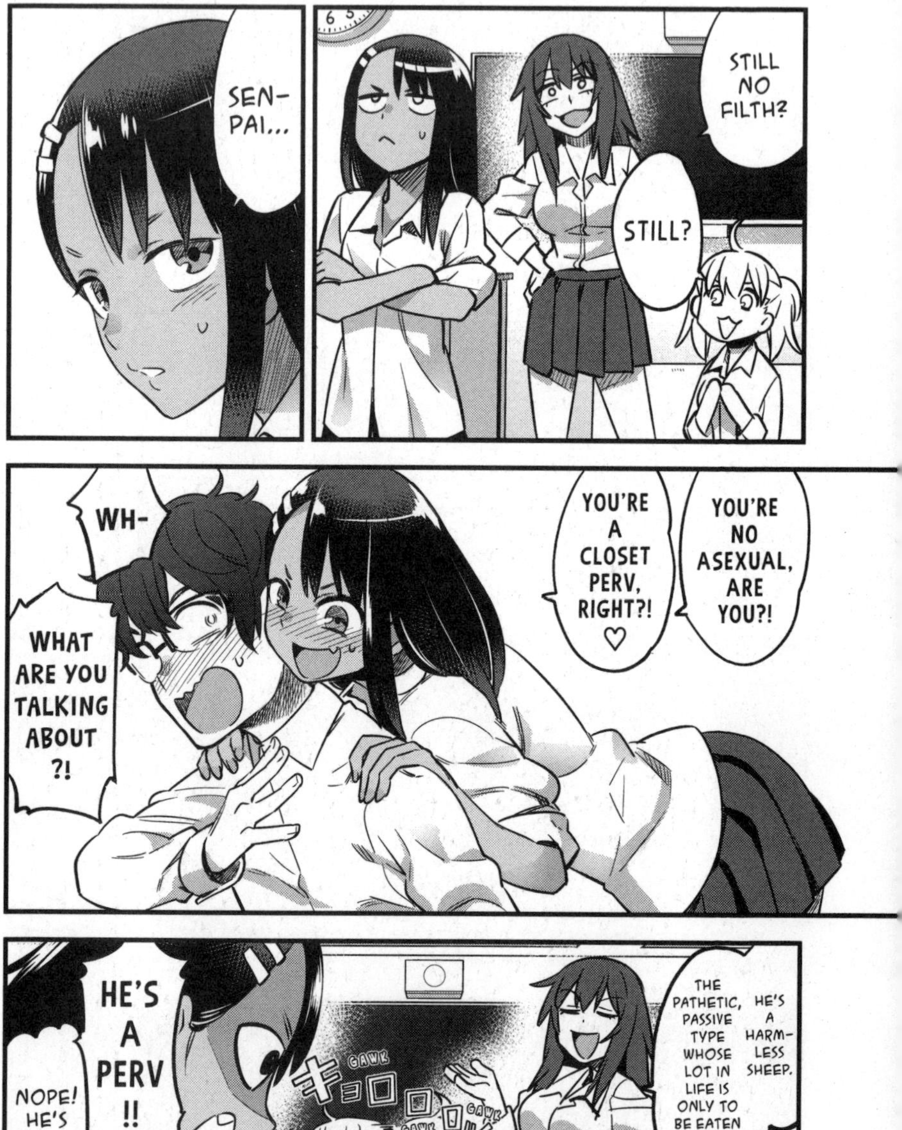
STILL NO FILTH?
STILL?
SEN-PAI...
YOU'RE NO ASEXUAL, ARE YOU?!
YOU'RE A CLOSET PERV, RIGHT?! ♡
WH-
WHAT ARE YOU TALKING ABOUT ?!
HE'S A HARMLESS SHEEP.
THE PATHETIC, PASSIVE TYPE WHOSE LOT IN LIFE IS ONLY TO BE EATEN BY A WOLF.
GAWK
GAWK
GAWK
HE'S A PERV !!
NOPE! HE'S A SHEEP.

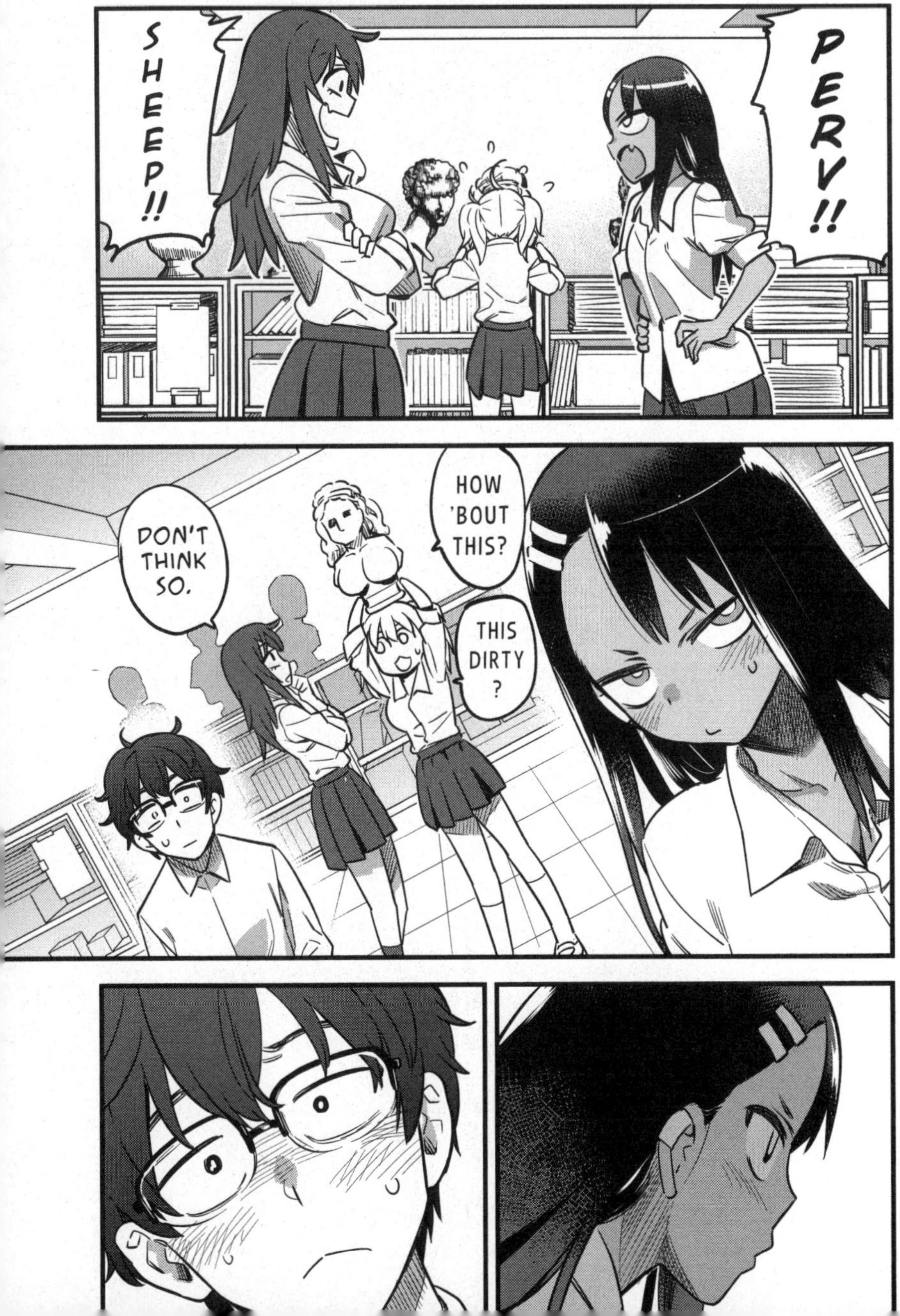
PERV!!
SHEEP!!
HOW 'BOUT THIS?
THIS DIRTY ?
DON'T THINK SO.

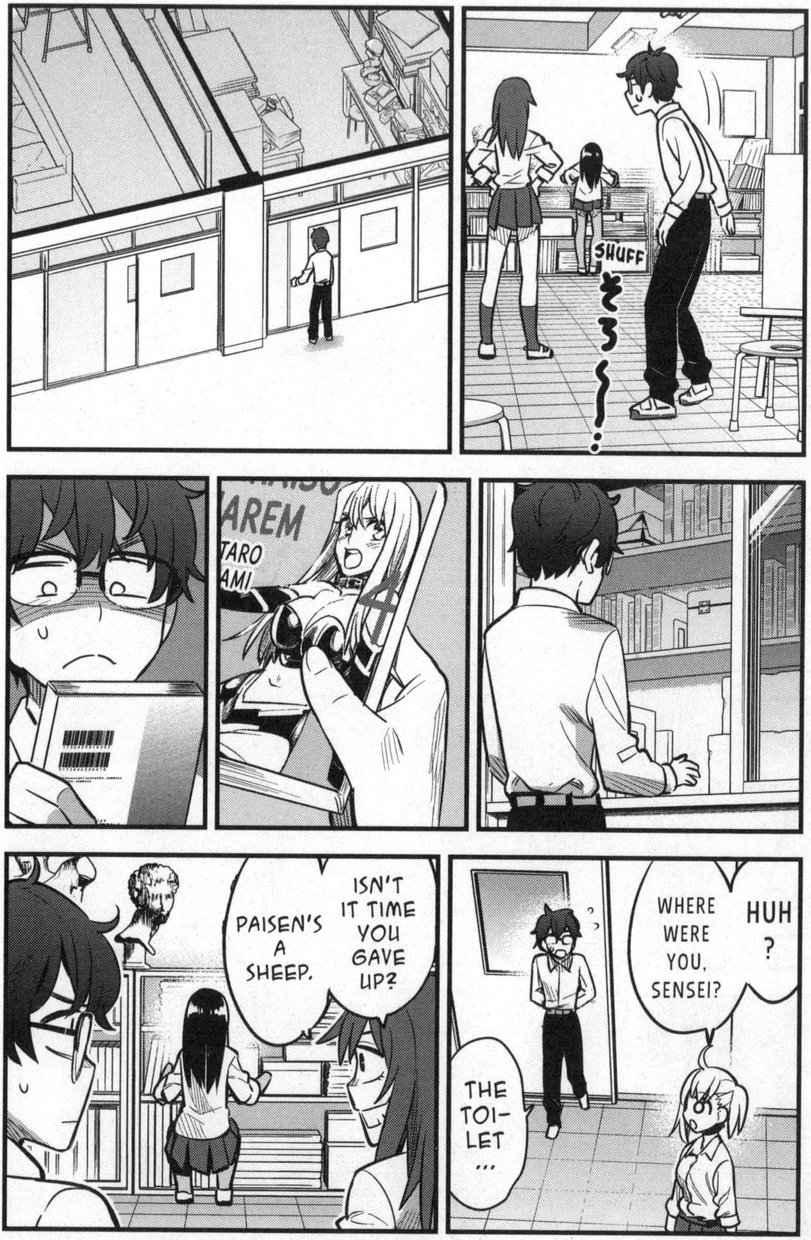
SHUFF
そろ〜…
HUH?
WHERE WERE YOU, SENSEI?
THE TOI-LET…
ISN'T IT TIME YOU GAVE UP?
PAISEN'S A SHEEP.

SHFF

7...

TOO BAD FOR YOU, NAGA-TORO !!

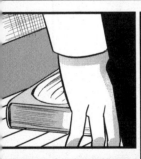

THERE ARE NO DIRTY BOOKS IN THIS ROOM !!

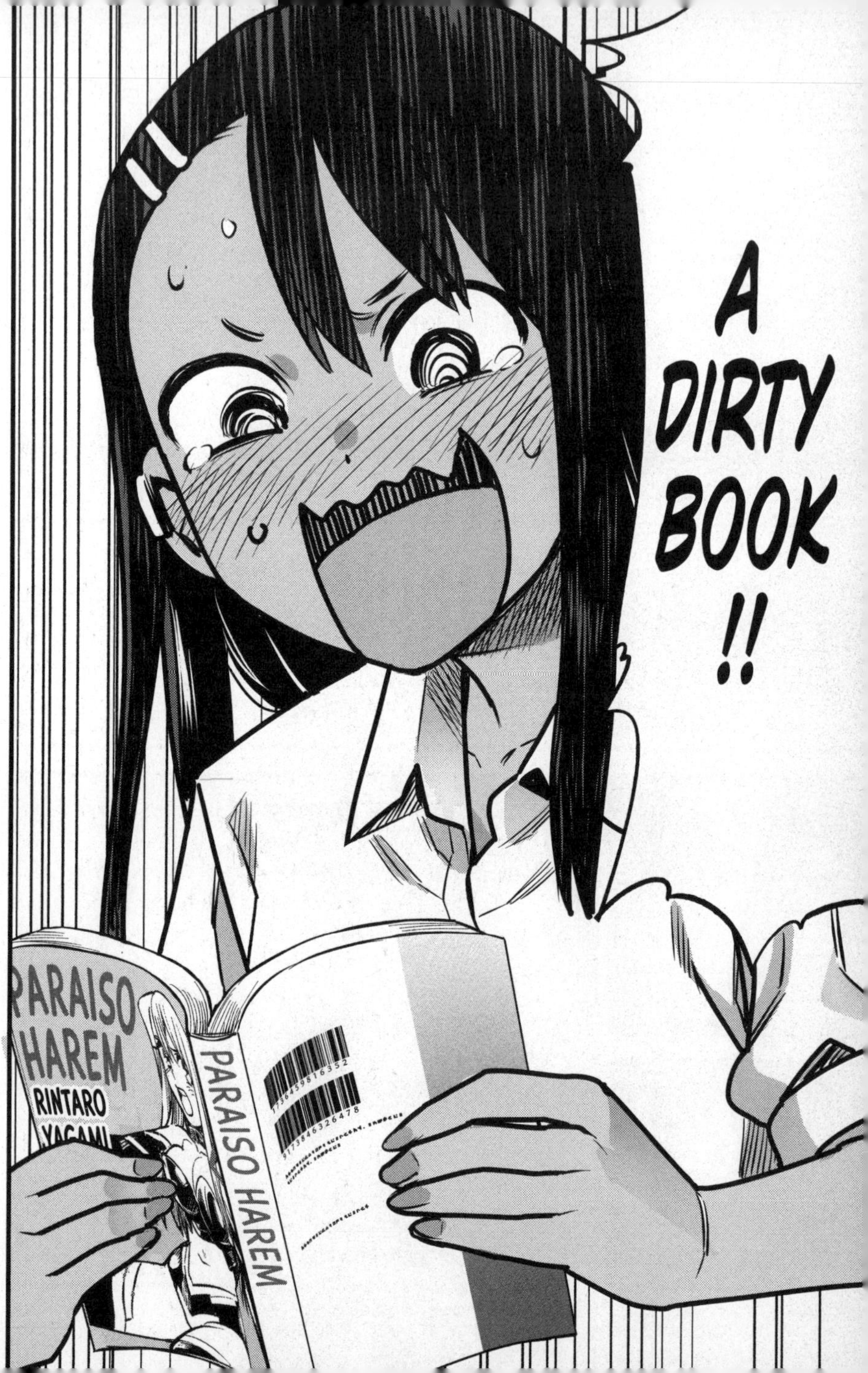
A DIRTY BOOK !!
PARAISO HAREM
PARAISO HAREM
RINTARO YAGAMI

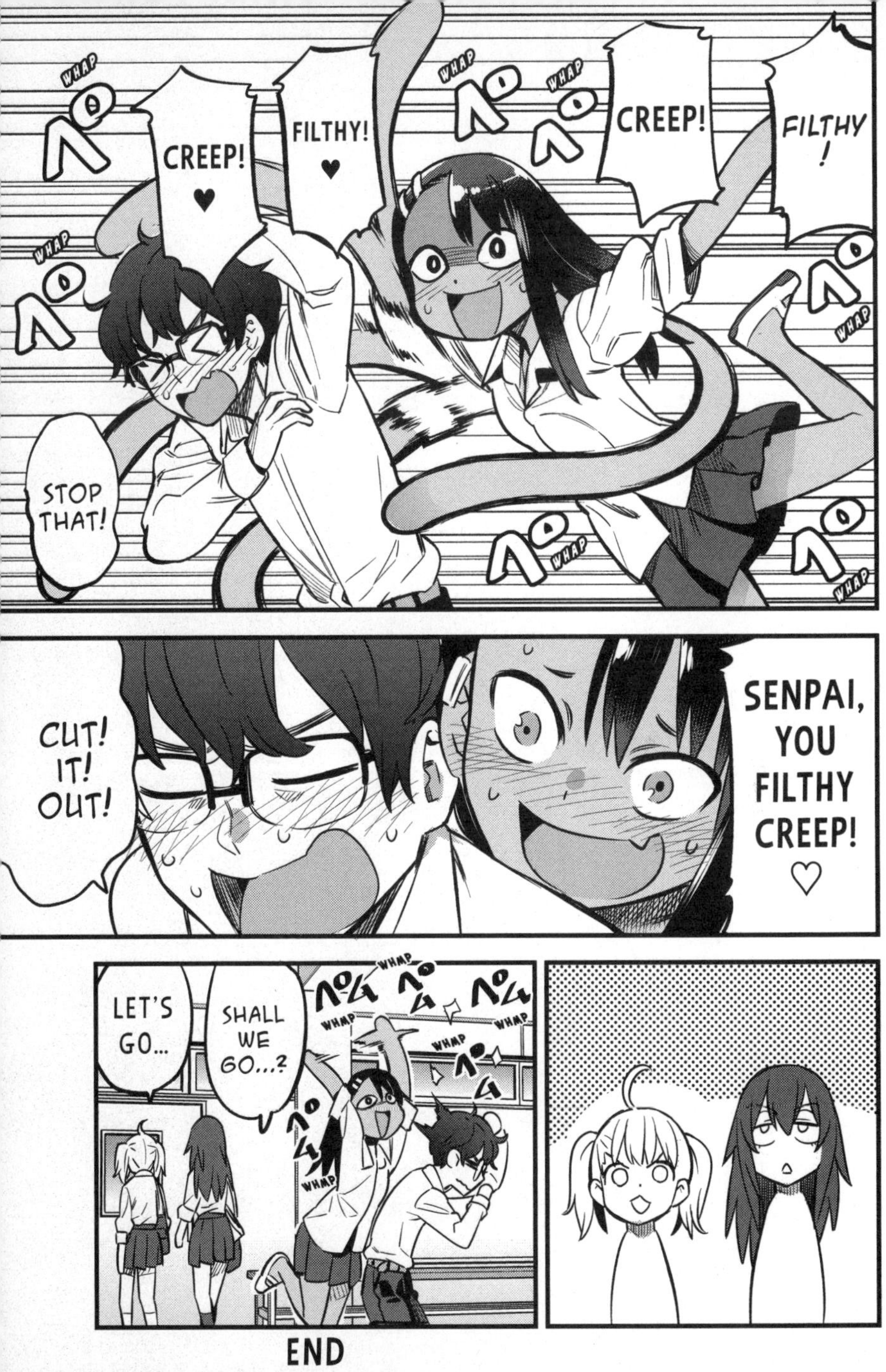

FILTHY!
CREEP!
WHAP
WHAP
FILTHY! ♥
CREEP! ♥
WHAP
WHAP
WHAP
STOP THAT!
WHAP
WHAP
SENPAI, YOU FILTHY CREEP! ♡
CUT! IT! OUT!
WHMP
WHMP
WHMP
WHMP
WHMP
SHALL WE GO...?
LET'S GO...

END

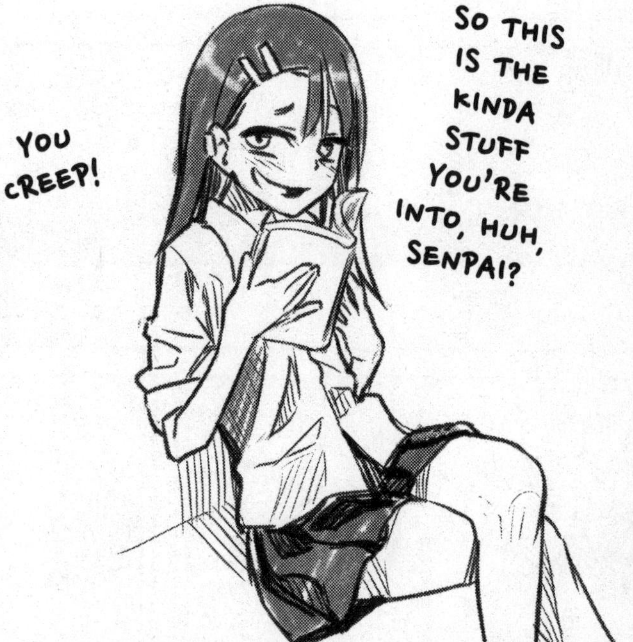
SO THIS IS THE KINDA STUFF YOU'RE INTO, HUH, SENPAI?
YOU CREEP!

Chapter 33: Senpai, What's in Your Bento Lunch?

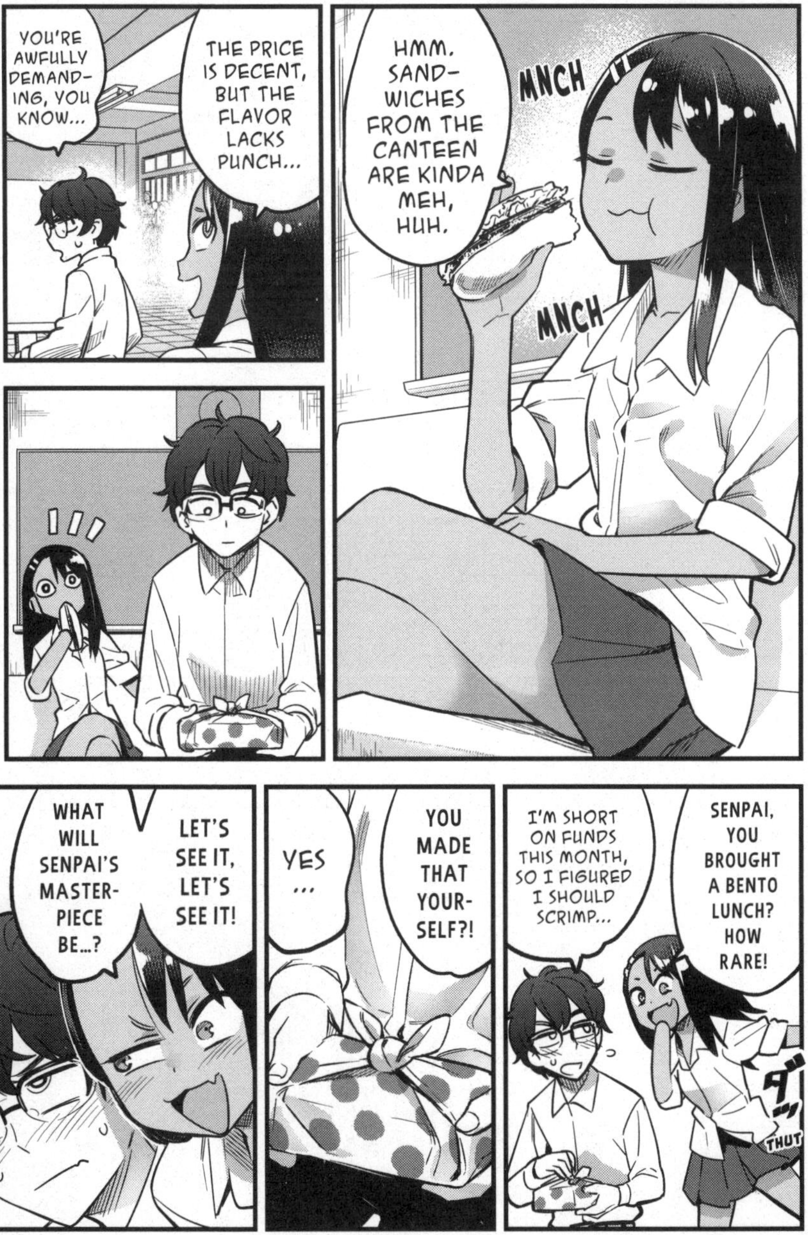
MNCH
HMM. SAND-WICHES FROM THE CANTEEN ARE KINDA MEH, HUH.
MNCH
THE PRICE IS DECENT, BUT THE FLAVOR LACKS PUNCH...
YOU'RE AWFULLY DEMAND-ING, YOU KNOW...
SENPAI, YOU BROUGHT A BENTO LUNCH? HOW RARE!
THUT
I'M SHORT ON FUNDS THIS MONTH, SO I FIGURED I SHOULD SCRIMP...
YOU MADE THAT YOUR-SELF?!
YES ...
LET'S SEE IT, LET'S SEE IT!
WHAT WILL SENPAI'S MASTER-PIECE BE...?

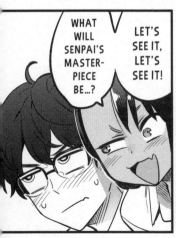

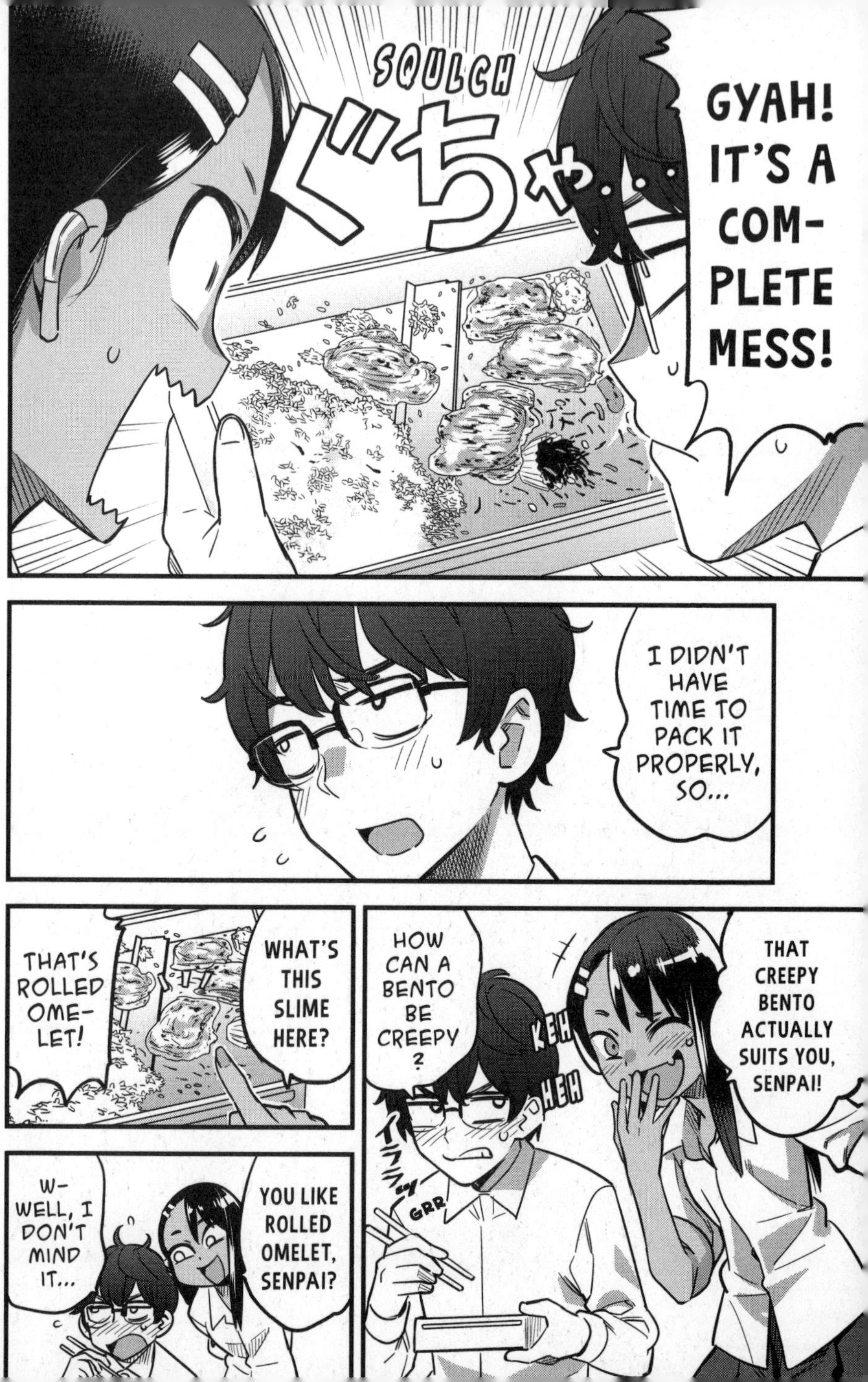

SQULCH
ぐちゃ
GYAH! IT'S A COM-PLETE MESS!
I DIDN'T HAVE TIME TO PACK IT PROPERLY, SO...
THAT CREEPY BENTO ACTUALLY SUITS YOU, SENPAI!
KEH HEH
HOW CAN A BENTO BE CREEPY?
GRR
WHAT'S THIS SLIME HERE?
THAT'S ROLLED OME-LET!
YOU LIKE ROLLED OMELET, SENPAI?
W-WELL, I DON'T MIND IT...

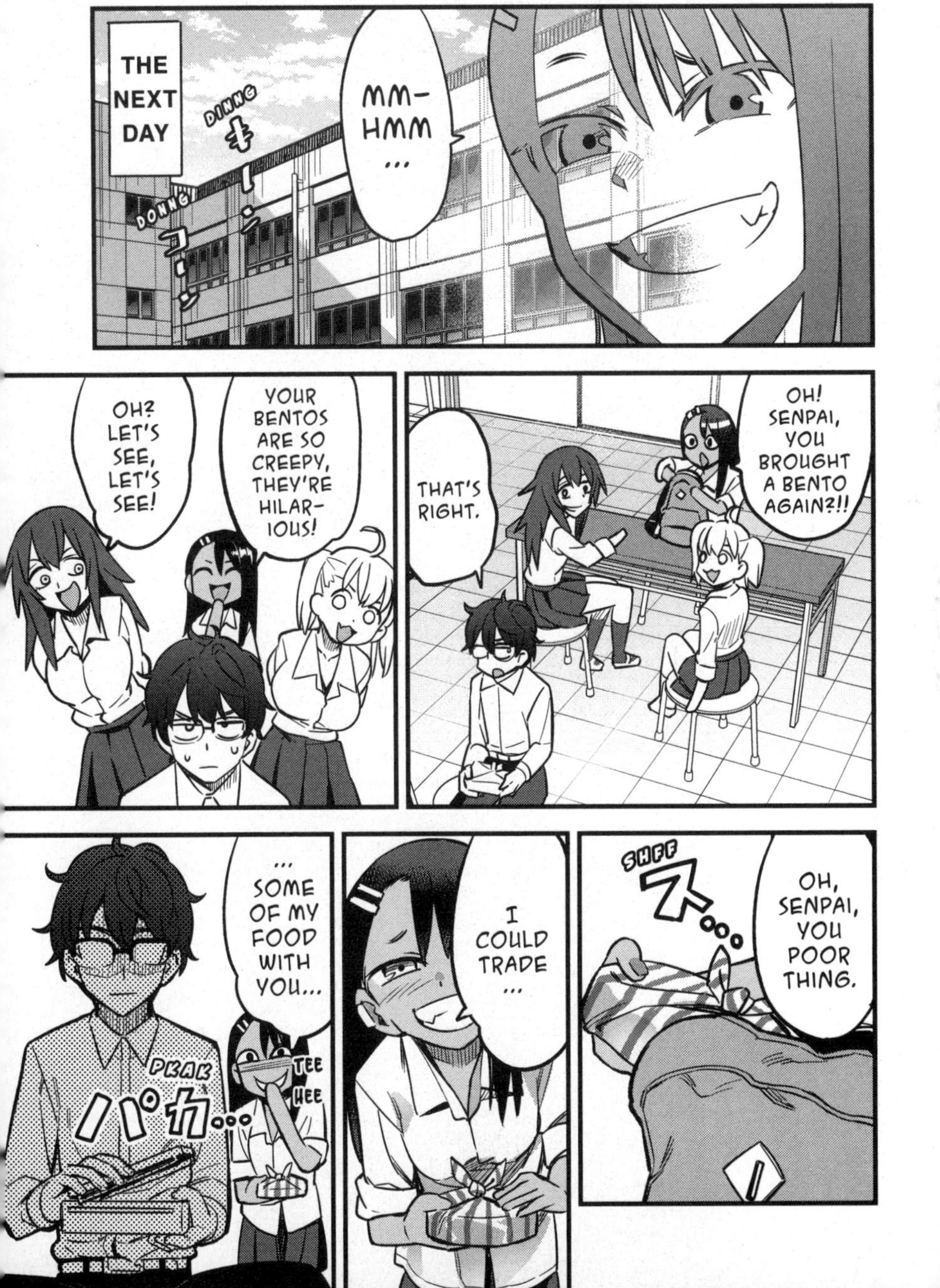
MM-HMM ...
THE NEXT DAY
DINNG
DONNG
OH! SENPAI, YOU BROUGHT A BENTO AGAIN?!!
THAT'S RIGHT.
YOUR BENTOS ARE SO CREEPY, THEY'RE HILARIOUS!
OH? LET'S SEE, LET'S SEE!
SHFF
OH, SENPAI, YOU POOR THING.
I COULD TRADE ...
... SOME OF MY FOOD WITH YOU...
TEE HEE
PKAK

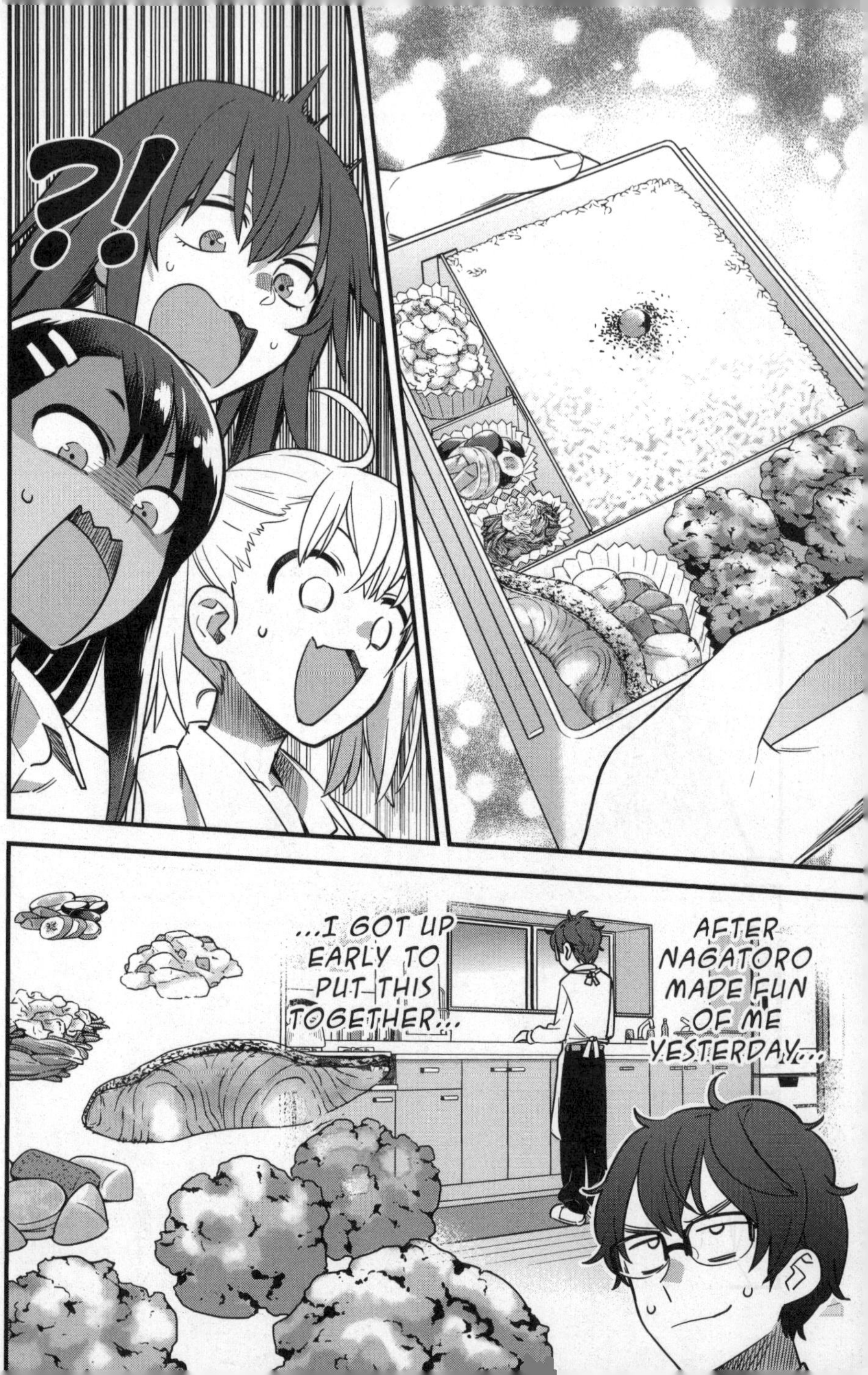
?!
AFTER NAGATORO MADE FUN OF ME YESTERDAY...
...I GOT UP EARLY TO PUT THIS TOGETHER...

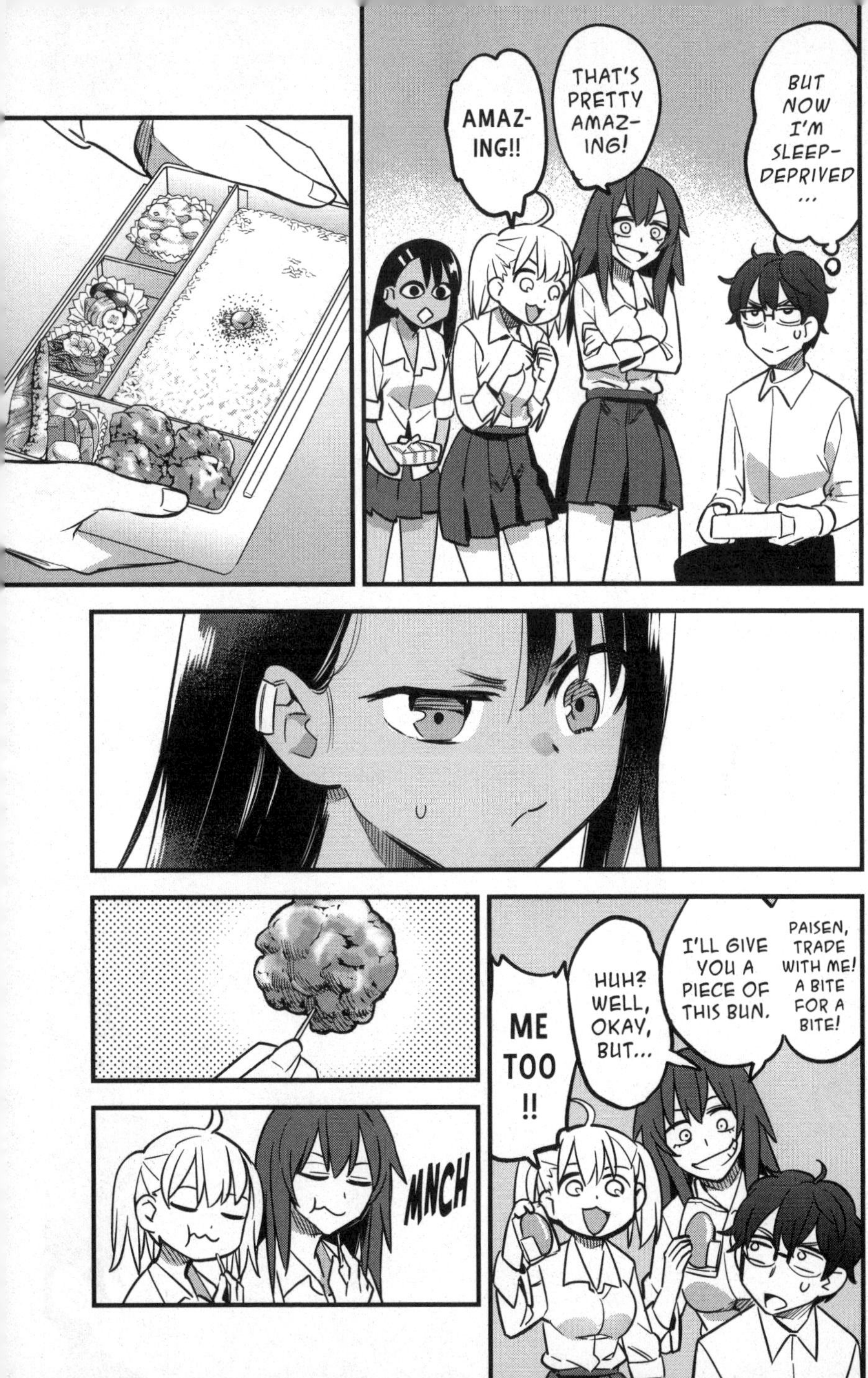
BUT NOW I'M SLEEP-DEPRIVED...
THAT'S PRETTY AMAZ-ING!
AMAZ-ING!!
PAISEN, TRADE WITH ME! A BITE FOR A BITE!
I'LL GIVE YOU A PIECE OF THIS BUN.
HUH? WELL, OKAY, BUT...
ME TOO!!
MNCH

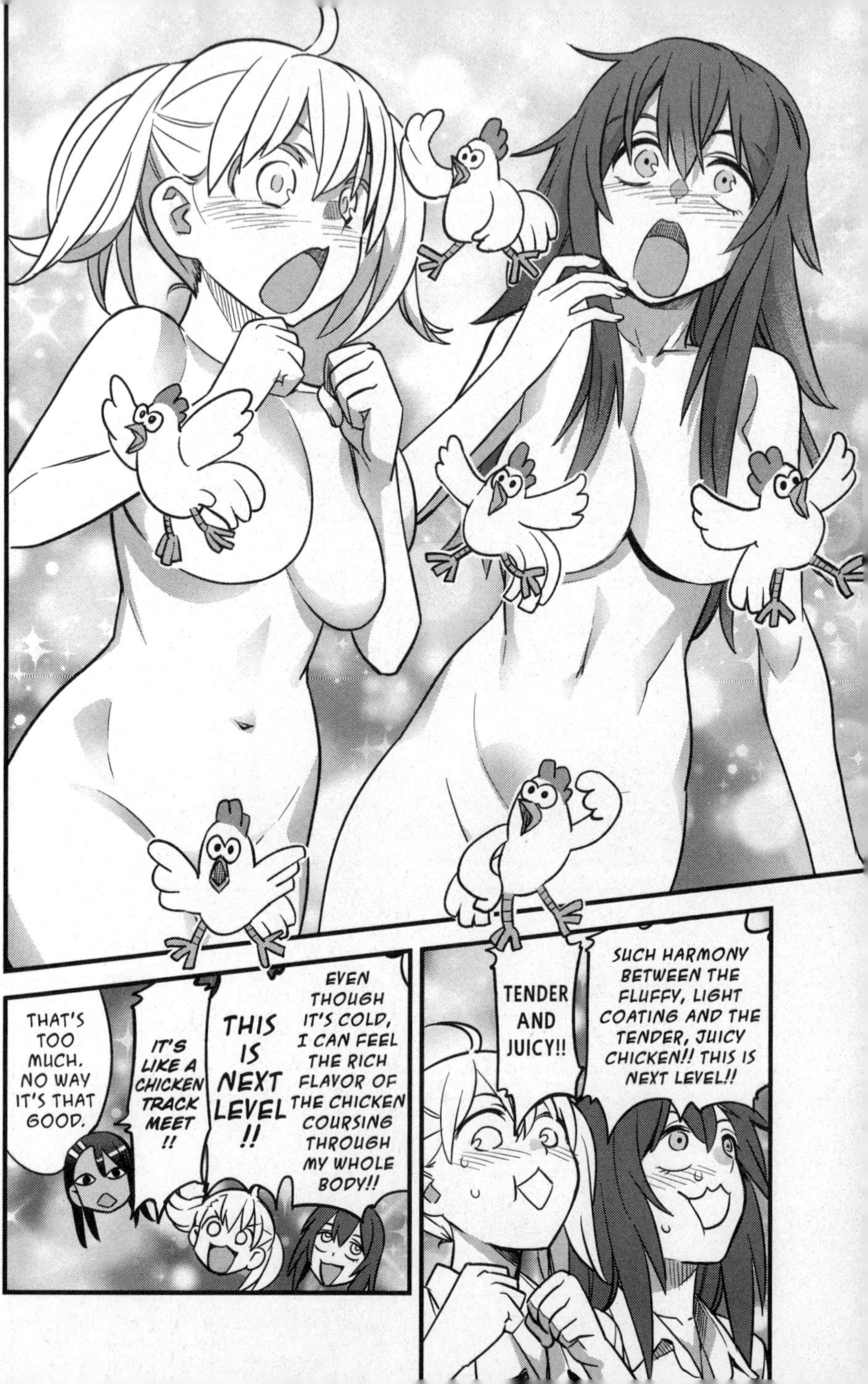
SUCH HARMONY BETWEEN THE FLUFFY, LIGHT COATING AND THE TENDER, JUICY CHICKEN!! THIS IS NEXT LEVEL!!
TENDER AND JUICY!!
EVEN THOUGH IT'S COLD, I CAN FEEL THE RICH FLAVOR OF THE CHICKEN COURSING THROUGH MY WHOLE BODY!!
THIS IS NEXT LEVEL !!
IT'S LIKE A CHICKEN TRACK MEET !!
THAT'S TOO MUCH. NO WAY IT'S THAT GOOD.

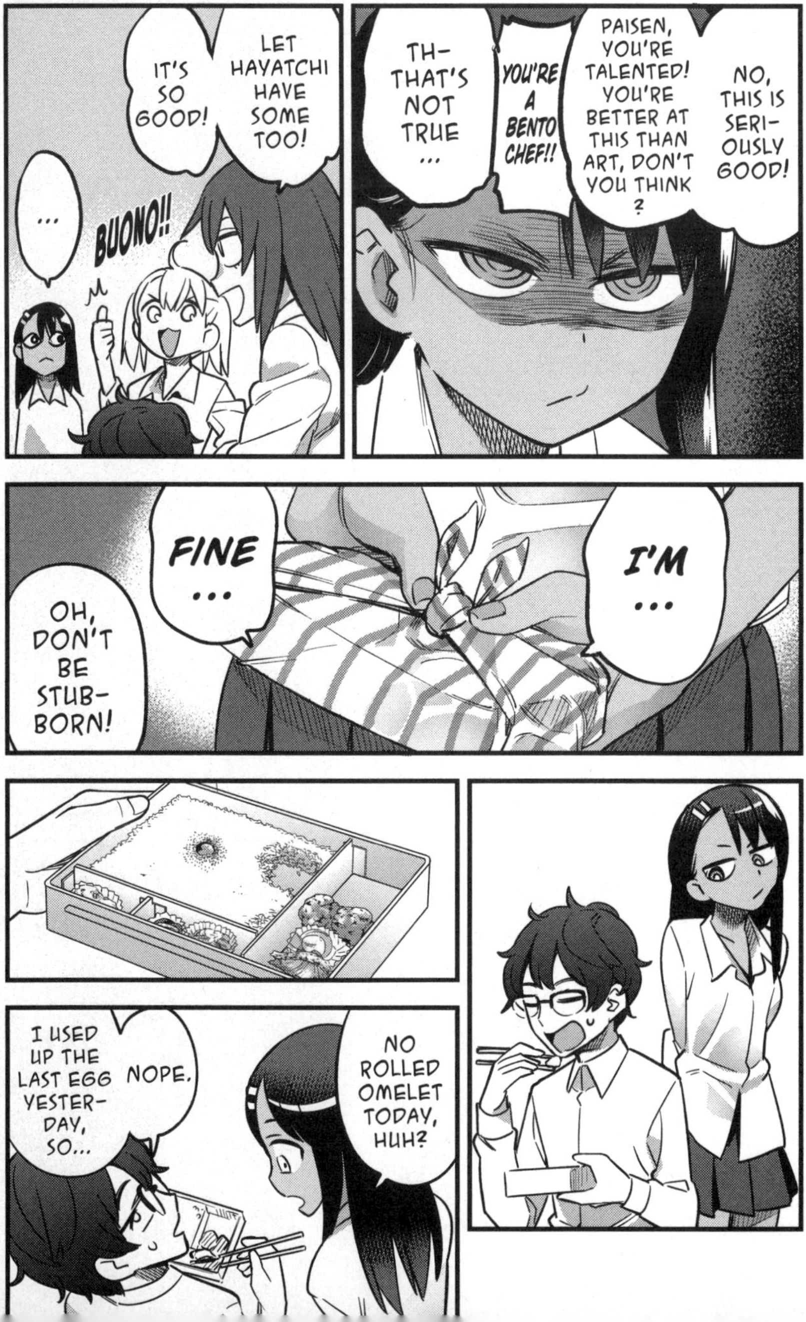
NO, THIS IS SERIOUSLY GOOD!
PAISEN, YOU'RE TALENTED! YOU'RE BETTER AT THIS THAN ART, DON'T YOU THINK?
YOU'RE A BENTO CHEF!!
TH-THAT'S NOT TRUE...
LET HAYATCHI HAVE SOME TOO!
IT'S SO GOOD!
BUONO!!
...
I'M...
FINE...
OH, DON'T BE STUBBORN!
NO ROLLED OMELET TODAY, HUH?
NOPE.
I USED UP THE LAST EGG YESTERDAY, SO...

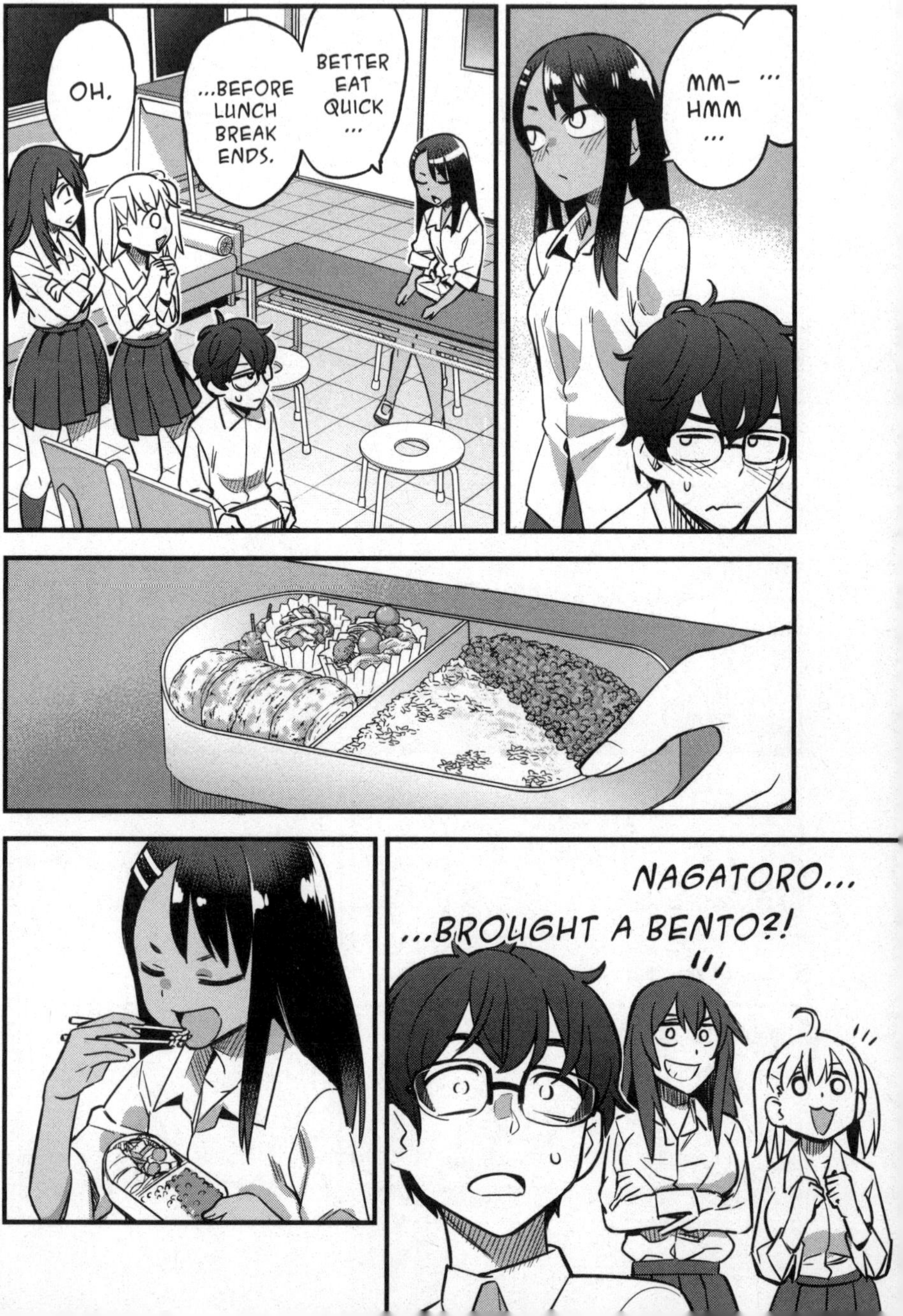
MM-HMM... ...
BETTER EAT QUICK...
...BEFORE LUNCH BREAK ENDS.
OH.
NAGATORO...
...BROUGHT A BENTO?!

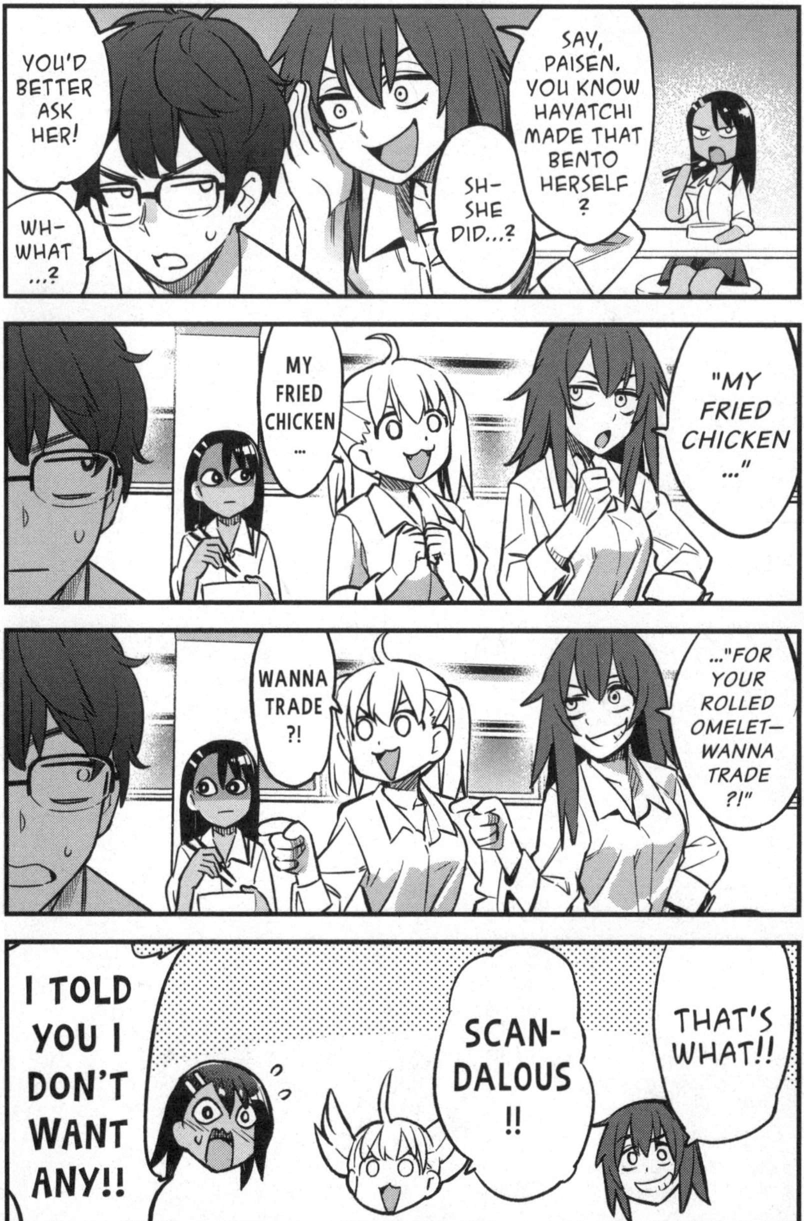
SAY, PAISEN. YOU KNOW HAYATCHI MADE THAT BENTO HERSELF?
SH-SHE DID...?
YOU'D BETTER ASK HER!
WH-WHAT...?
"MY FRIED CHICKEN..."
MY FRIED CHICKEN...
..."FOR YOUR ROLLED OMELET—WANNA TRADE?!"
WANNA TRADE?!
THAT'S WHAT!!
SCAN-DALOUS!!
I TOLD YOU I DON'T WANT ANY!!

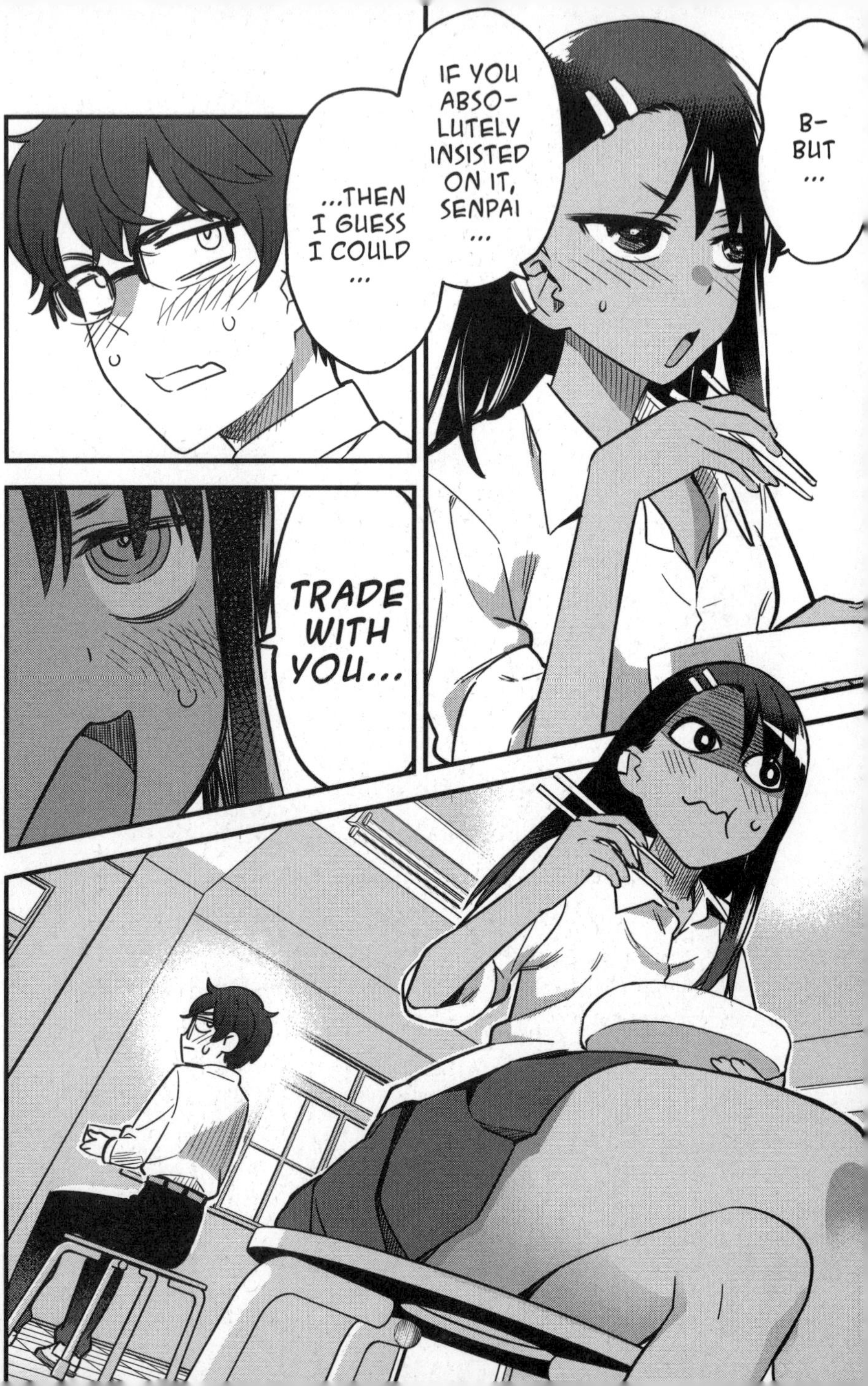
B-BUT...
IF YOU ABSO-LUTELY INSISTED ON IT, SENPAI...
...THEN I GUESS I COULD...
TRADE WITH YOU...

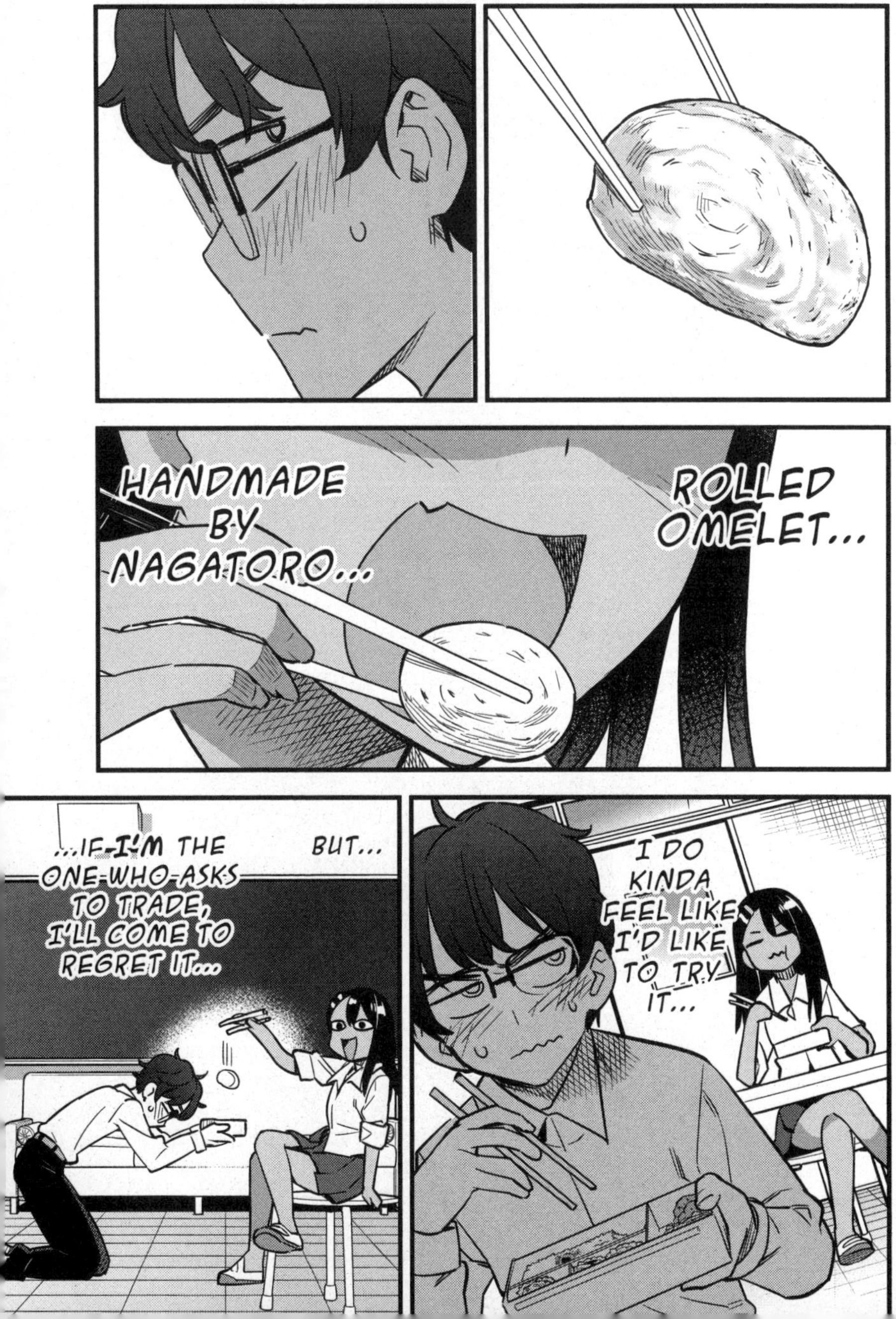
ROLLED OMELET...
HANDMADE BY NAGATORO...
I DO KINDA FEEL LIKE I'D LIKE TO TRY IT...
BUT...
...IF I'M THE ONE WHO ASKS TO TRADE, I'LL COME TO REGRET IT...

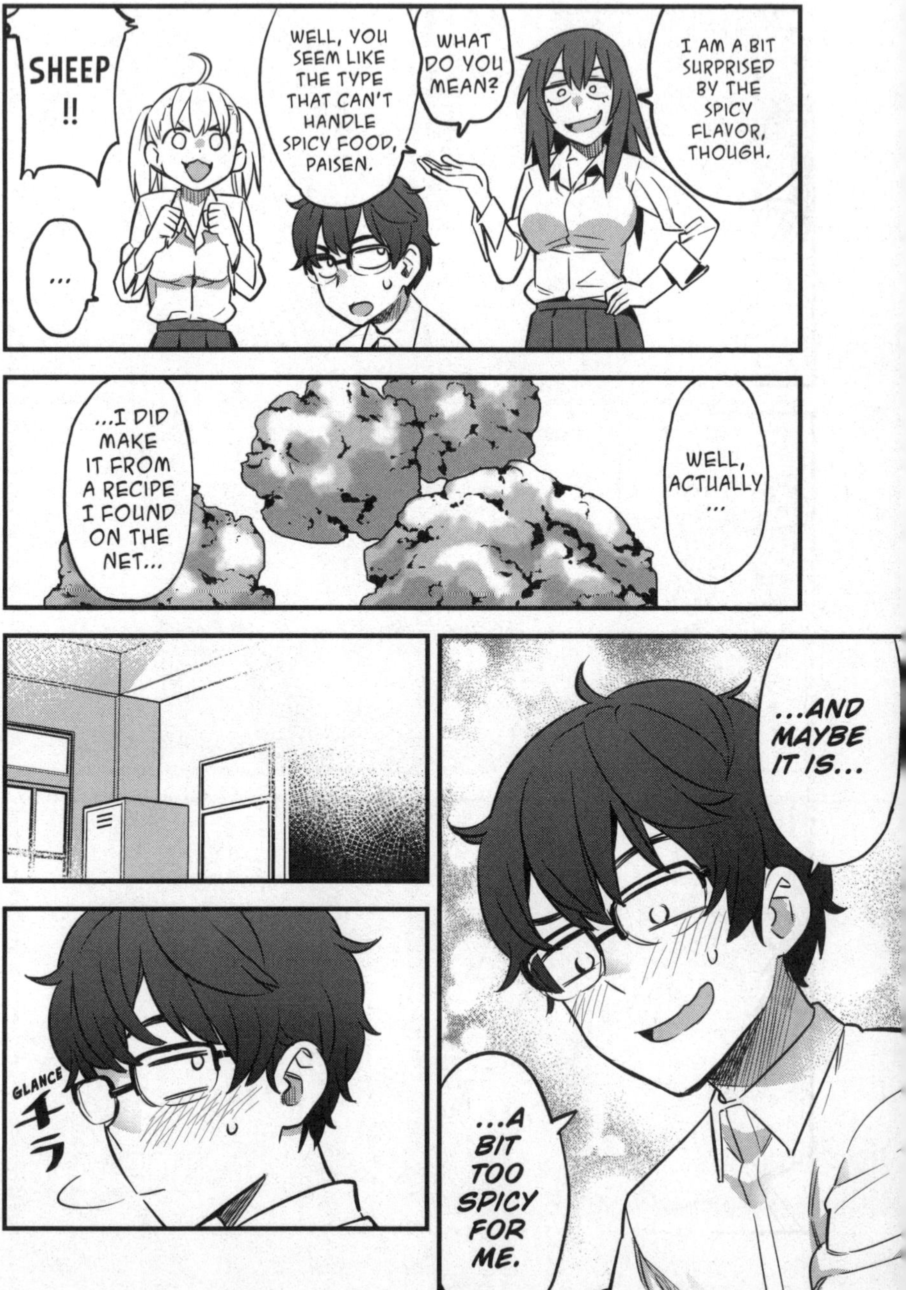
I AM A BIT SURPRISED BY THE SPICY FLAVOR, THOUGH.
WHAT DO YOU MEAN?
WELL, YOU SEEM LIKE THE TYPE THAT CAN'T HANDLE SPICY FOOD, PAISEN.
SHEEP!!
...
WELL, ACTUALLY...
...I DID MAKE IT FROM A RECIPE I FOUND ON THE NET...
...AND MAYBE IT IS...
...A BIT TOO SPICY FOR ME.
GLANCE
チラ

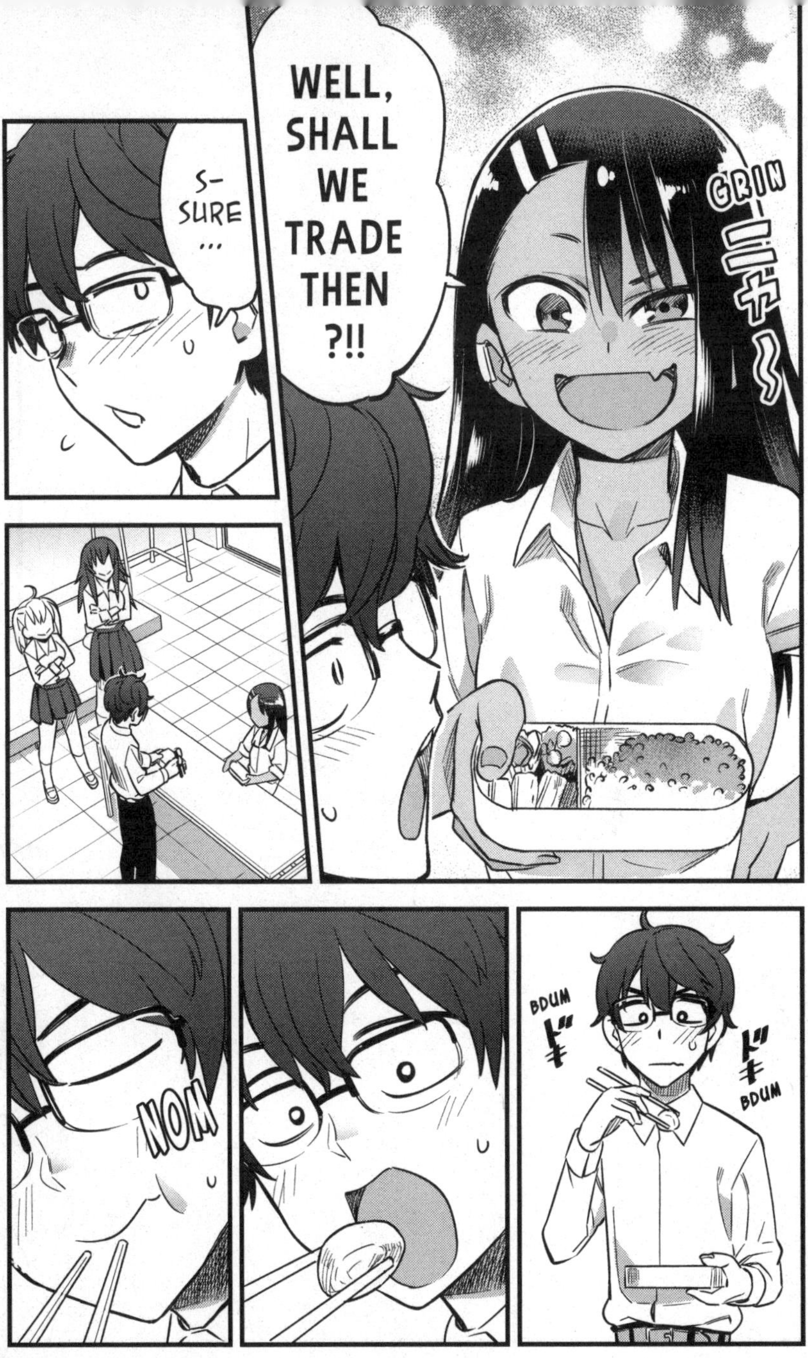
WELL, SHALL WE TRADE THEN?!!
GRIN
ニヤ〜
S-SURE...
ドキ
BDUM
BDUM
ドキ
NOM

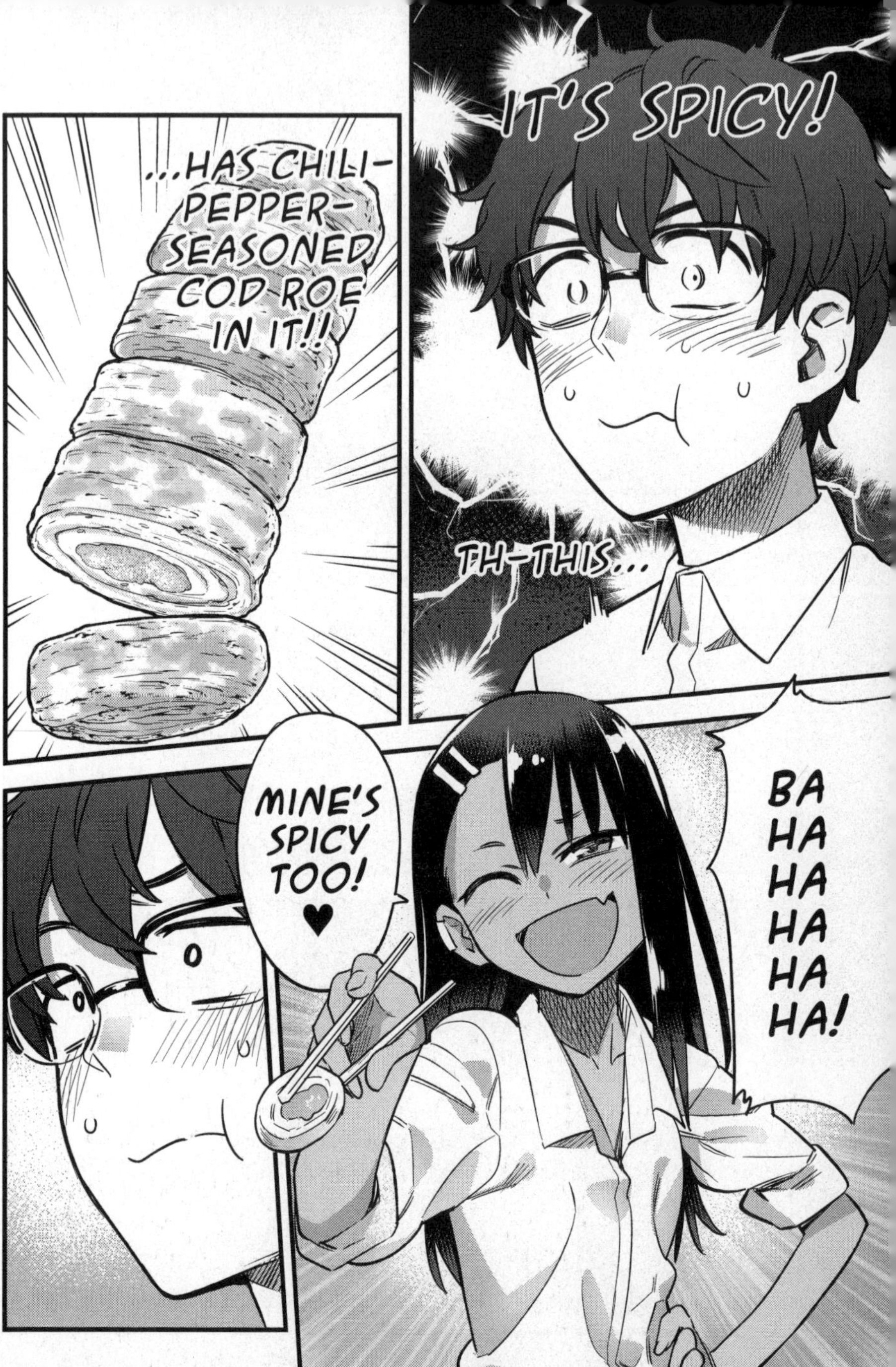
IT'S SPICY!
TH-THIS...
...HAS CHILI-PEPPER-SEASONED COD ROE IN IT!!
BA HA HA HA HA HA HA!
MINE'S SPICY TOO! ♥

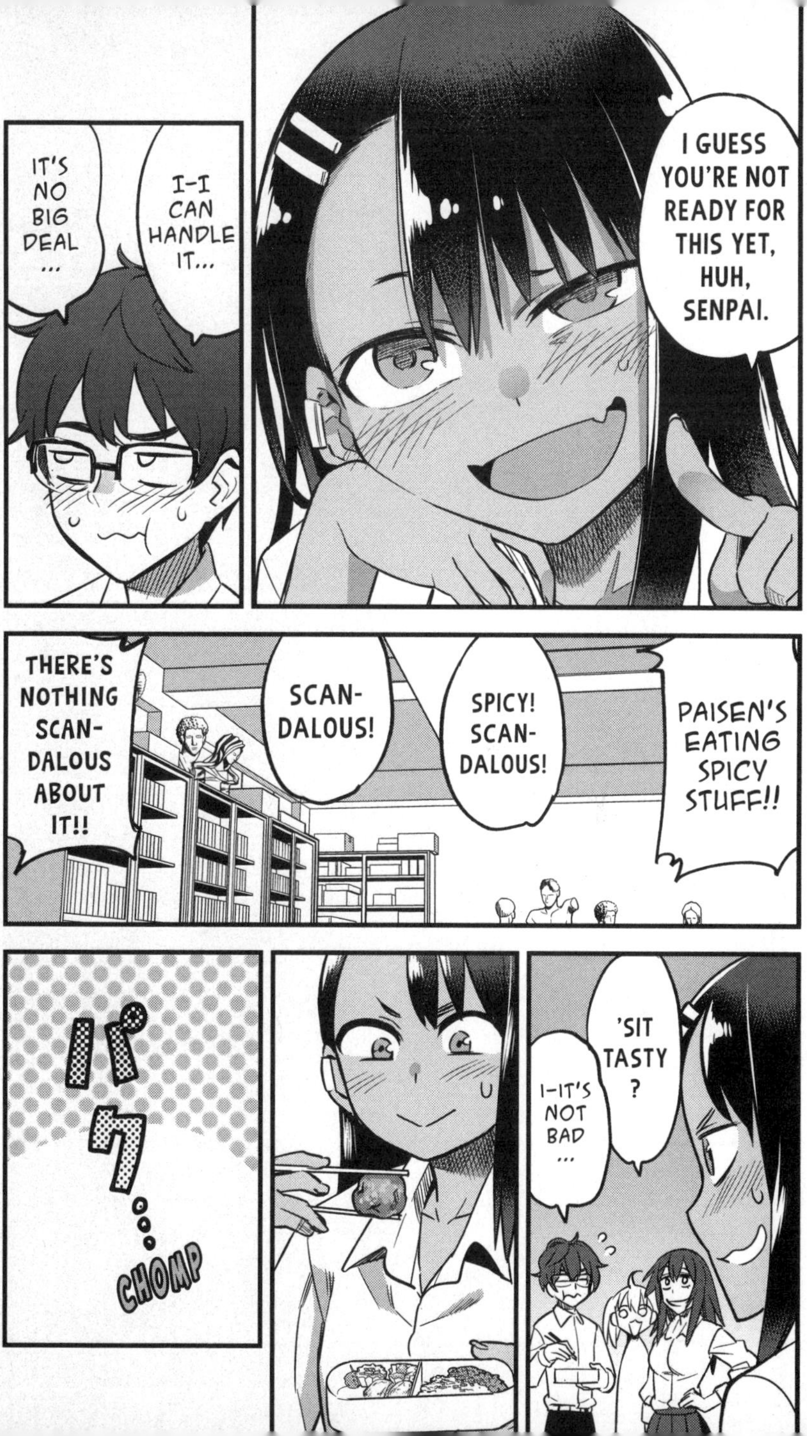
I GUESS YOU'RE NOT READY FOR THIS YET, HUH, SENPAI.
I-I CAN HANDLE IT...
IT'S NO BIG DEAL ...
PAISEN'S EATING SPICY STUFF!!
SPICY! SCAN-DALOUS!
SCAN-DALOUS!
THERE'S NOTHING SCAN-DALOUS ABOUT IT!!
'SIT TASTY ?
I-IT'S NOT BAD ...
パク...
CHOMP

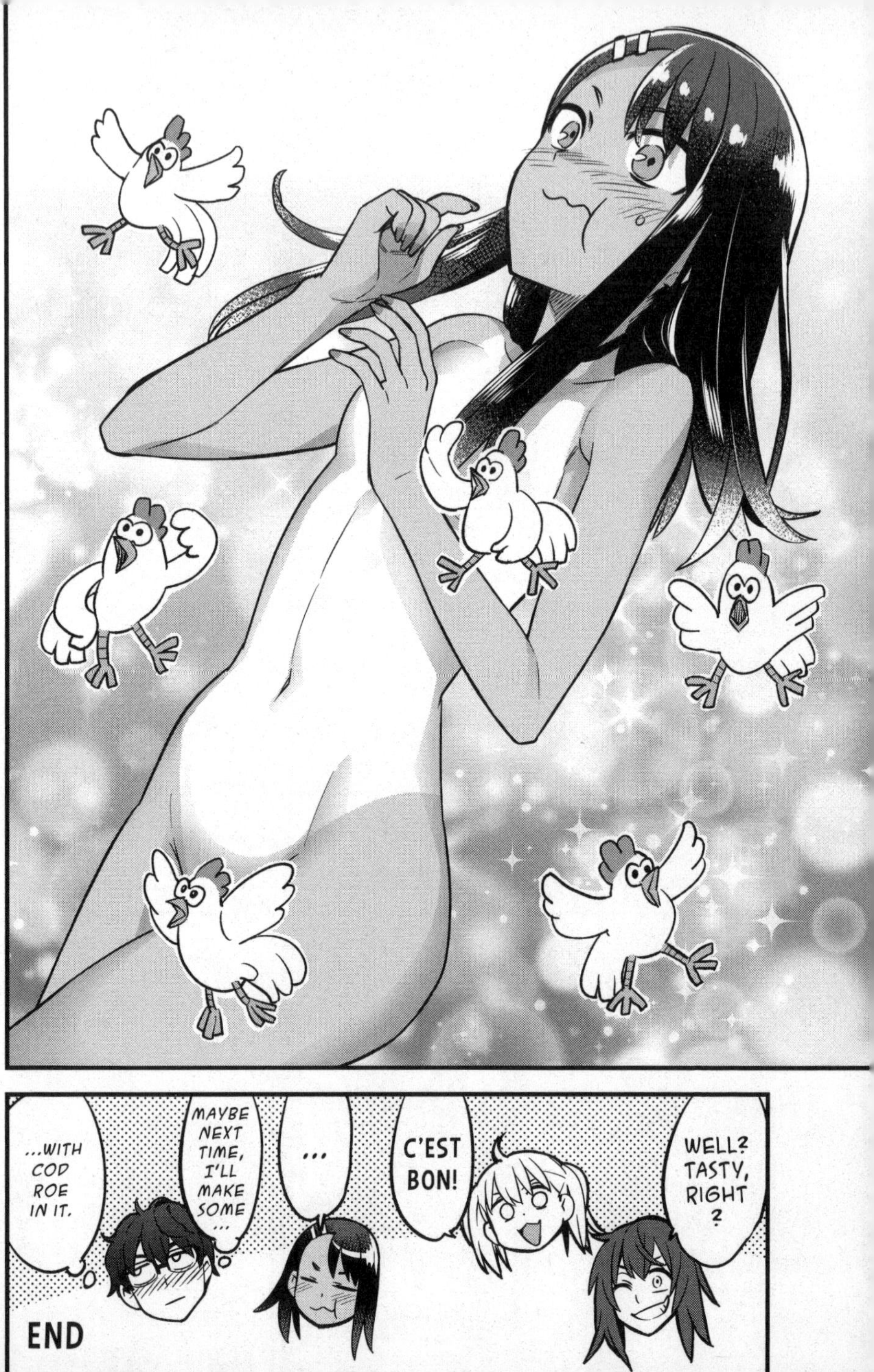
WELL? TASTY, RIGHT?
C'EST BON!
...
MAYBE NEXT TIME, I'LL MAKE SOME...
...WITH COD ROE IN IT.
END

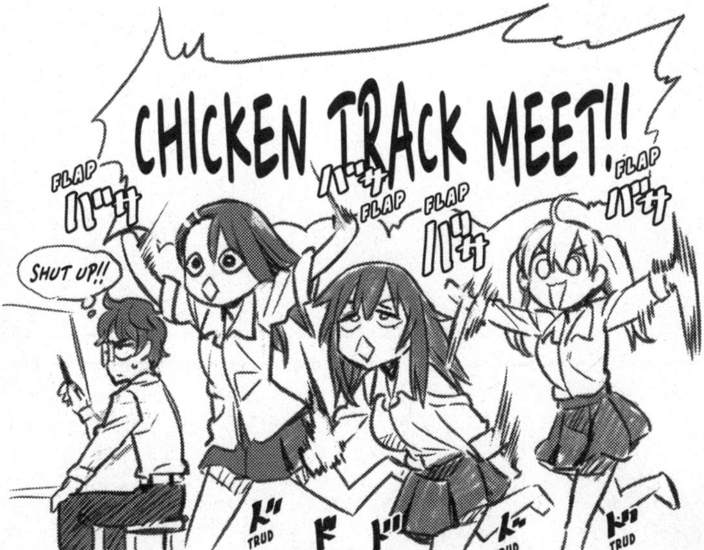
CHICKEN TRACK MEET!!
FLAP
FLAP
FLAP
FLAP
SHUT UP!!
TRUD
TRUD
TRUD
TRUD
TRUD

DON'T TOY WITH ME,
MISS NAGATORO

CHAPTER 34: AS IF A CREEP LIKE SENPAI COULD GO ON A PROPER DATE!!

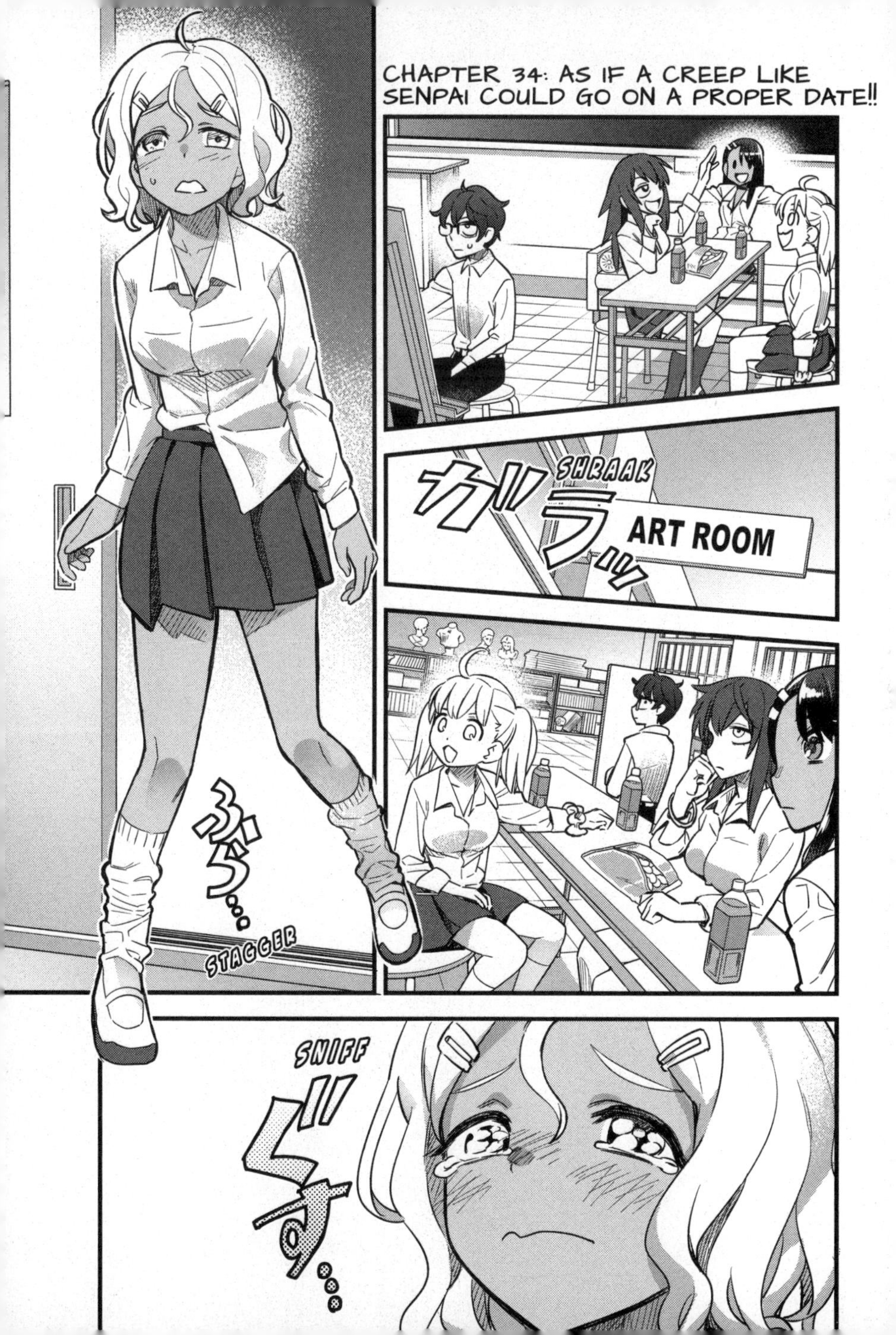
SHRAAK
ART ROOM
STAGGER
SNIFF

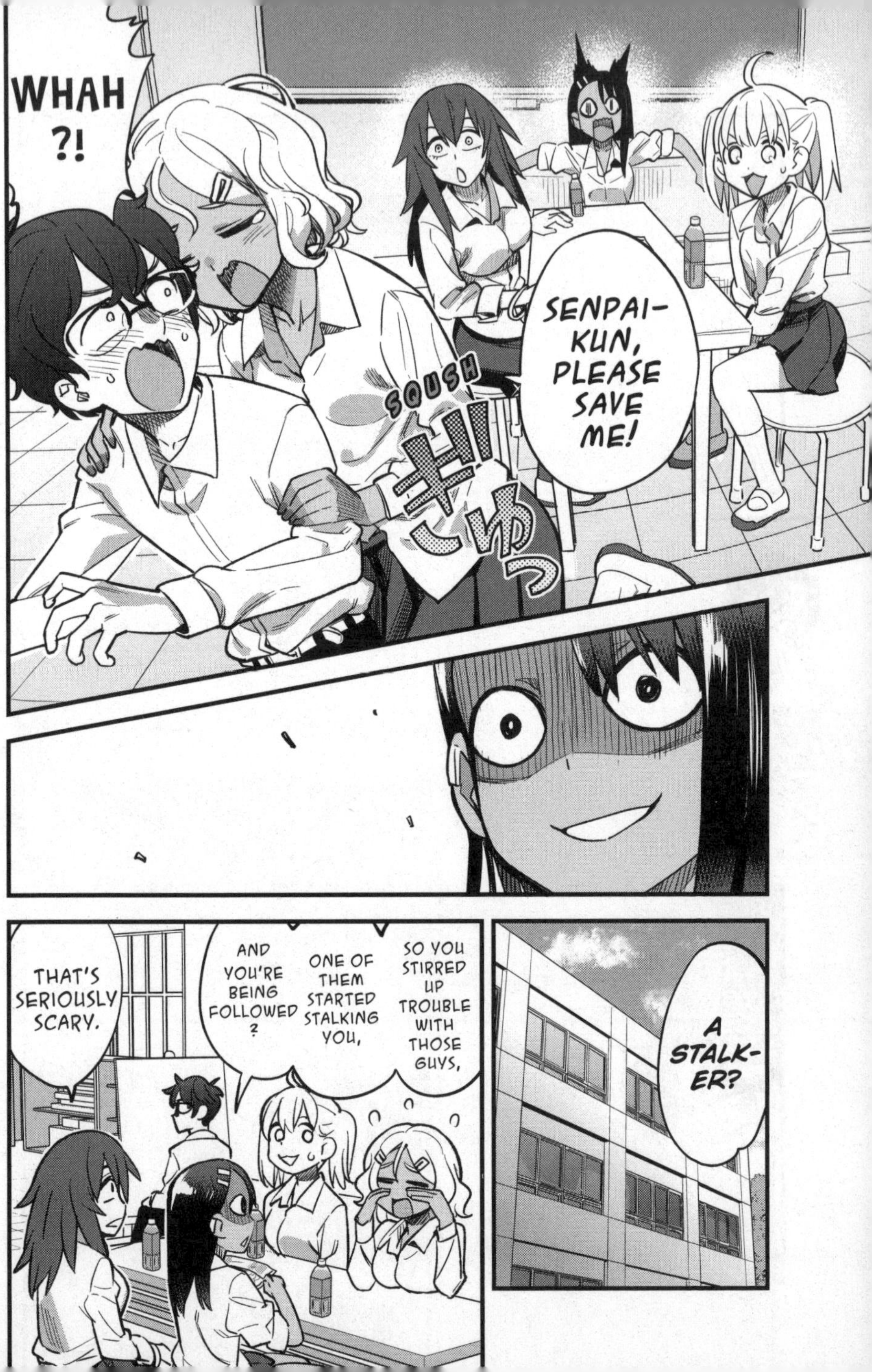
SENPAI-KUN, PLEASE SAVE ME!
SQUSH
ぎゅっ
WHAH ?!
A STALKER?
SO YOU STIRRED UP TROUBLE WITH THOSE GUYS,
ONE OF THEM STARTED STALKING YOU,
AND YOU'RE BEING FOLLOWED?
THAT'S SERIOUSLY SCARY.

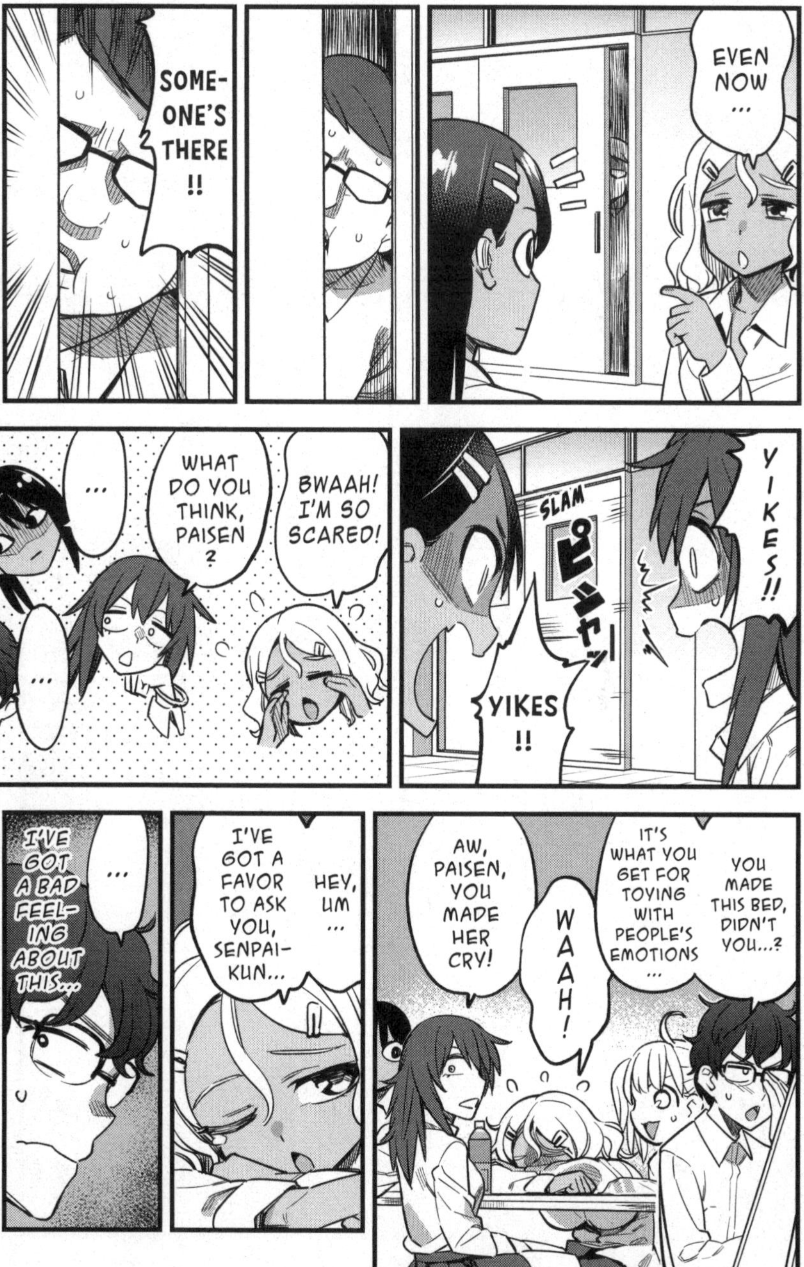
EVEN NOW ...
SOME-ONE'S THERE !!
YIKES!!
SLAM
ピシャッ
YIKES !!
BWAAH! I'M SO SCARED!
WHAT DO YOU THINK, PAISEN ?
...
...
YOU MADE THIS BED, DIDN'T YOU...?
IT'S WHAT YOU GET FOR TOYING WITH PEOPLE'S EMOTIONS ...
WAAH!
AW, PAISEN, YOU MADE HER CRY!
HEY, UM ...
I'VE GOT A FAVOR TO ASK YOU, SENPAI-KUN...
...
I'VE GOT A BAD FEELING ABOUT THIS...

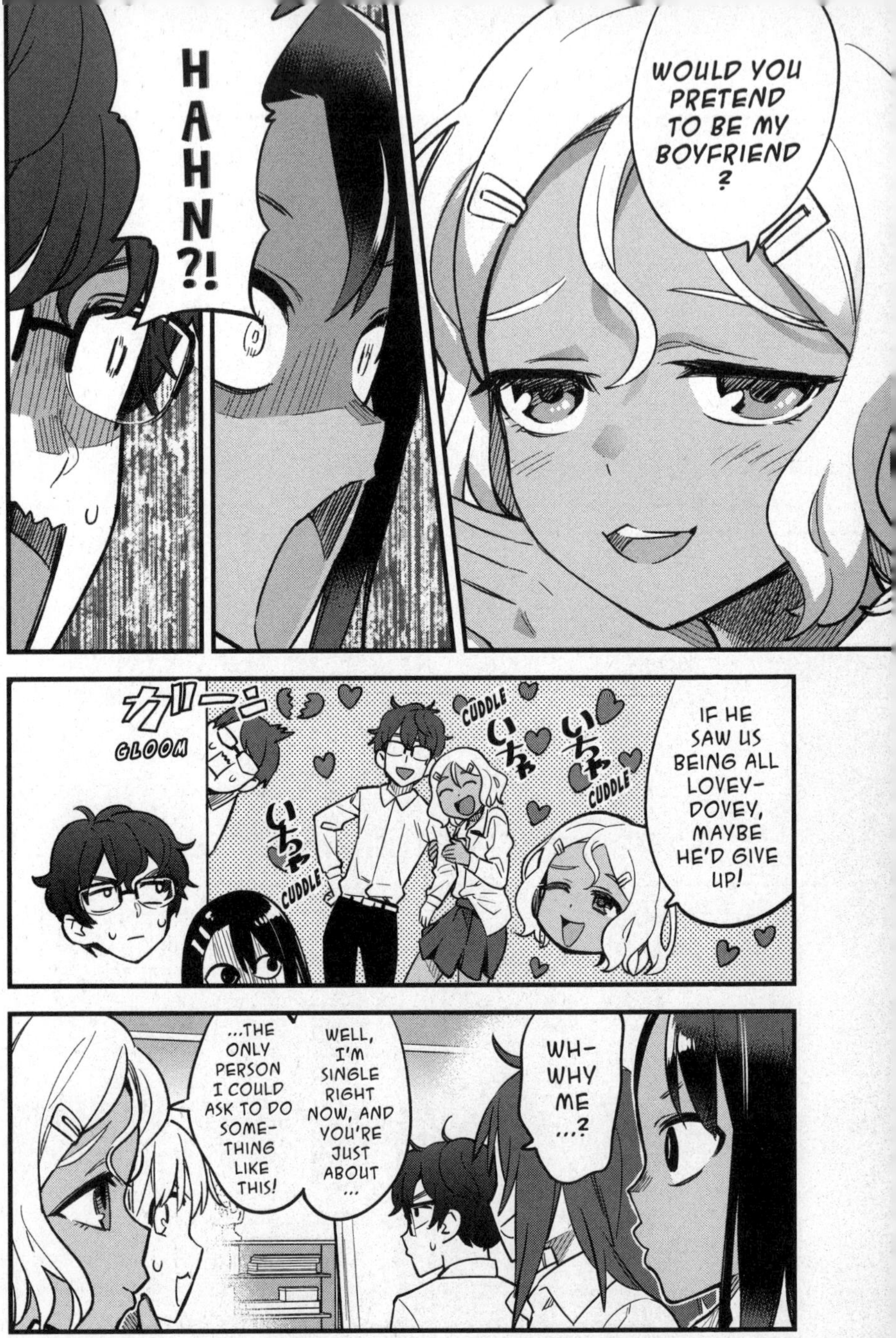
WOULD YOU PRETEND TO BE MY BOYFRIEND?
HAHN?!
IF HE SAW US BEING ALL LOVEY-DOVEY, MAYBE HE'D GIVE UP!
いちゃ
CUDDLE
いちゃ
CUDDLE
いちゃ
CUDDLE
GLOOM
WH-WHY ME...?
WELL, I'M SINGLE RIGHT NOW, AND YOU'RE JUST ABOUT...
...THE ONLY PERSON I COULD ASK TO DO SOME-THING LIKE THIS!

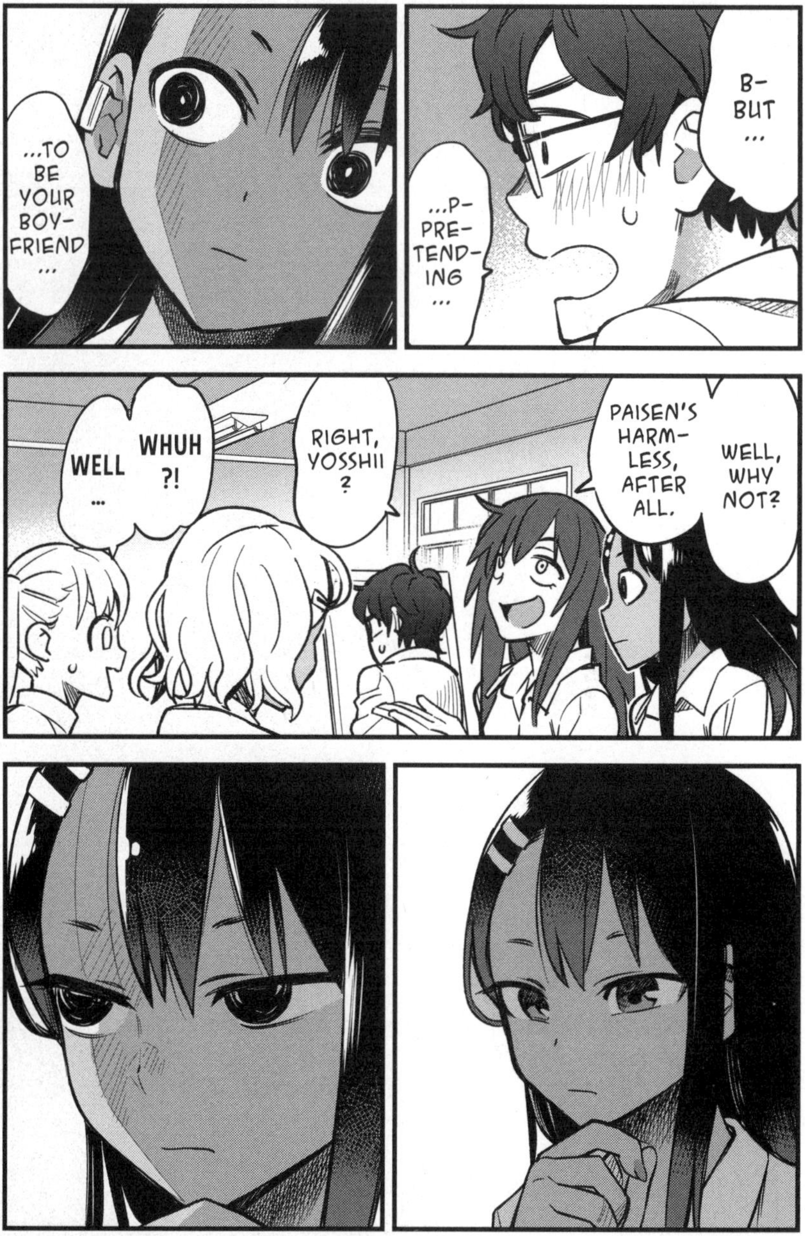

B- BUT ...
...P- PRE- TEND- ING ...
...TO BE YOUR BOY- FRIEND ...
WELL, WHY NOT?
PAISEN'S HARM- LESS, AFTER ALL.
RIGHT, YOSSHII?
WHUH ?!
WELL ...

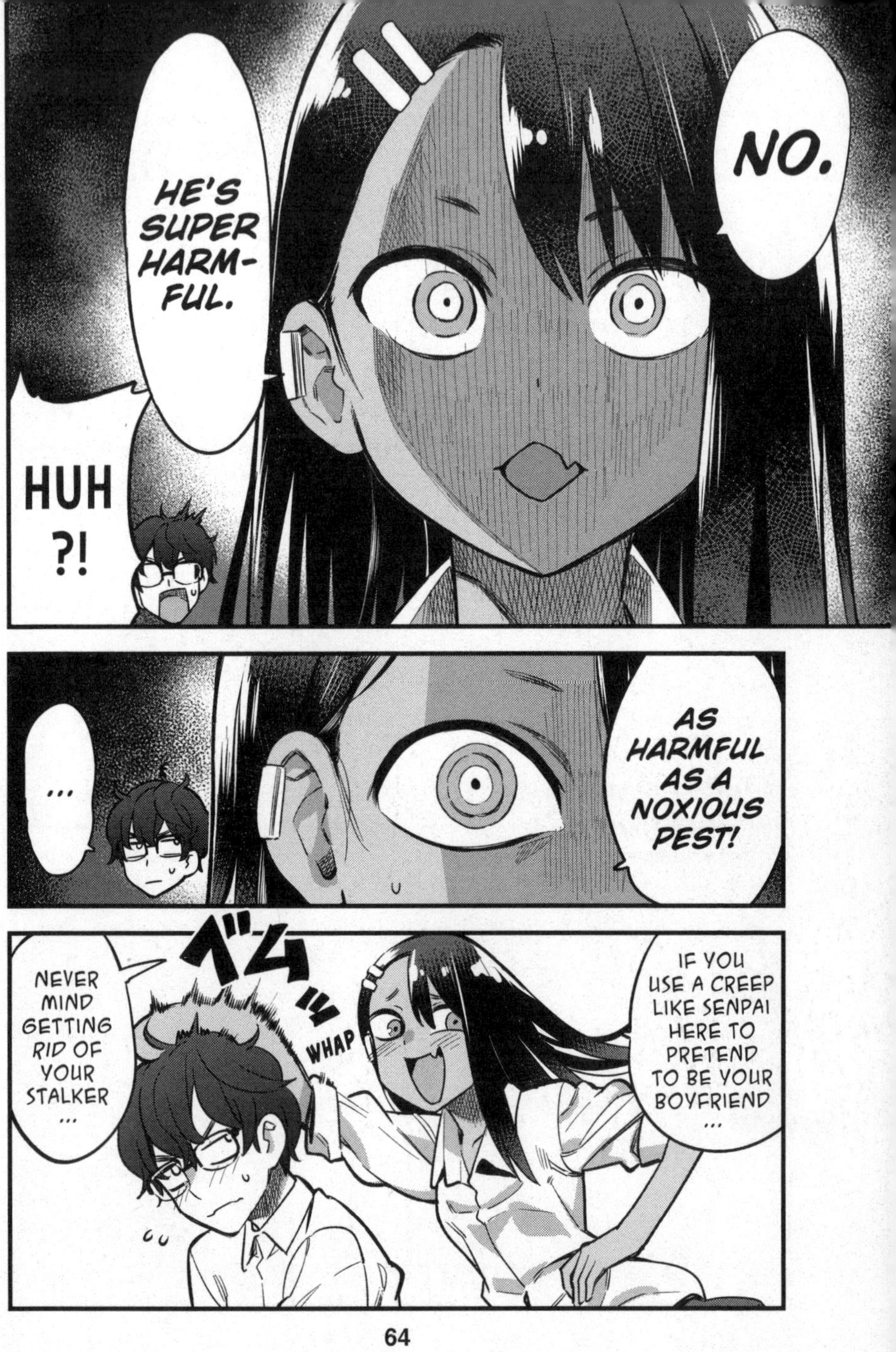
NO.
HE'S SUPER HARMFUL.
HUH ?!
AS HARMFUL AS A NOXIOUS PEST!
...
IF YOU USE A CREEP LIKE SENPAI HERE TO PRETEND TO BE YOUR BOYFRIEND ...
WHAP
NEVER MIND GETTING RID OF YOUR STALKER ...

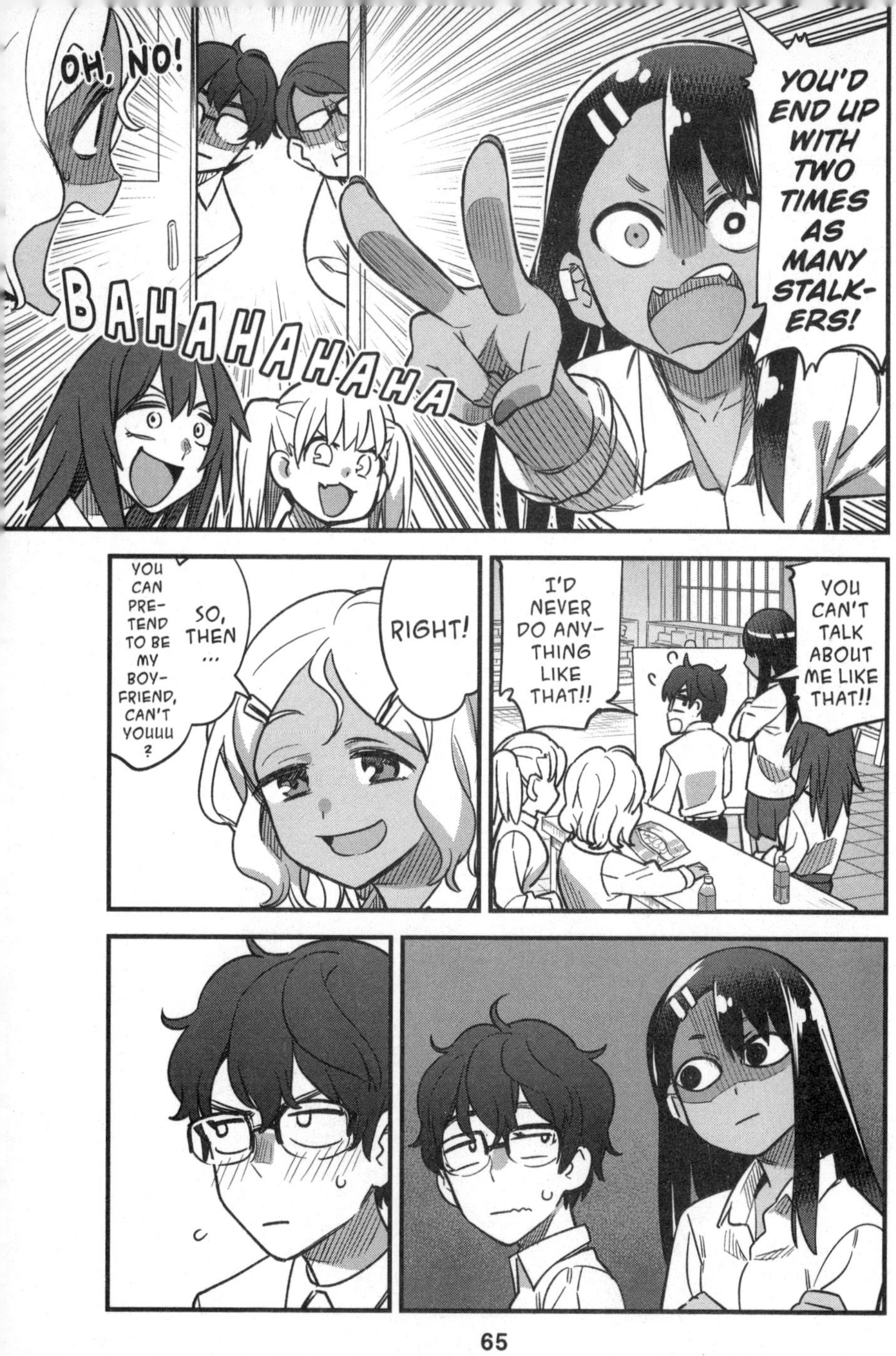
YOU'D END UP WITH TWO TIMES AS MANY STALK-ERS!
BAHAHAHAHAHA
OH, NO!
YOU CAN'T TALK ABOUT ME LIKE THAT!!
I'D NEVER DO ANY-THING LIKE THAT!!
RIGHT!
SO, THEN ...
YOU CAN PRE-TEND TO BE MY BOY-FRIEND, CAN'T YOUUU?

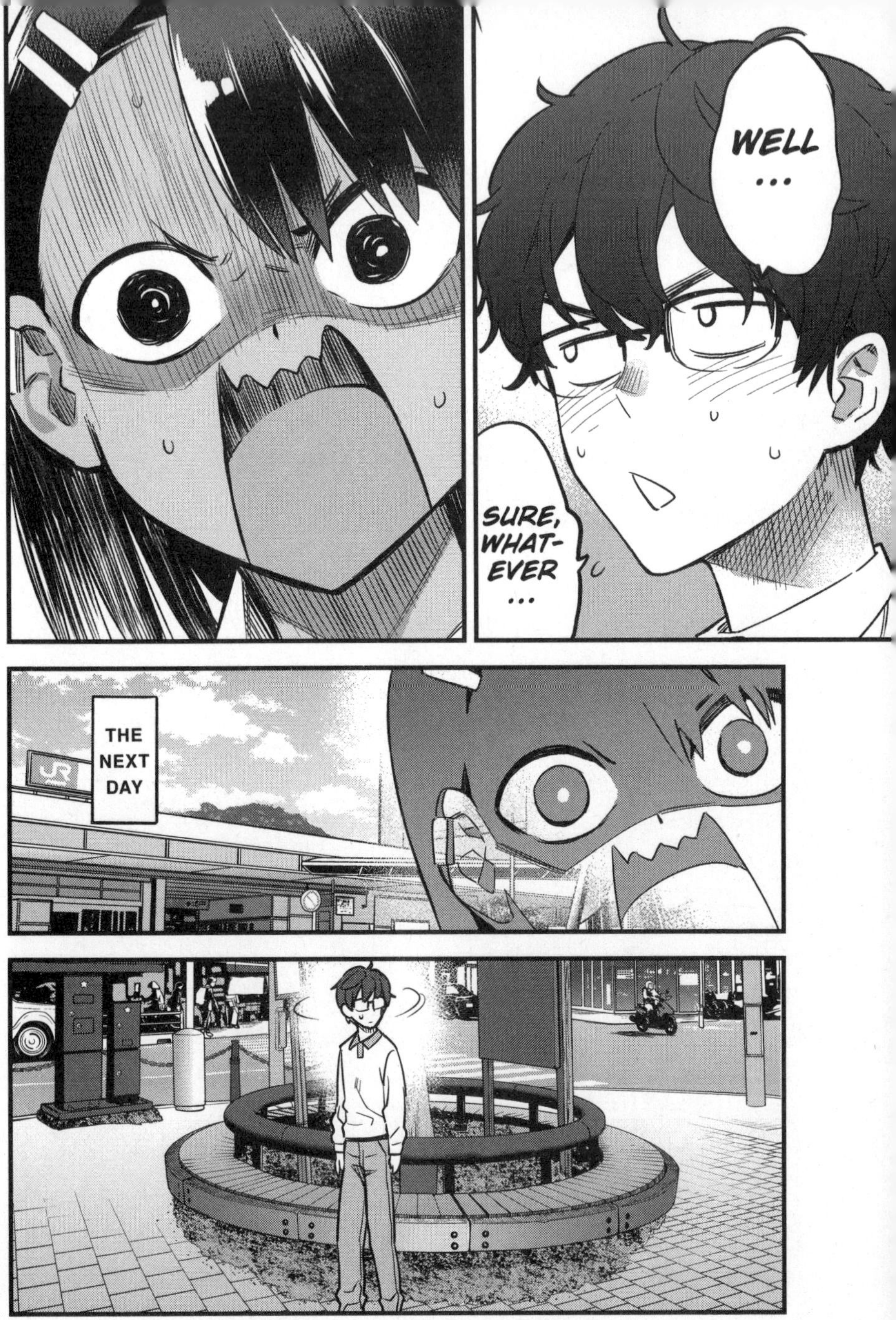
WELL ...
SURE, WHAT-EVER ...
THE NEXT DAY

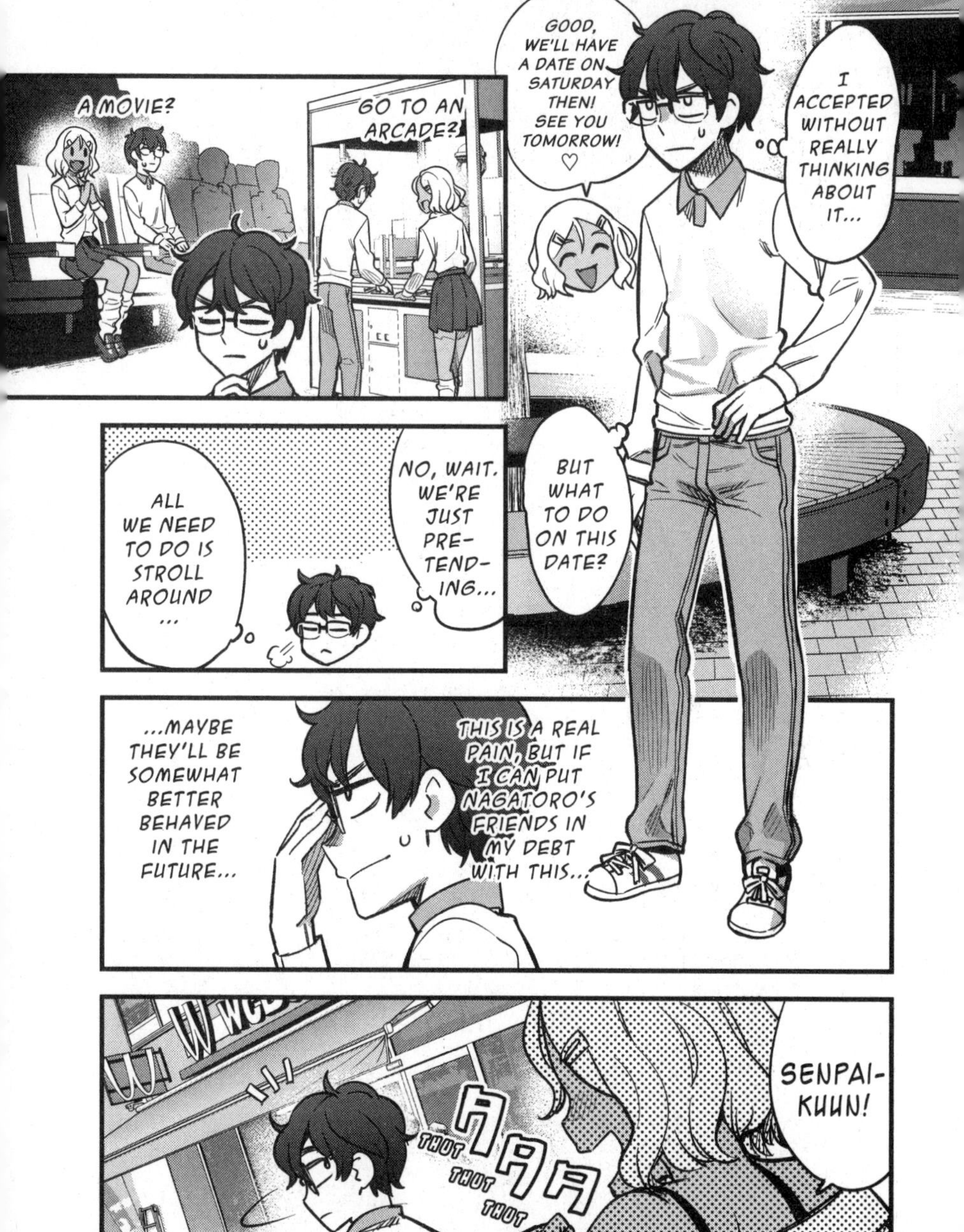
I ACCEPTED WITHOUT REALLY THINKING ABOUT IT...
GOOD, WE'LL HAVE A DATE ON SATURDAY THEN! SEE YOU TOMORROW! ♡
BUT WHAT TO DO ON THIS DATE?
GO TO AN ARCADE?
A MOVIE?
NO, WAIT. WE'RE JUST PRE-TEND-ING...
ALL WE NEED TO DO IS STROLL AROUND ...
THIS IS A REAL PAIN, BUT IF I CAN PUT NAGATORO'S FRIENDS IN MY DEBT WITH THIS...
...MAYBE THEY'LL BE SOMEWHAT BETTER BEHAVED IN THE FUTURE...
SENPAI-KUUN!
THUT THUT THUT

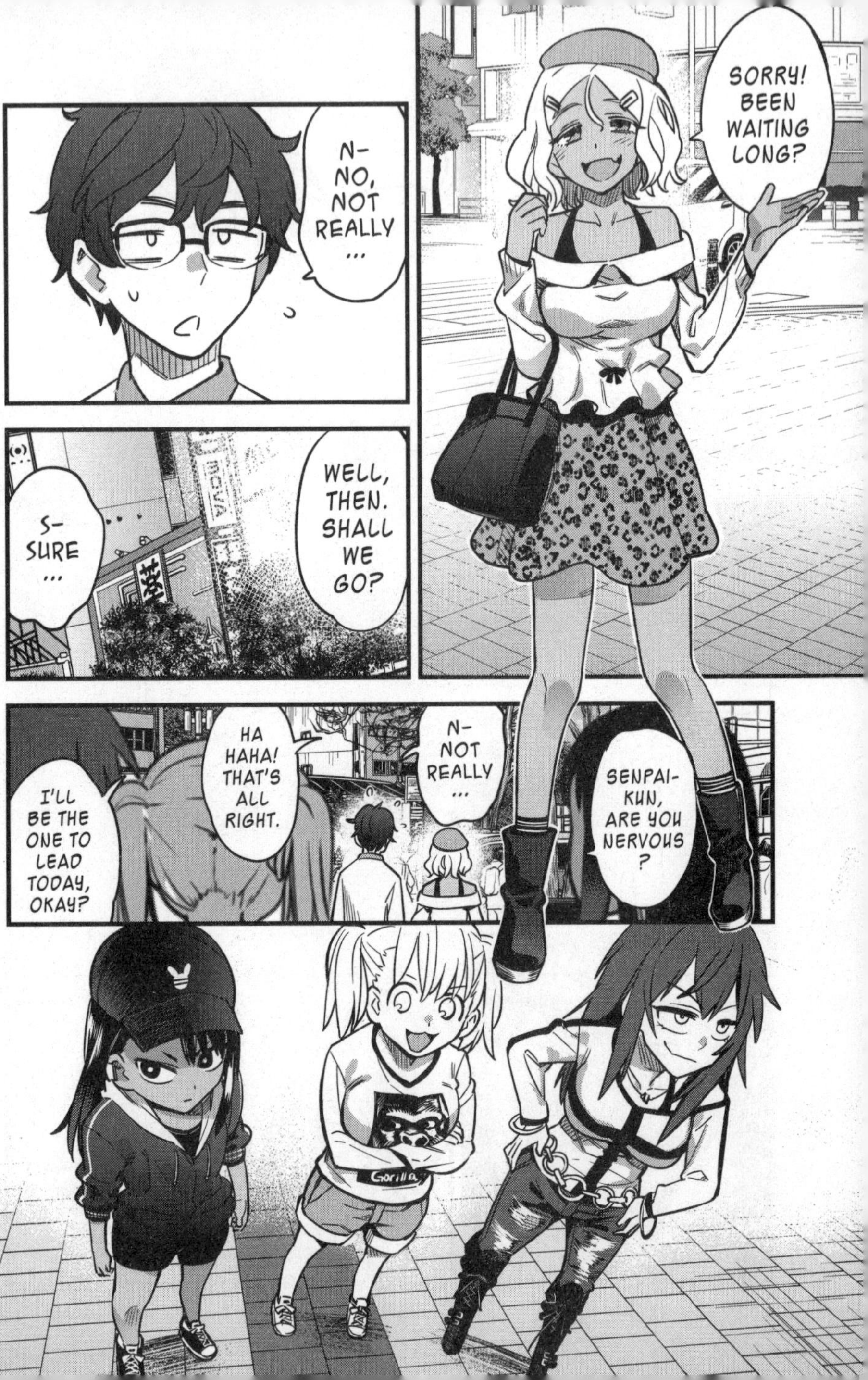
SORRY! BEEN WAITING LONG?
N-NO, NOT REALLY ...
WELL, THEN. SHALL WE GO?
S-SURE ...
SENPAI-KUN, ARE YOU NERVOUS?
N-NOT REALLY ...
HA HAHA! THAT'S ALL RIGHT.
I'LL BE THE ONE TO LEAD TODAY, OKAY?
Gorilla

PAISEN'S SUPER NERVOUS, HUH.
...
DOESN'T THIS SEEM LIKE THE KINDA THING THAT WOULD BE IN THE TYPE OF ANIME PAISEN PROBABLY LIKES?
IT *DOES* SEEM LIKE THAT!
WHERE TWO PEOPLE PRETEND TO BE ON A DATE FOR SOME REASON ...
SOME REASON !!
AND THEN IT'S, LIKE, THE LIE BRINGS OUT THE TRUTH.
AND THE VIBE STARTS TO GET BETTER AND BETTER ...

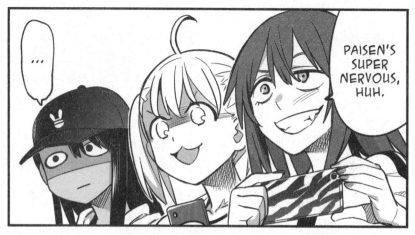

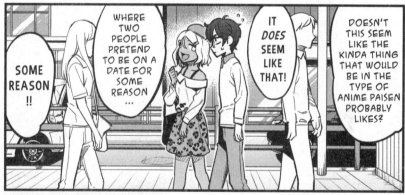

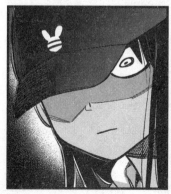

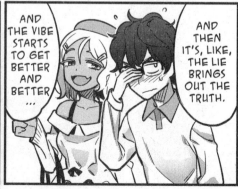

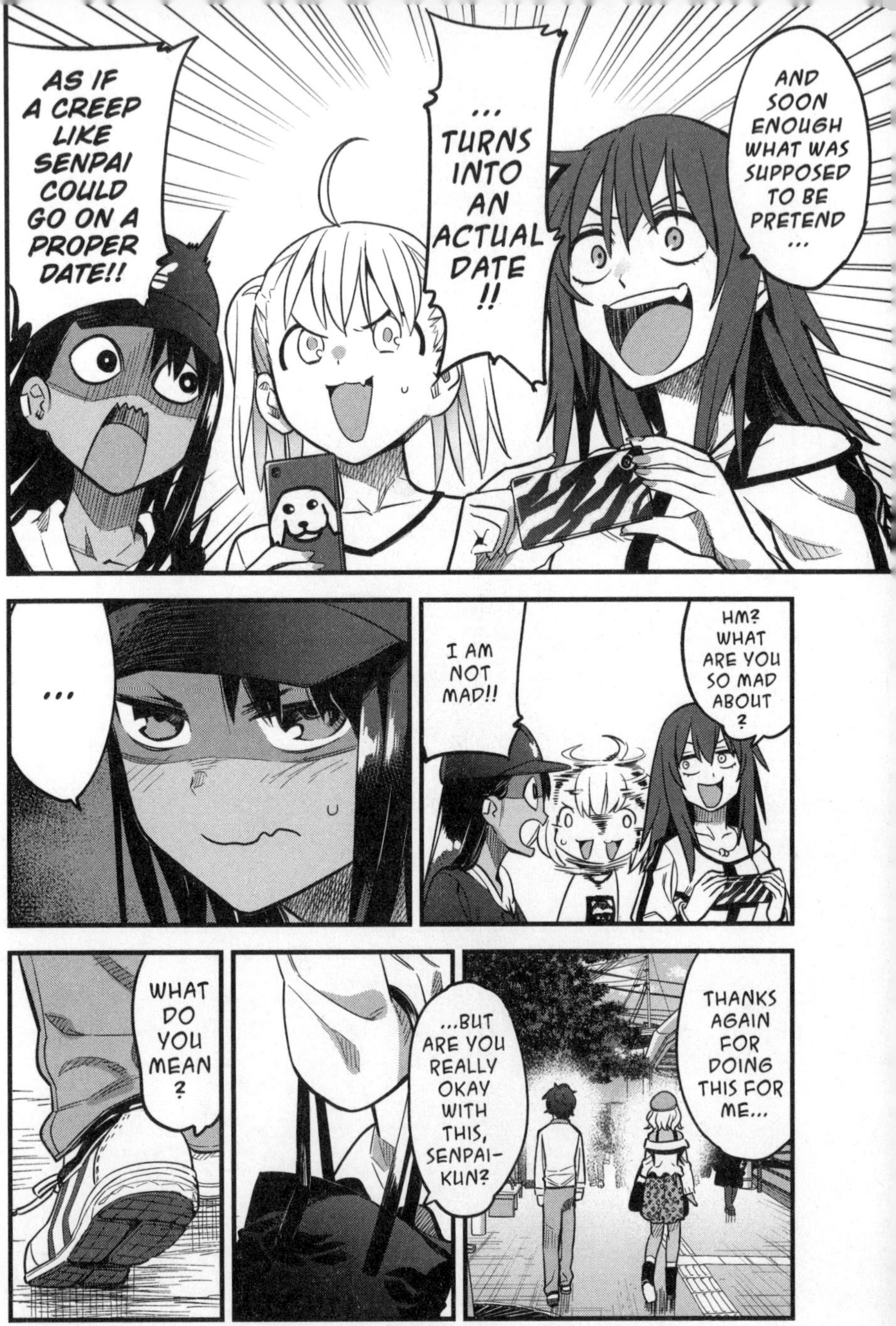
AND SOON ENOUGH WHAT WAS SUPPOSED TO BE PRETEND...
...TURNS INTO AN ACTUAL DATE!!
AS IF A CREEP LIKE SENPAI COULD GO ON A PROPER DATE!!
HM? WHAT ARE YOU SO MAD ABOUT?
I AM NOT MAD!!
...
THANKS AGAIN FOR DOING THIS FOR ME...
...BUT ARE YOU REALLY OKAY WITH THIS, SENPAI-KUN?
WHAT DO YOU MEAN?

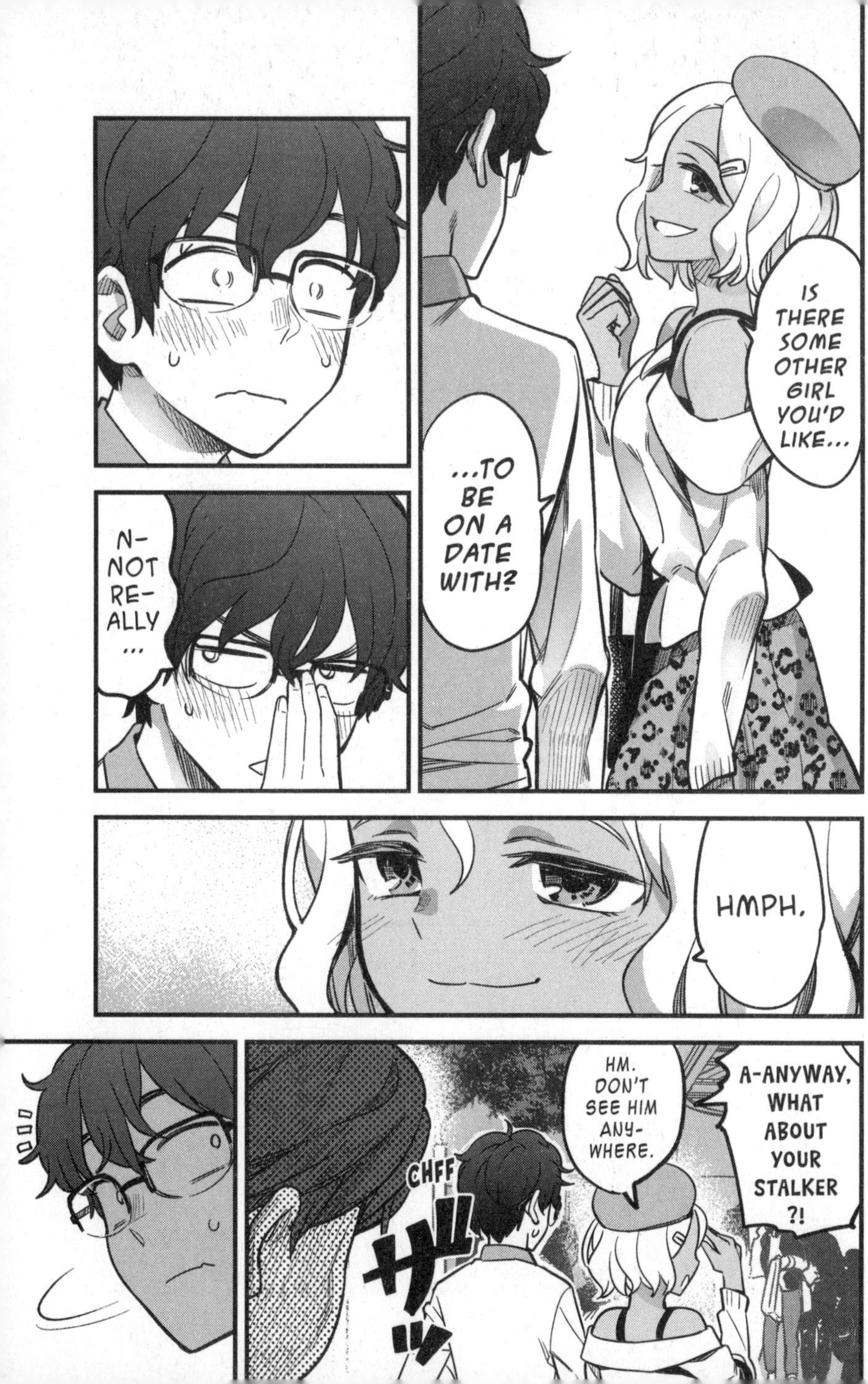
IS THERE SOME OTHER GIRL YOU'D LIKE...
...TO BE ON A DATE WITH?
N-NOT RE-ALLY...
HMPH.
A-ANYWAY, WHAT ABOUT YOUR STALKER?!
HM. DON'T SEE HIM ANY-WHERE.
CHFF

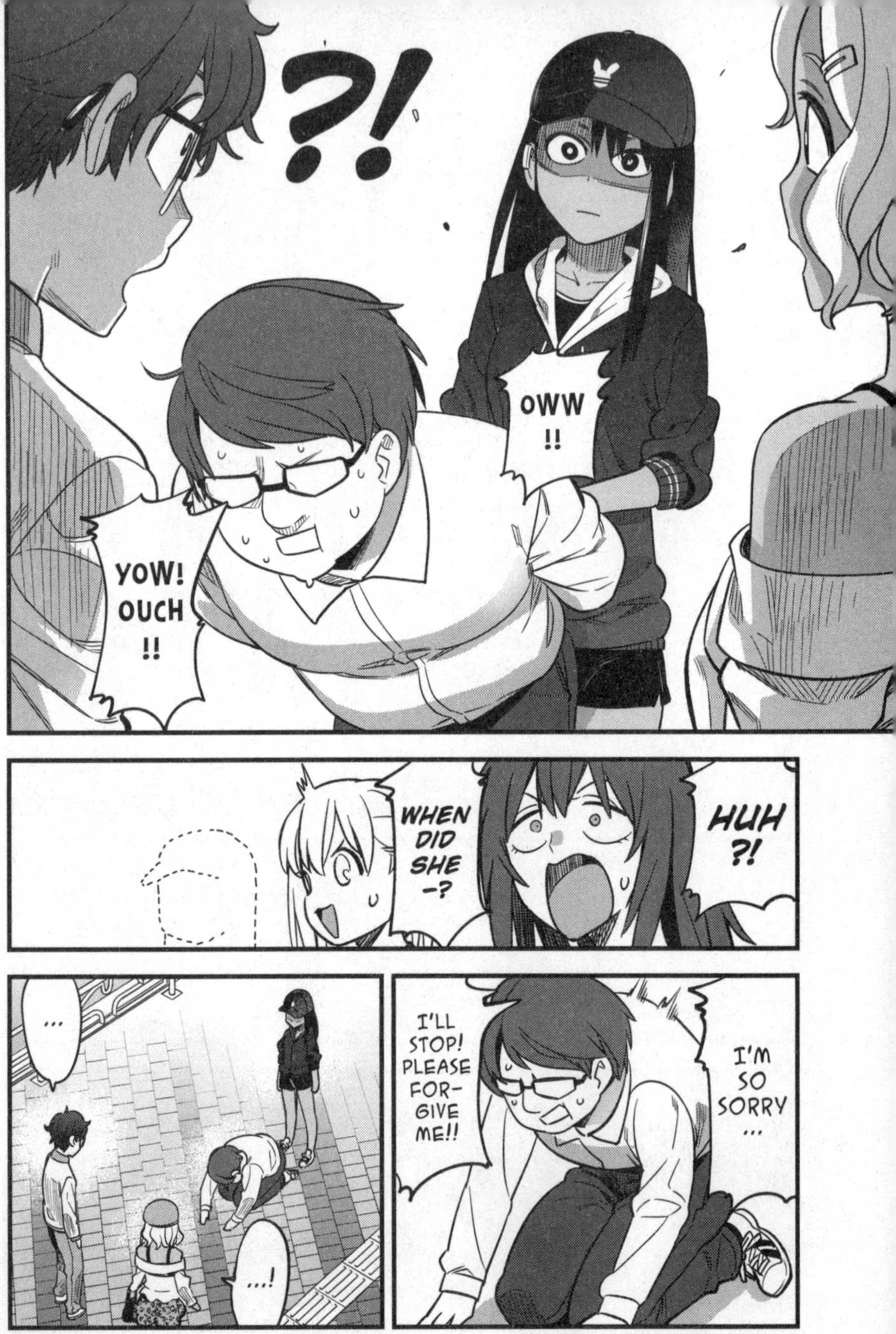
?!
OWW !!
YOW! OUCH !!
HUH ?!
WHEN DID SHE -?
I'M SO SORRY ...
I'LL STOP! PLEASE FOR-GIVE ME!!
...
...!

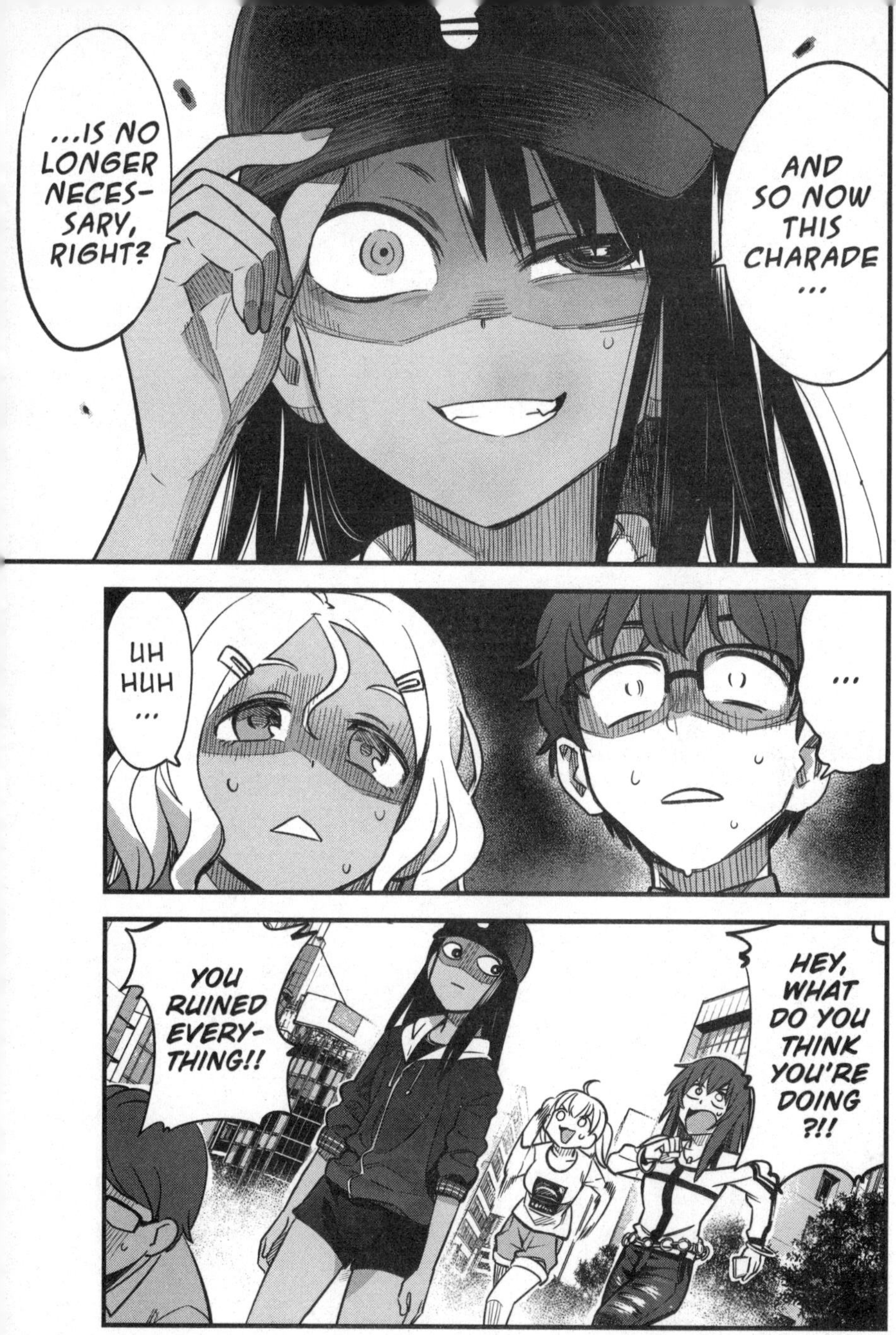
AND SO NOW THIS CHARADE...
...IS NO LONGER NECES-SARY, RIGHT?
...
UH HUH...
HEY, WHAT DO YOU THINK YOU'RE DOING?!!
YOU RUINED EVERY-THING!!

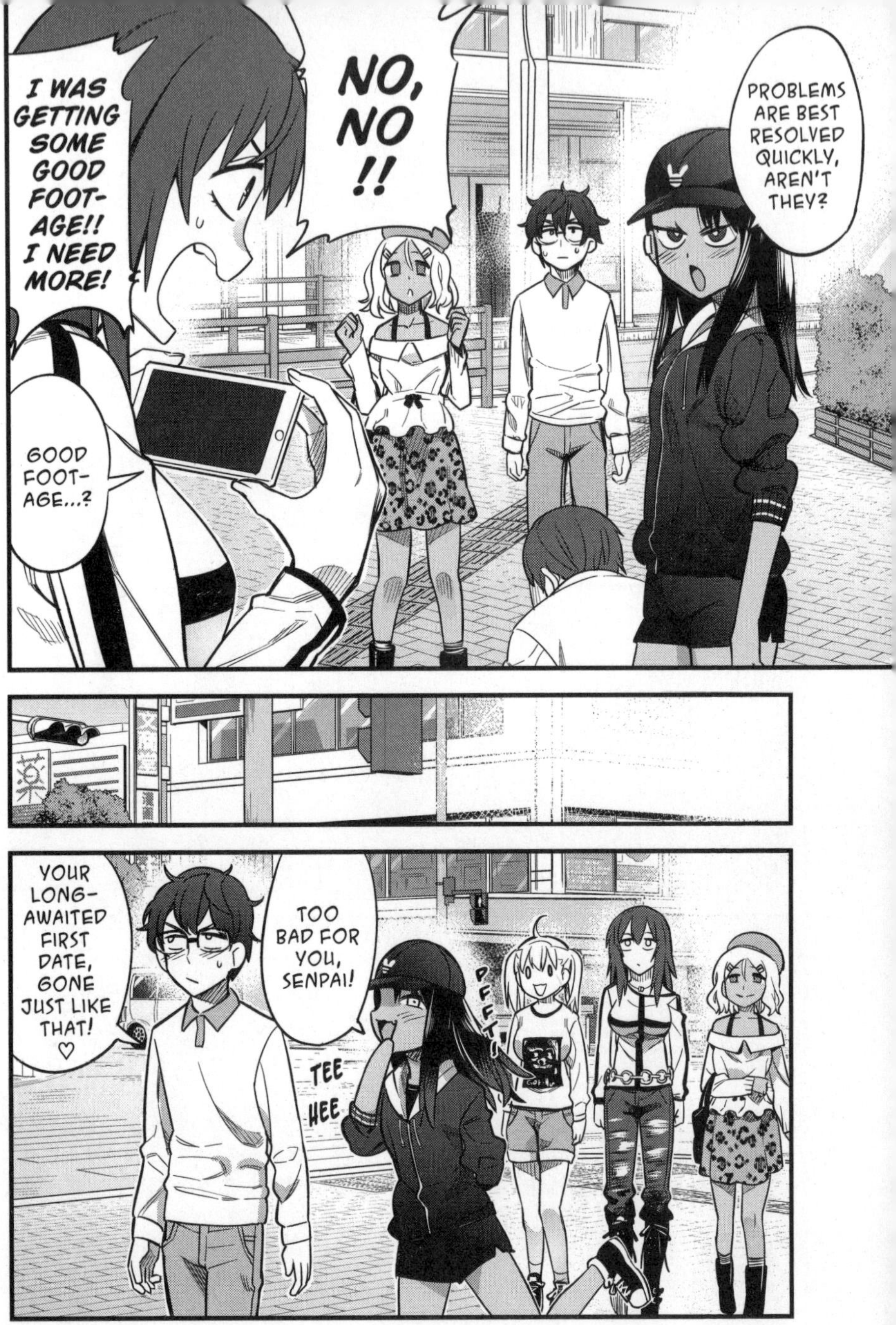
PROBLEMS ARE BEST RESOLVED QUICKLY, AREN'T THEY?
NO, NO!!
I WAS GETTING SOME GOOD FOOTAGE!! I NEED MORE!
GOOD FOOTAGE...?
PFFT
TOO BAD FOR YOU, SENPAI!
TEE HEE
YOUR LONG-AWAITED FIRST DATE, GONE JUST LIKE THAT! ♡

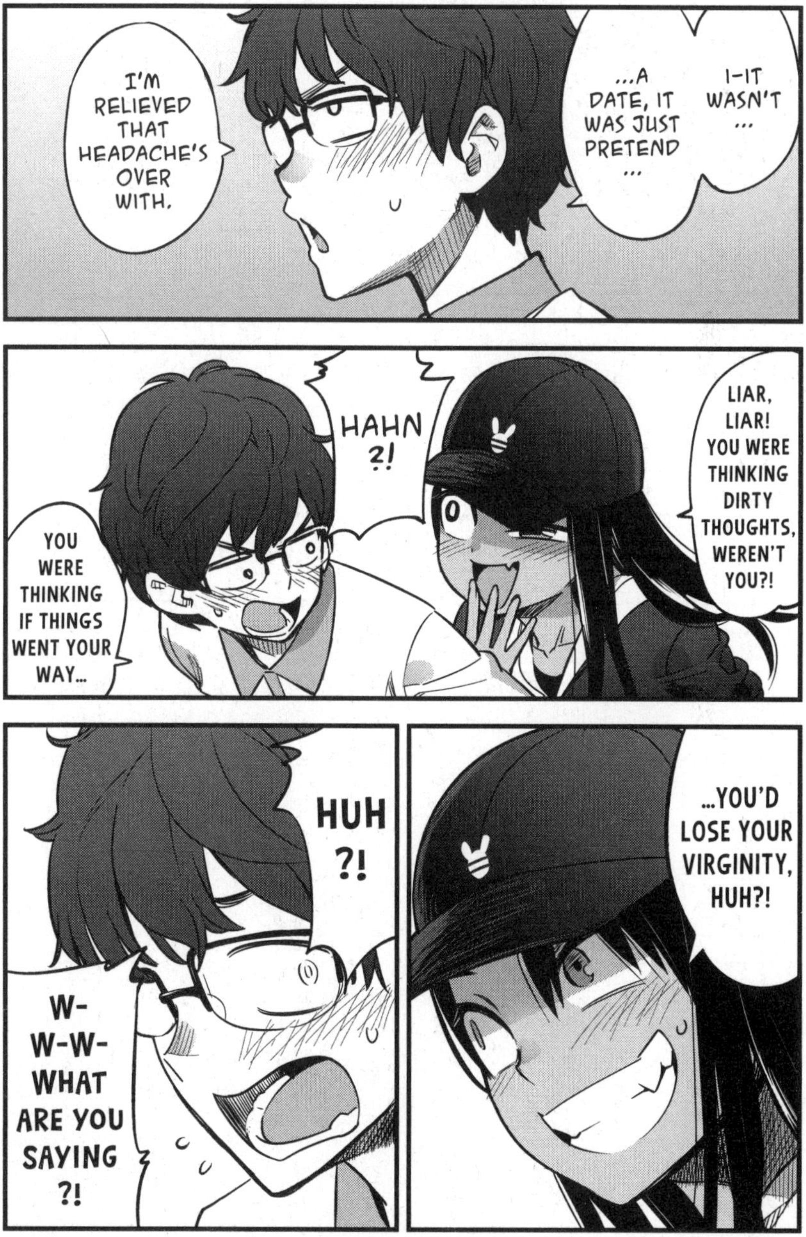
I-IT WASN'T ...
...A DATE, IT WAS JUST PRETEND ...
I'M RELIEVED THAT HEADACHE'S OVER WITH.
LIAR, LIAR! YOU WERE THINKING DIRTY THOUGHTS, WEREN'T YOU?!
HAHN ?!
YOU WERE THINKING IF THINGS WENT YOUR WAY...
...YOU'D LOSE YOUR VIRGINITY, HUH?!
HUH ?!
W-W-W-WHAT ARE YOU SAYING ?!

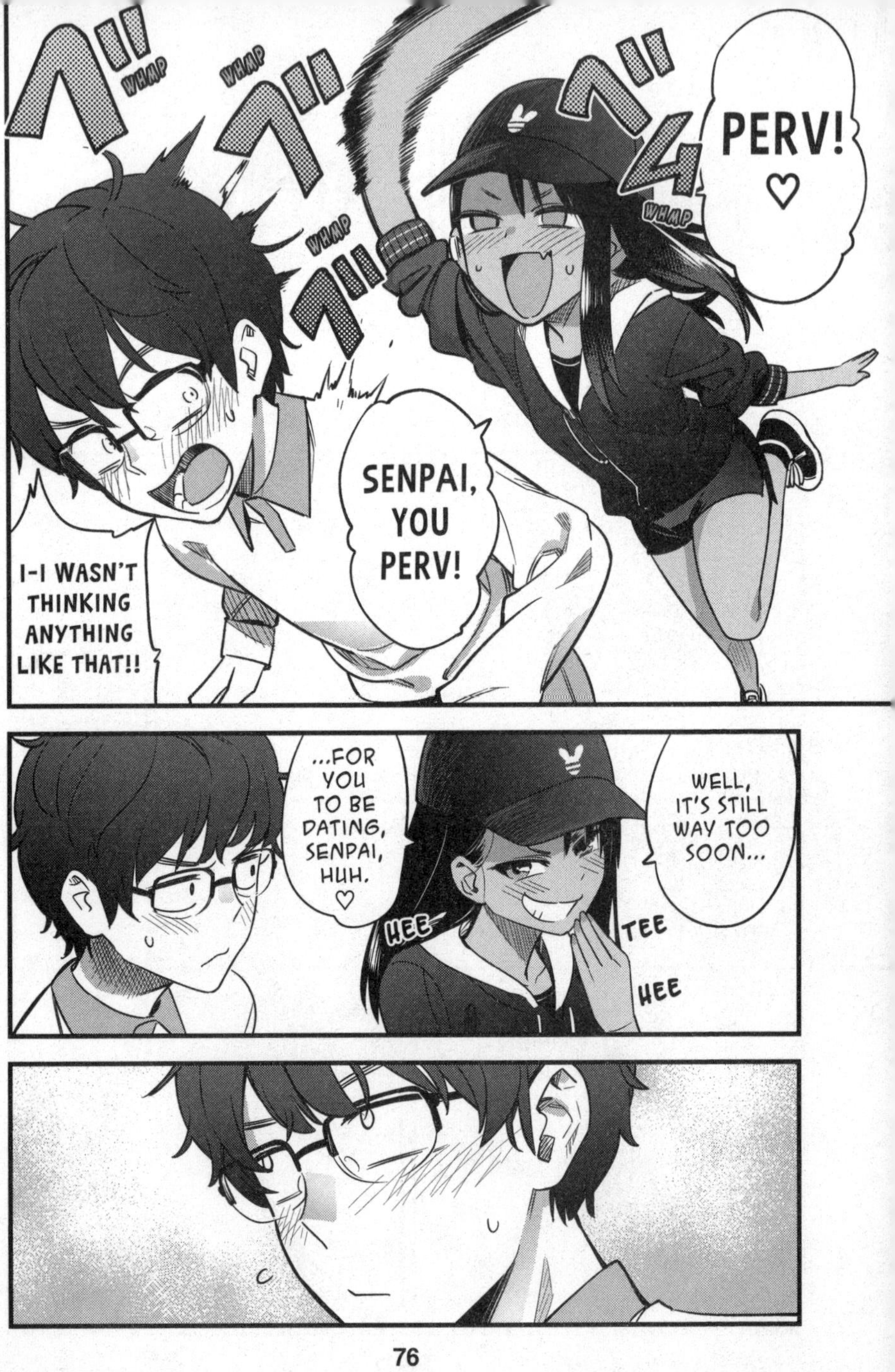
PERV! ♡
WHMP
WHMP
WHMP
WHMP
SENPAI, YOU PERV!
I-I WASN'T THINKING ANYTHING LIKE THAT!!
WELL, IT'S STILL WAY TOO SOON...
...FOR YOU TO BE DATING, SENPAI, HUH. ♡
TEE
HEE
HEE

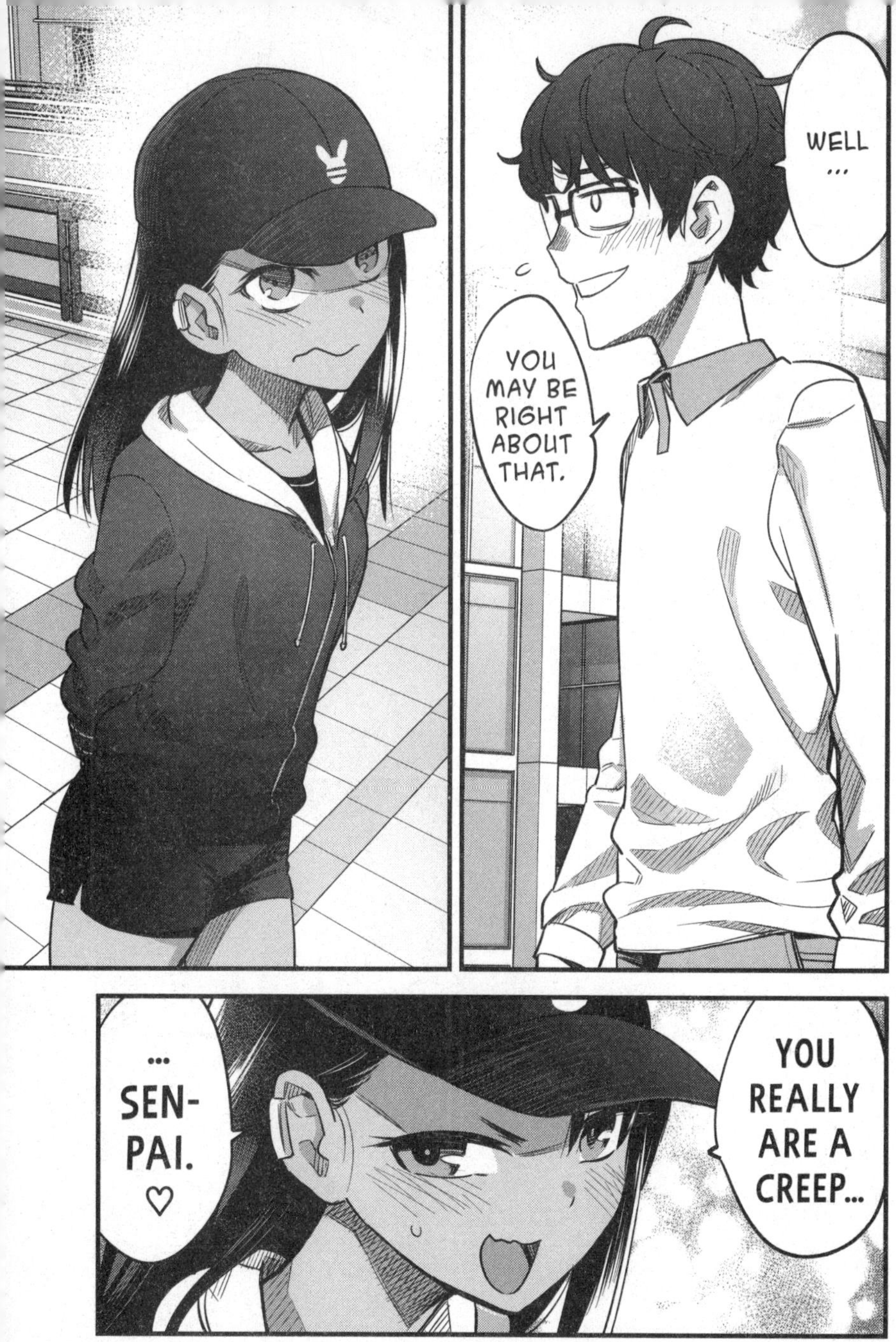
WELL ...
YOU MAY BE RIGHT ABOUT THAT.
YOU REALLY ARE A CREEP...
... SEN-PAI. ♡

END

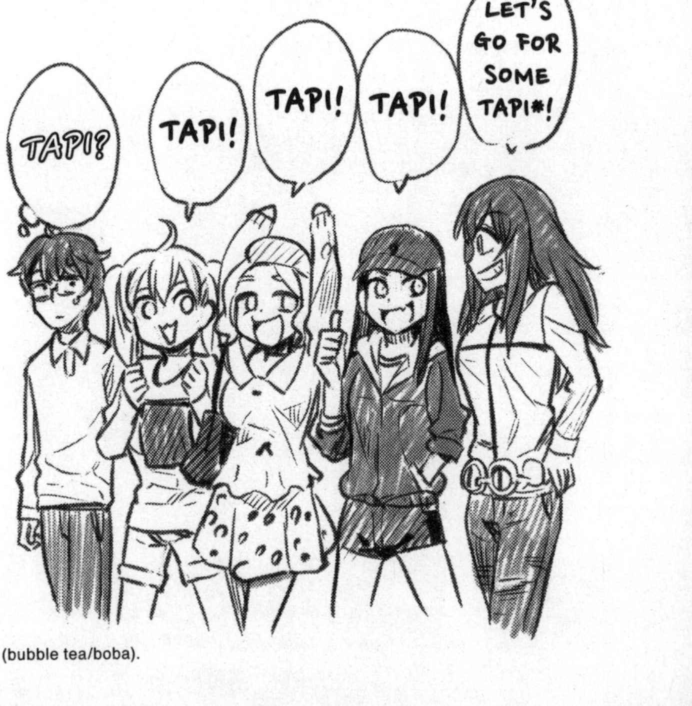
LET'S GO FOR SOME TAPI*!
TAPI!
TAPI!
TAPI!
TAPI?

*Short for "tapioca drink" (bubble tea/boba).

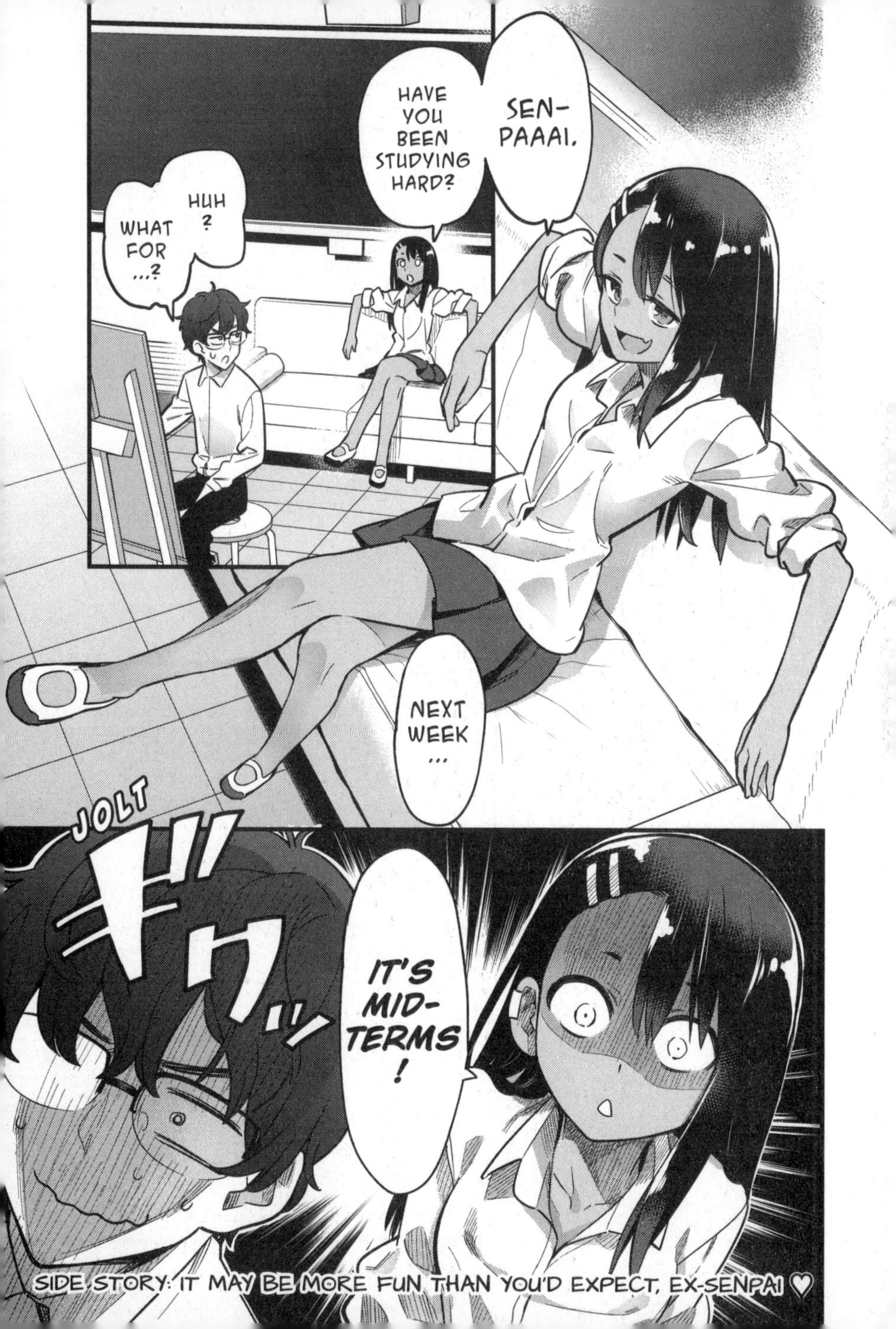
SEN-PAAAI.
HAVE YOU BEEN STUDYING HARD?
HUH?
WHAT FOR...?
NEXT WEEK...
IT'S MID-TERMS!
JOLT
SIDE STORY: IT MAY BE MORE FUN THAN YOU'D EXPECT, EX-SENPAI ♡

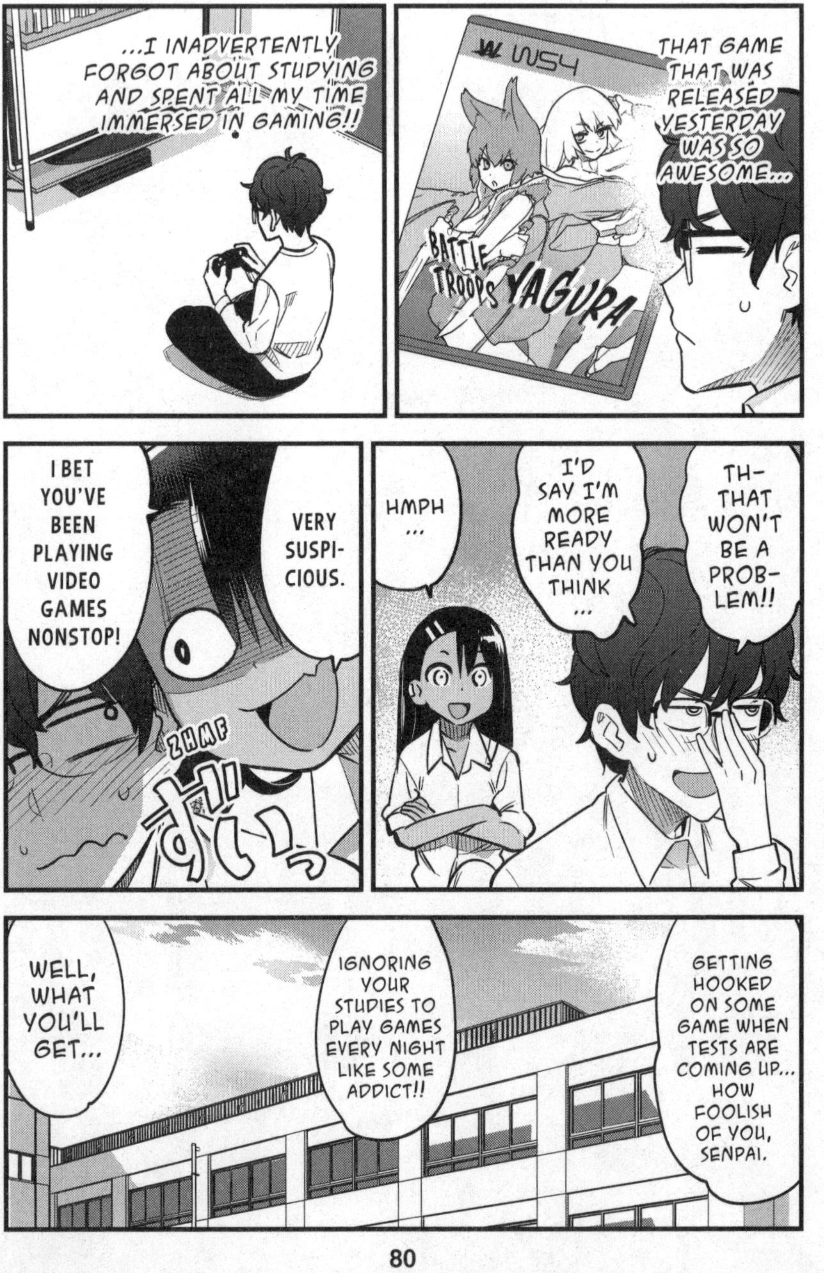
THAT GAME THAT WAS RELEASED YESTERDAY WAS SO AWESOME...
WS4
BATTLE TROOPS YAGURA
...I INADVERTENTLY FORGOT ABOUT STUDYING AND SPENT ALL MY TIME IMMERSED IN GAMING!!
TH-THAT WON'T BE A PROB-LEM!!
I'D SAY I'M MORE READY THAN YOU THINK...
HMPH...
VERY SUSPI-CIOUS.
I BET YOU'VE BEEN PLAYING VIDEO GAMES NONSTOP!
ZHMF
すいっ
GETTING HOOKED ON SOME GAME WHEN TESTS ARE COMING UP... HOW FOOLISH OF YOU, SENPAI.
IGNORING YOUR STUDIES TO PLAY GAMES EVERY NIGHT LIKE SOME ADDICT!!
WELL, WHAT YOU'LL GET...

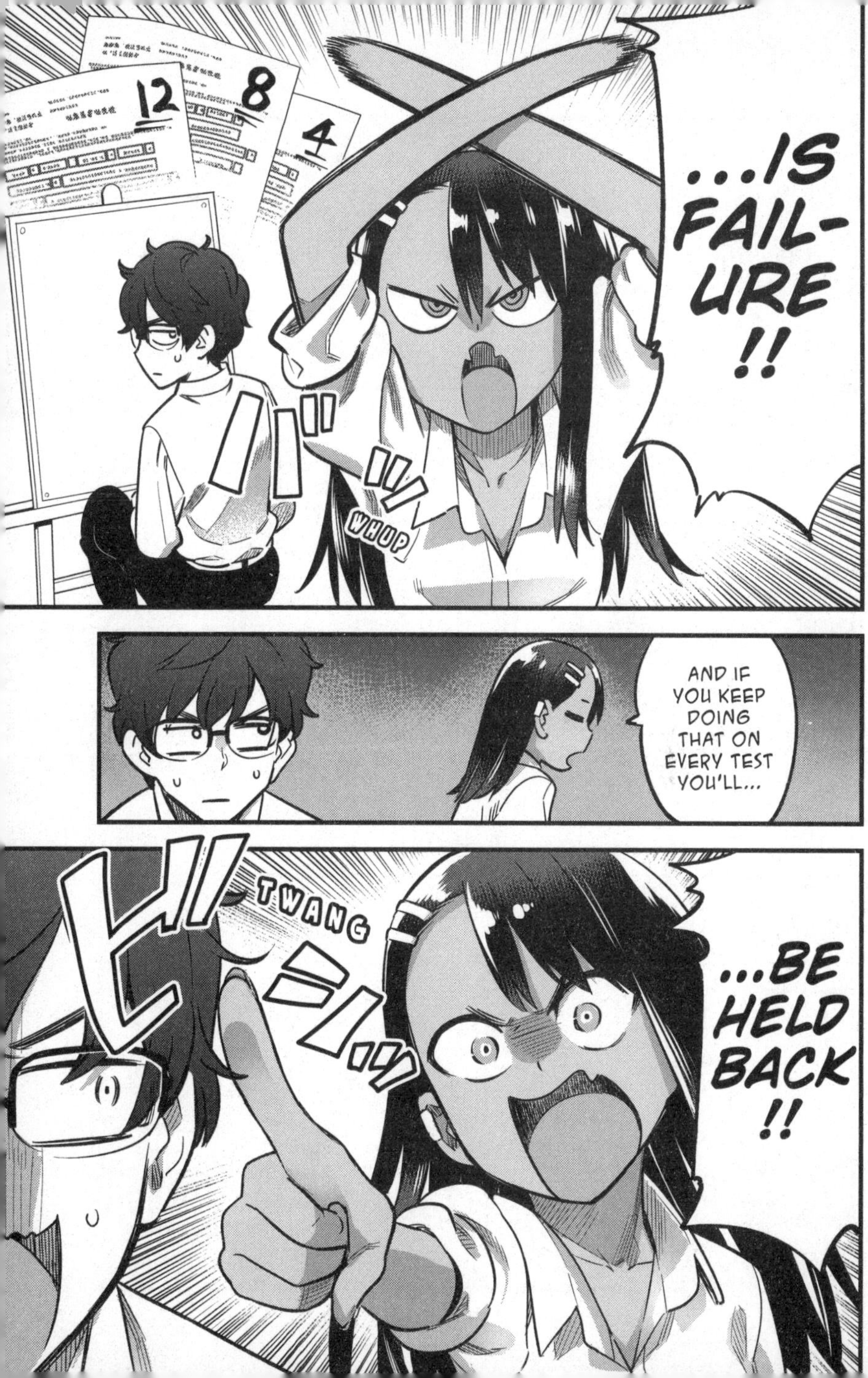
12
8
4
...IS FAIL-URE !!
WHUP
AND IF YOU KEEP DOING THAT ON EVERY TEST YOU'LL...
TWANG
...BE HELD BACK !!

THERE'S NO WAY I'D EVER BE HELD BACK!!

FWIP

FWIP

NO, NO, NO!!

YOU COOL? YOU COOL WITH BEING HELD BACK?

BEING HELD BACK?

I TOLD YOU, I WON'T...

YOU COOL WITH BEING HELD BACK?

WHMP

YOU COOL? YOU COOL WITH THAT?

WHMP

WHMP

WHMP

WHMP

E-EVEN IF THAT WERE TO HAPPEN, IT WOULDN'T BOTHER ME.

GRR

HUH, HUH, HUH?

HUH, SENPAI, HUH?

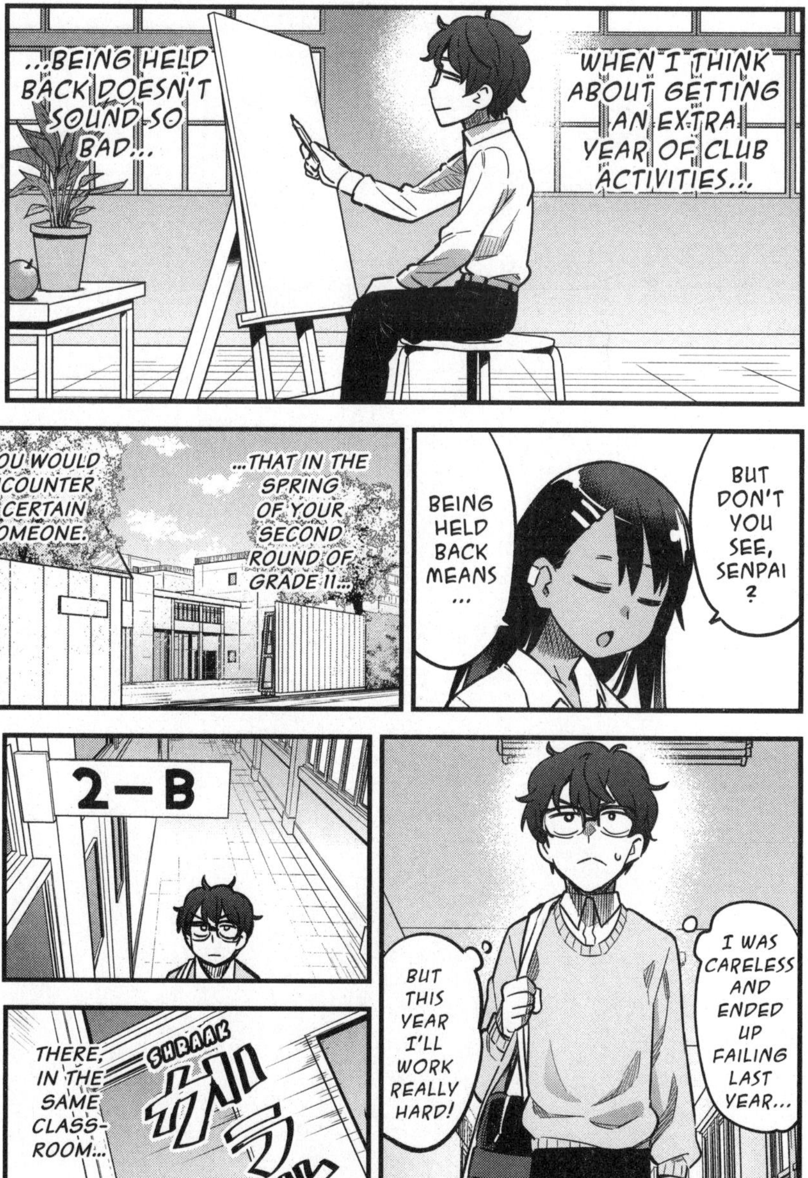
WHEN I THINK ABOUT GETTING AN EXTRA YEAR OF CLUB ACTIVITIES...
...BEING HELD BACK DOESN'T SOUND SO BAD...
BUT DON'T YOU SEE, SENPAI?
BEING HELD BACK MEANS...
...THAT IN THE SPRING OF YOUR SECOND ROUND OF GRADE 11...
...YOU WOULD ENCOUNTER A CERTAIN SOMEONE.
I WAS CARELESS AND ENDED UP FAILING LAST YEAR...
BUT THIS YEAR I'LL WORK REALLY HARD!
2-B
SHRAAK
THERE, IN THE SAME CLASS-ROOM...

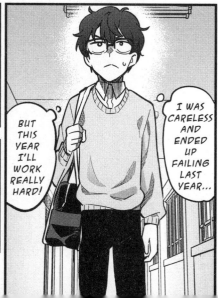

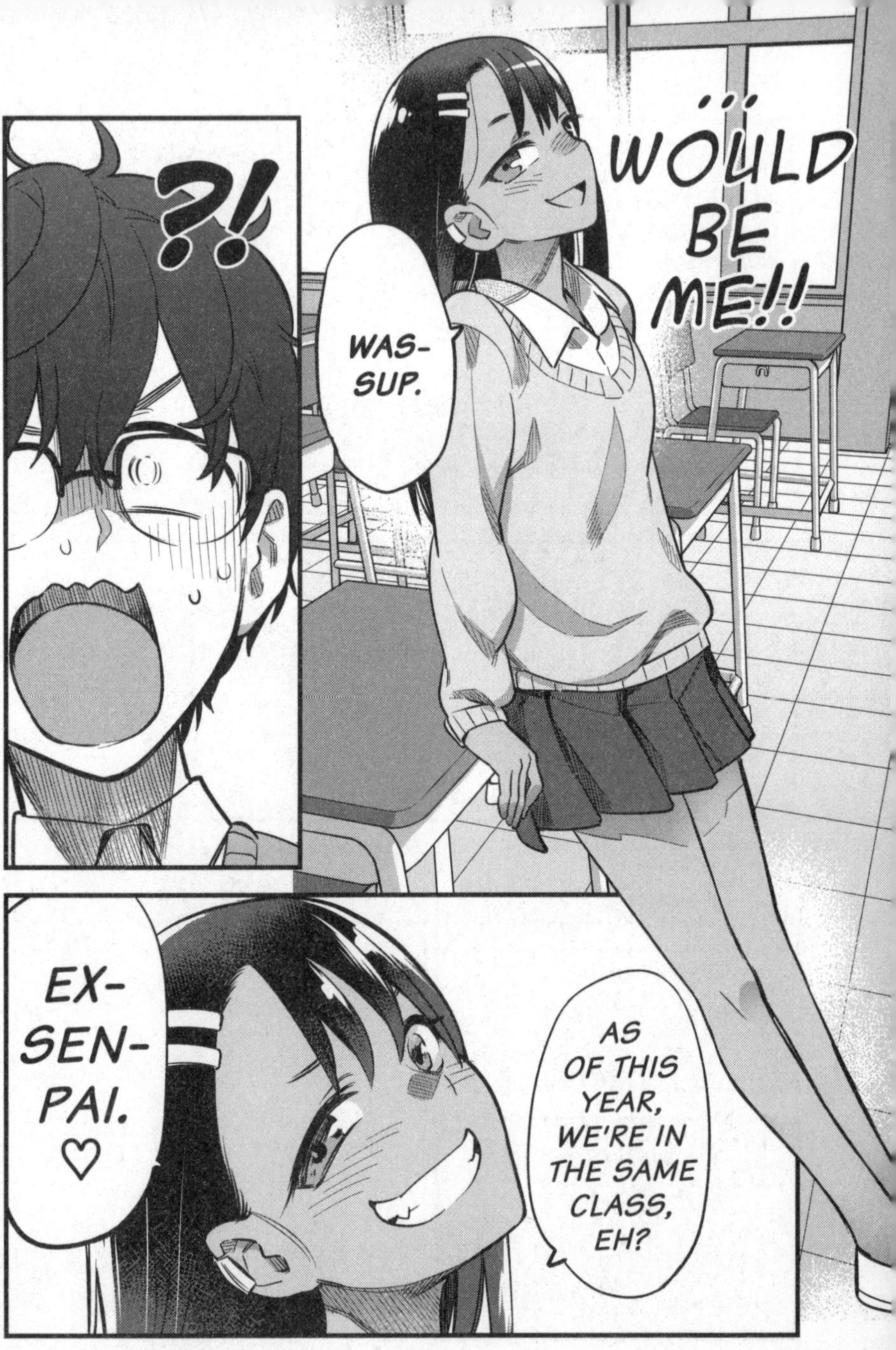
...WOULD BE ME!!
WAS-SUP.
?!
AS OF THIS YEAR, WE'RE IN THE SAME CLASS, EH?
EX-SEN-PAI. ♡

HM? YOU FORGOT YOUR TEXTBOOK AGAIN?
YOU REALLY ARE HOPELESS, HUH, EX-SENPAI. ♡
HERE, I'LL LET YOU LOOK AT MINE. PUSH OUR DESKS TOGETHER.
HA HA HA!
CATCH YA LATER!
MUST SUCK GETTING PASSED BY A FORMER KOHAI, HUH? PUSH HARDER!
HUFF
HUFF
EX-SEN-PAI! ♡
I DON'T REALLY GET THIS QUES-TION.
HUH? YOU DON'T GET IT EITHER, EX-SENPAI?
KEH
HEH
HEH
WHOA, WHOA. THIS IS YOUR SECOND TIME AROUND, ISN'T IT?
YOU NEED TO GET IT TO-GETHER, EX-SENPAI.

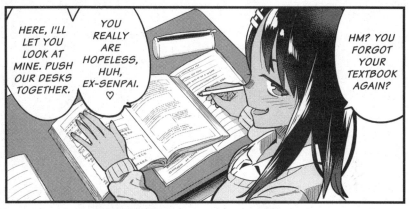

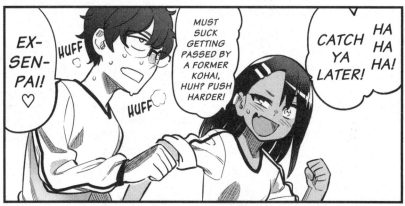

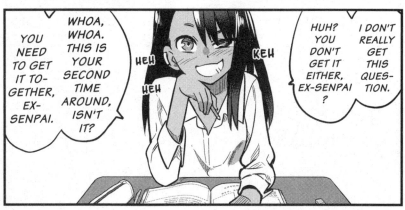

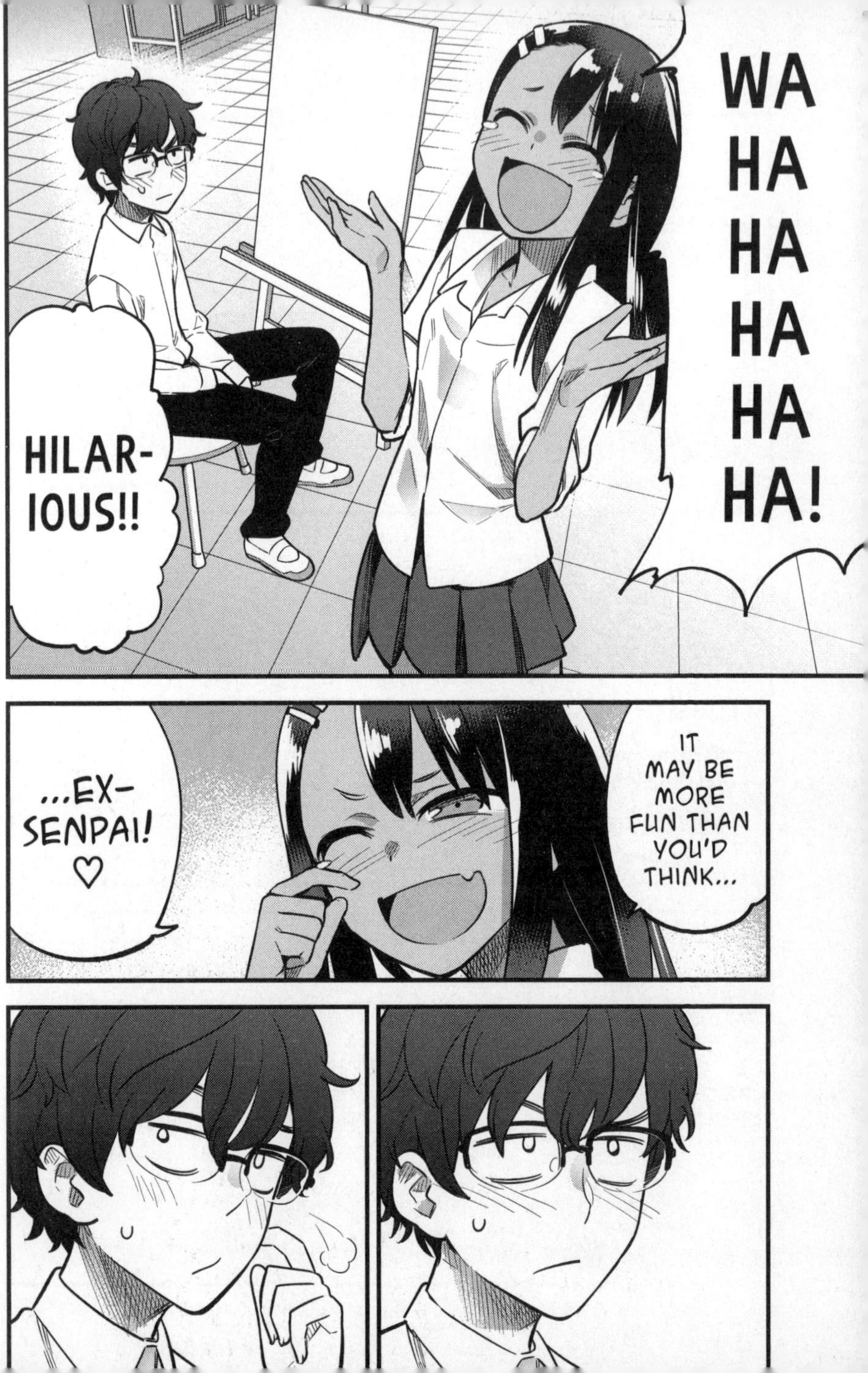
WA HA HA HA HA HA HA!
HILAR-IOUS!!
IT MAY BE MORE FUN THAN YOU'D THINK...
...EX-SENPAI! ♡

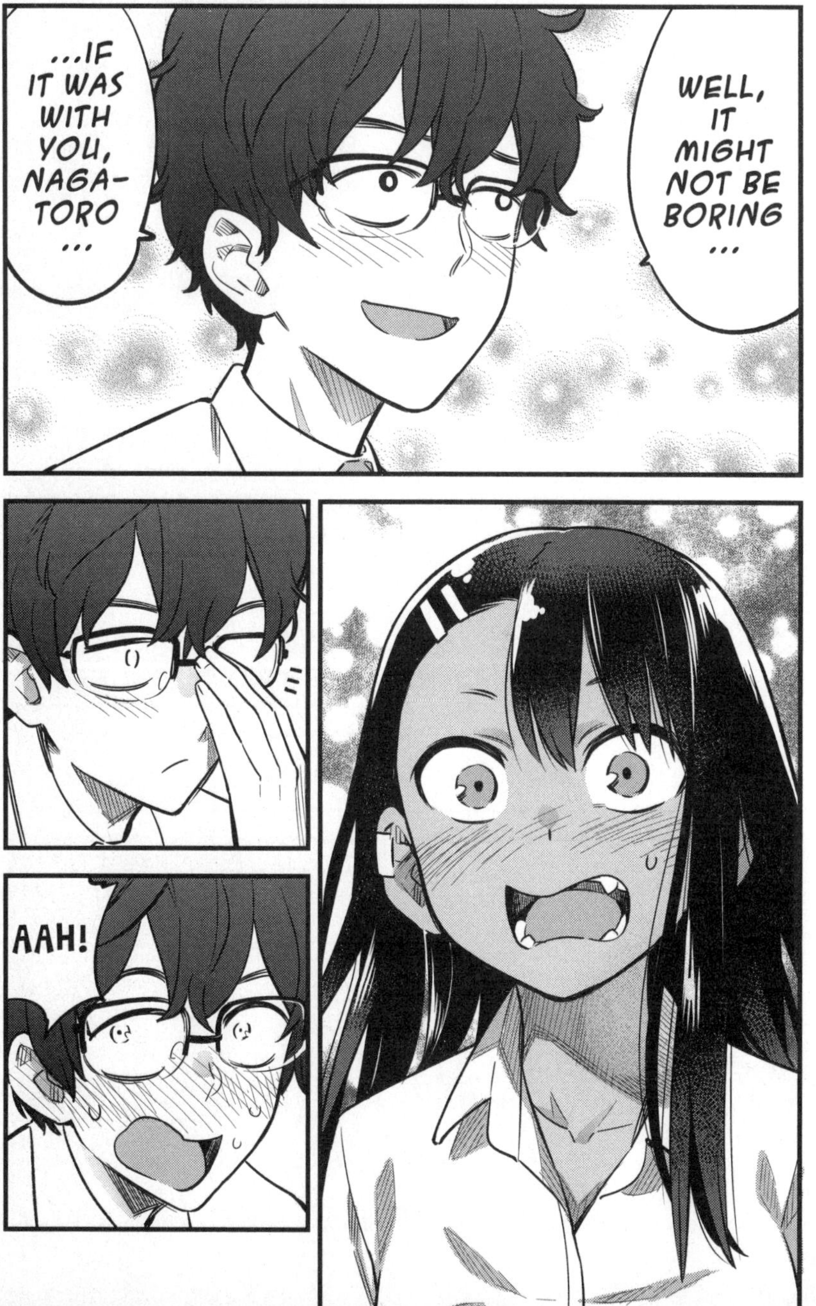
WELL, IT MIGHT NOT BE BORING...
...IF IT WAS WITH YOU, NAGA-TORO...
AAH!

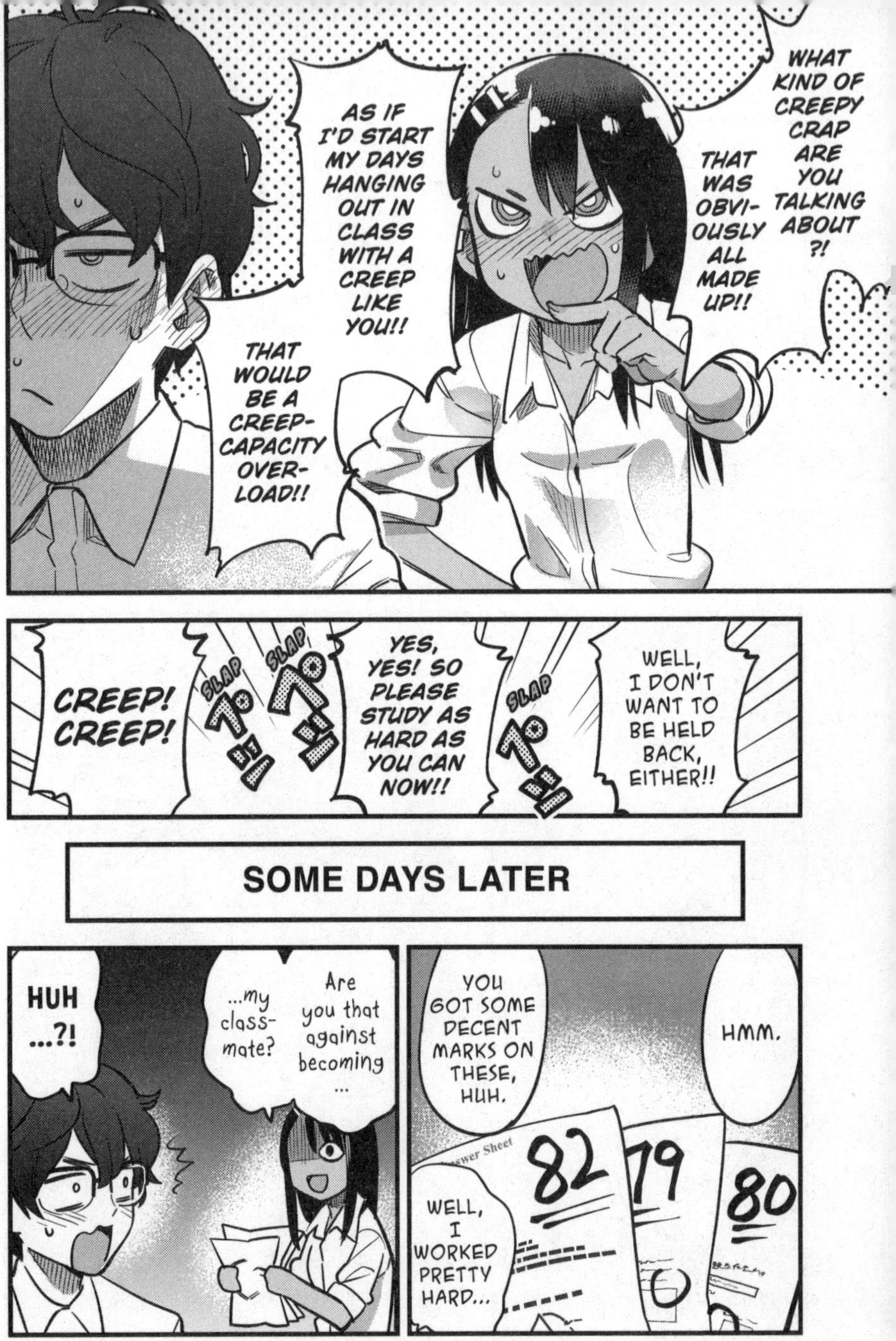
WHAT KIND OF CREEPY CRAP ARE YOU TALKING ABOUT?!
THAT WAS OBVI-OUSLY ALL MADE UP!!
AS IF I'D START MY DAYS HANGING OUT IN CLASS WITH A CREEP LIKE YOU!!
THAT WOULD BE A CREEP-CAPACITY OVER-LOAD!!
WELL, I DON'T WANT TO BE HELD BACK, EITHER!!
SLAP
YES, YES! SO PLEASE STUDY AS HARD AS YOU CAN NOW!!
SLAP
SLAP
CREEP! CREEP!
SOME DAYS LATER
HMM.
YOU GOT SOME DECENT MARKS ON THESE, HUH.
82
79
80
WELL, I WORKED PRETTY HARD...
Are you that against becoming ...
...my class-mate?
HUH ...?!

END

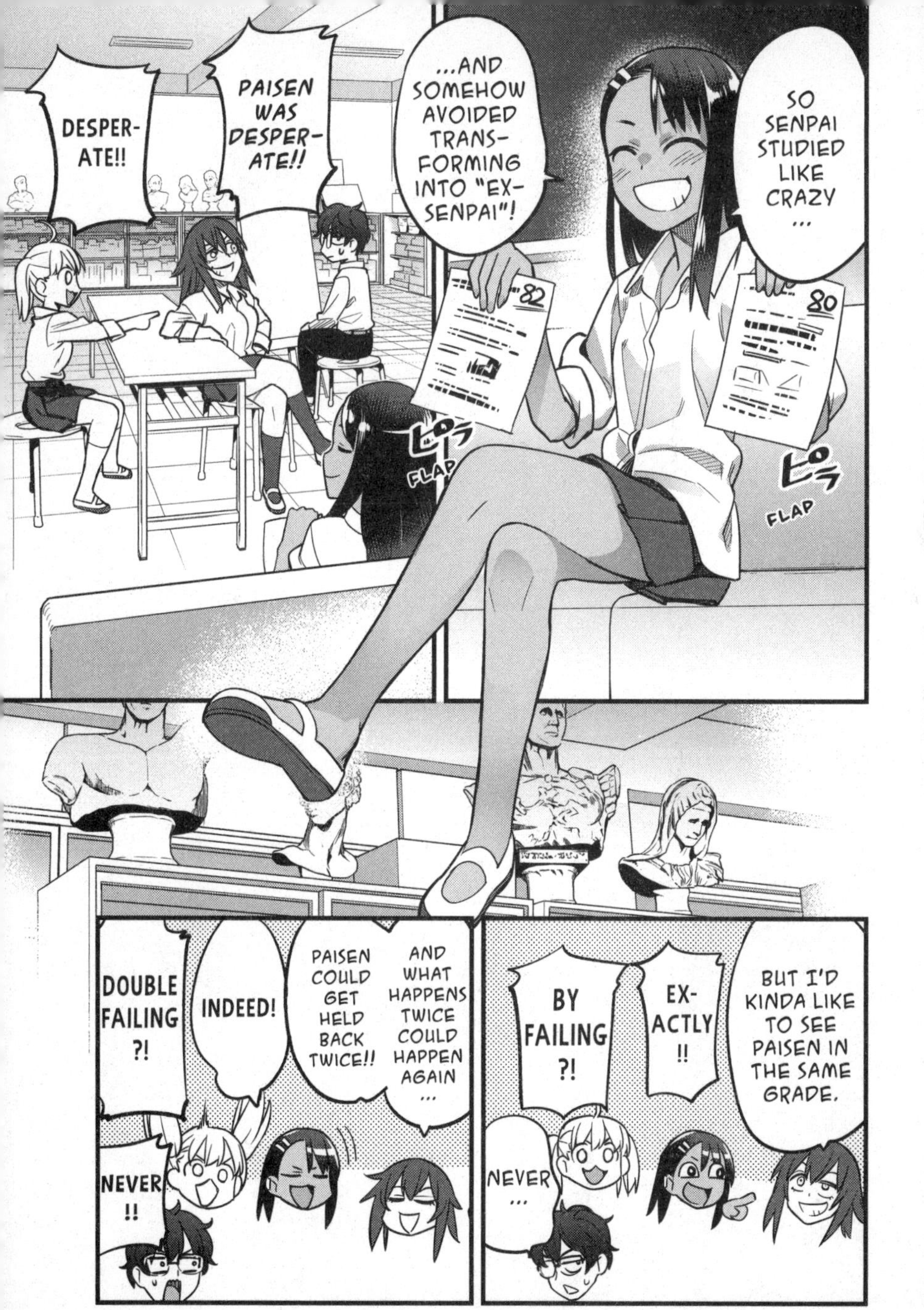
SO SENPAI STUDIED LIKE CRAZY...
...AND SOMEHOW AVOIDED TRANS-FORMING INTO "EX-SENPAI"!
PAISEN WAS DESPER-ATE!!
DESPER-ATE!!
ピラ FLAP
ピラ FLAP
BUT I'D KINDA LIKE TO SEE PAISEN IN THE SAME GRADE.
EX-ACTLY!!
BY FAILING?!
NEVER...
AND WHAT HAPPENS TWICE COULD HAPPEN AGAIN...
PAISEN COULD GET HELD BACK TWICE!!
INDEED!
DOUBLE FAILING?!
NEVER!!

CHAPTER 35: WE'D END UP BECOMING YOUR SENPAIS, RIGHT, PAISEN?

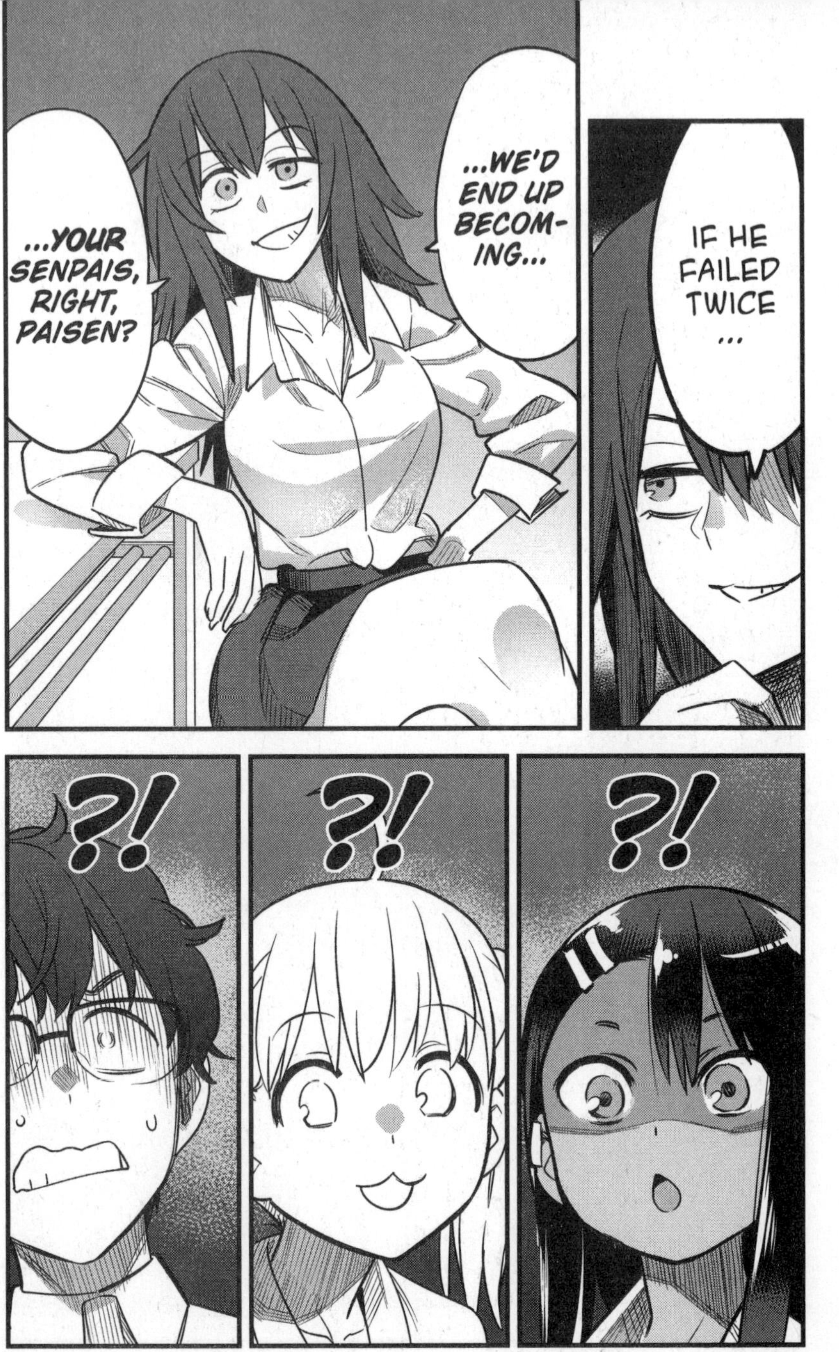
IF HE FAILED TWICE ...
...WE'D END UP BECOMING...
...YOUR SENPAIS, RIGHT, PAISEN?
?!
?!
?!

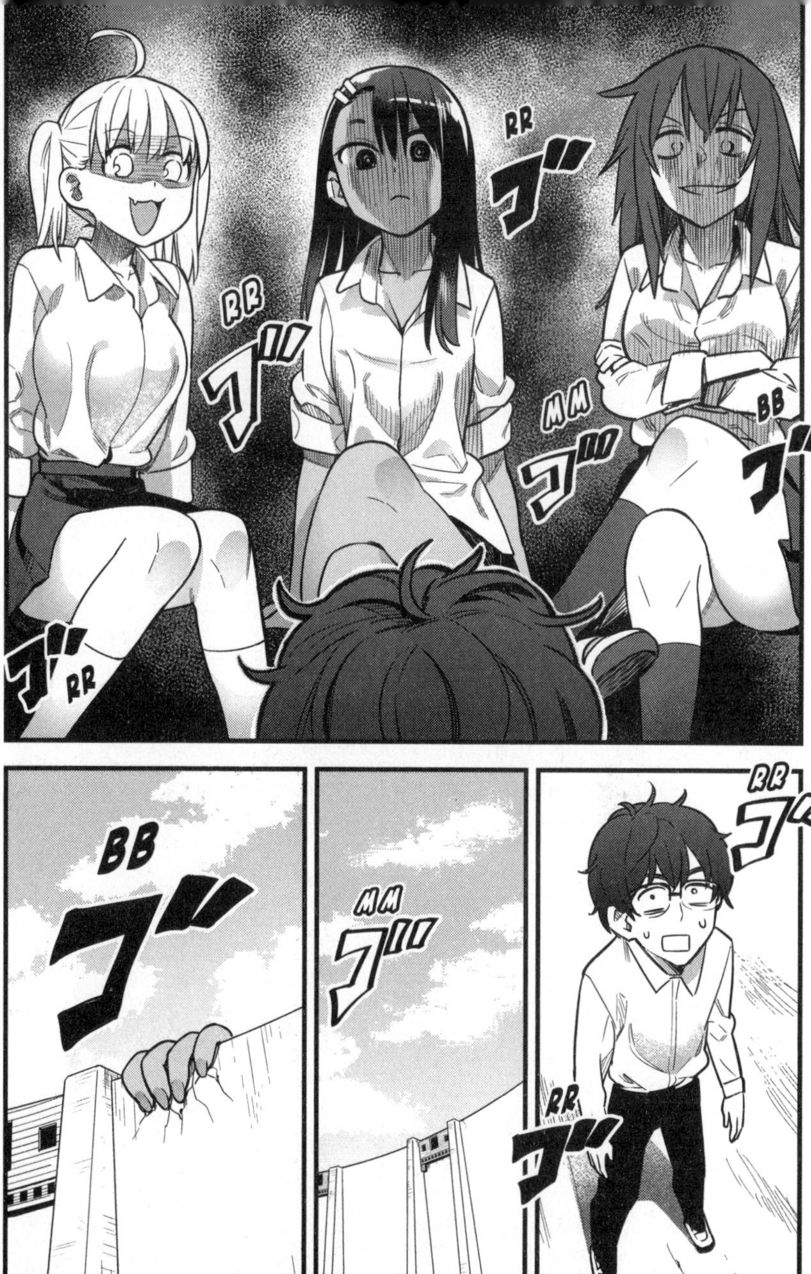
RR
BB
MM
RR
RR
RR
RR
MM
BB

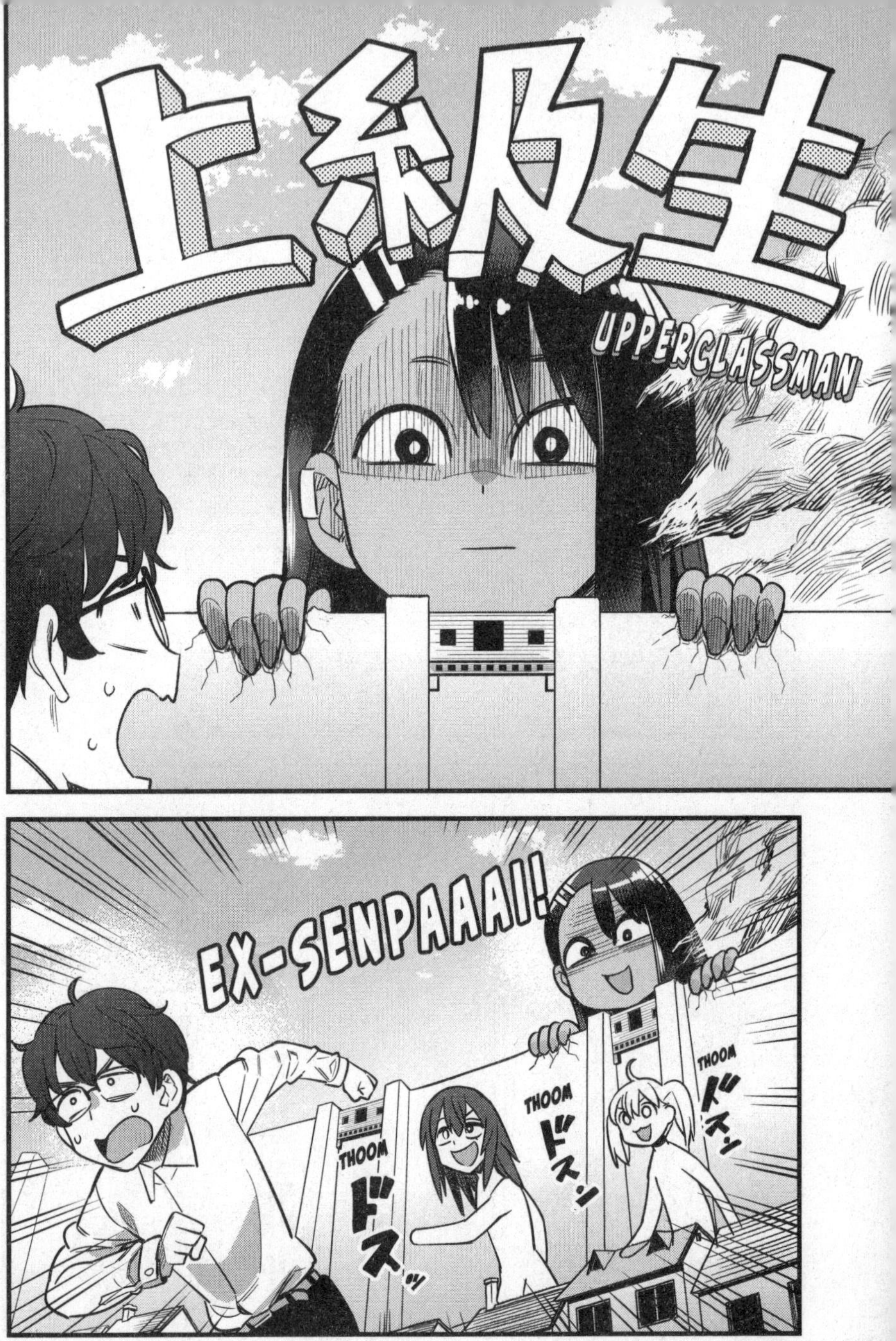
上級生
UPPERCLASSMAN
EX-SENPAAAI!
THOOM
ドスン
THOOM
ドスン
THOOM
ドスッ

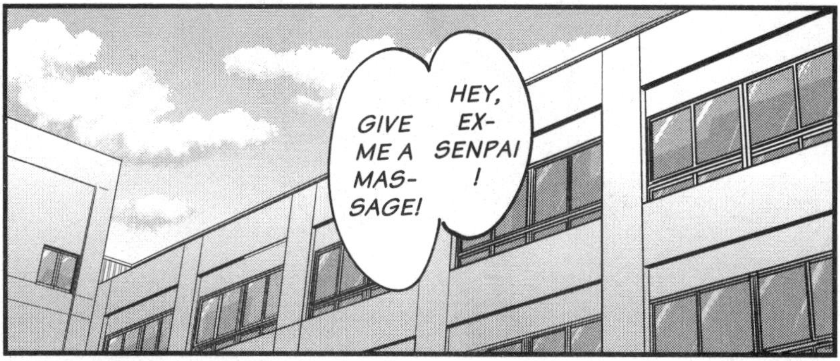
HEY, EX-SENPAI!
GIVE ME A MAS-SAGE!

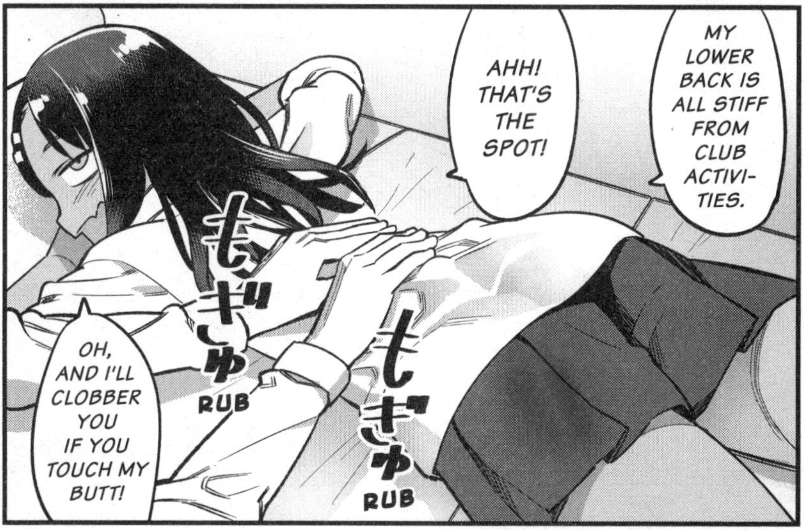
MY LOWER BACK IS ALL STIFF FROM CLUB ACTIVI-TIES.
AHH! THAT'S THE SPOT!
RUB
RUB
OH, AND I'LL CLOBBER YOU IF YOU TOUCH MY BUTT!

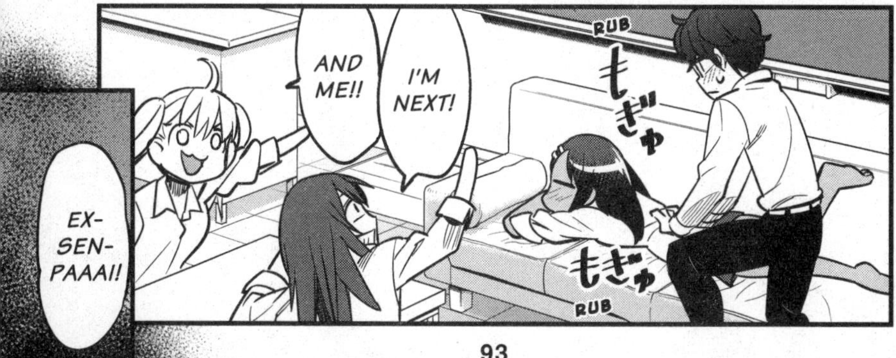
RUB
RUB
I'M NEXT!
AND ME!!
EX-SEN-PAAAI!

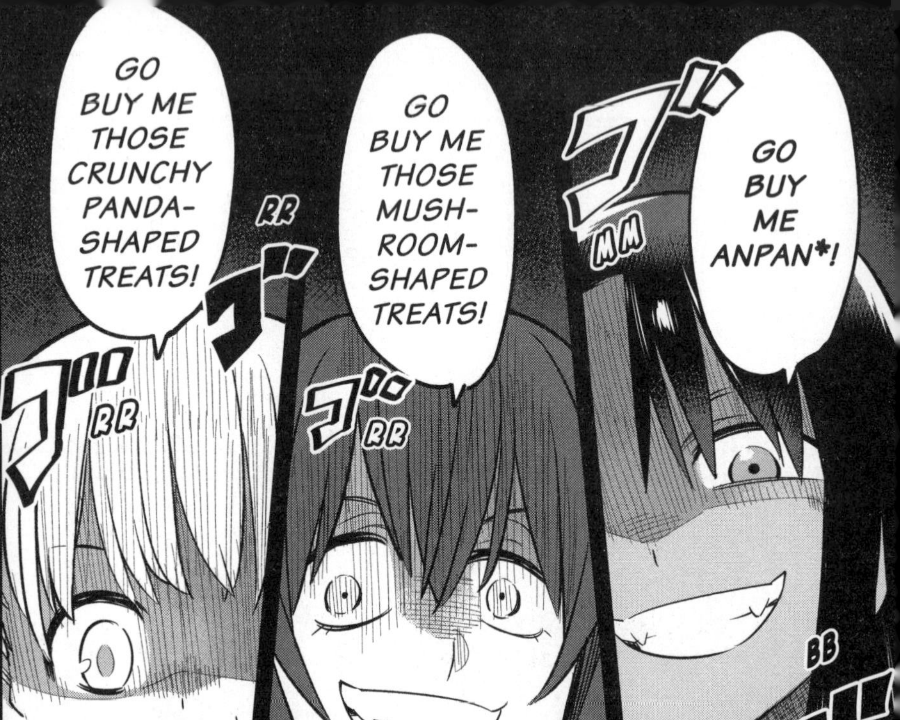
GO BUY ME ANPAN*!
MM
BB
GO BUY ME THOSE MUSH-ROOM-SHAPED TREATS!
RR
GO BUY ME THOSE CRUNCHY PANDA-SHAPED TREATS!
RR
RR
RR
MM

*pastry filled with sweet red bean paste

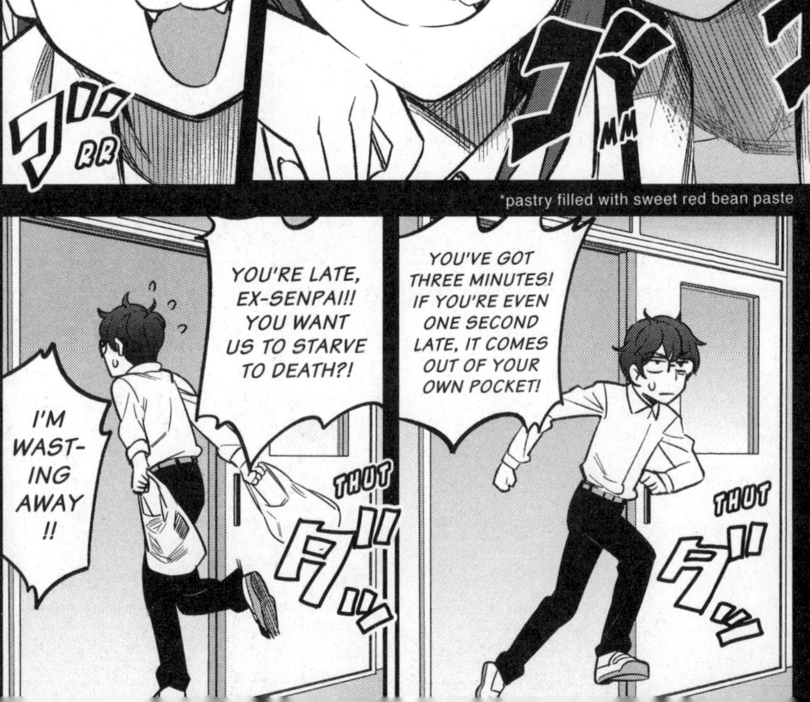
YOU'VE GOT THREE MINUTES! IF YOU'RE EVEN ONE SECOND LATE, IT COMES OUT OF YOUR OWN POCKET!
THUT
YOU'RE LATE, EX-SENPAI!! YOU WANT US TO STARVE TO DEATH?!
I'M WAST-ING AWAY !!
THUT

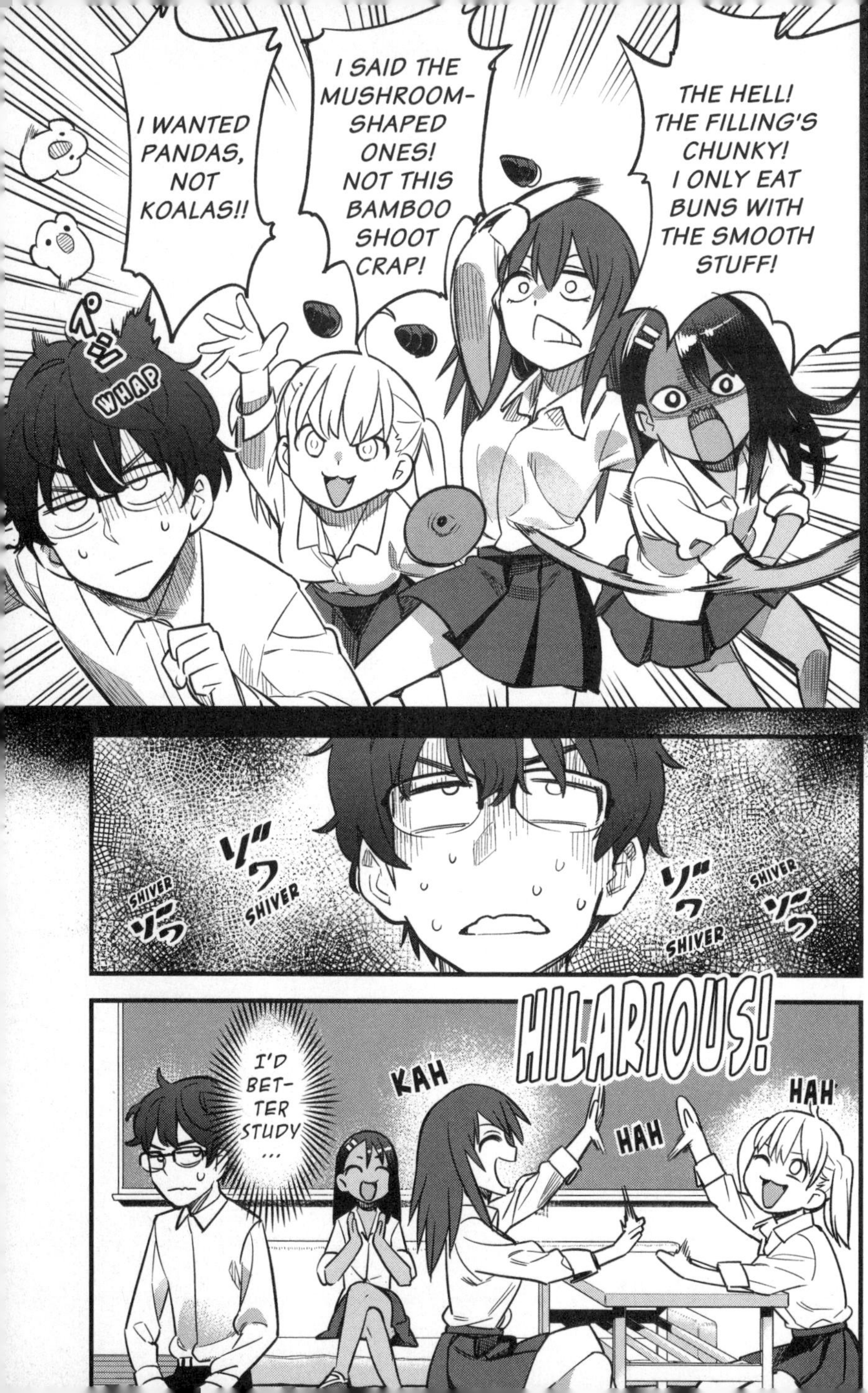
THE HELL! THE FILLING'S CHUNKY! I ONLY EAT BUNS WITH THE SMOOTH STUFF!
I SAID THE MUSHROOM-SHAPED ONES! NOT THIS BAMBOO SHOOT CRAP!
I WANTED PANDAS, NOT KOALAS!!
WHAP
SHIVER
SHIVER
SHIVER
SHIVER
HILARIOUS!
HAH
HAH
KAH
I'D BET-TER STUDY ...

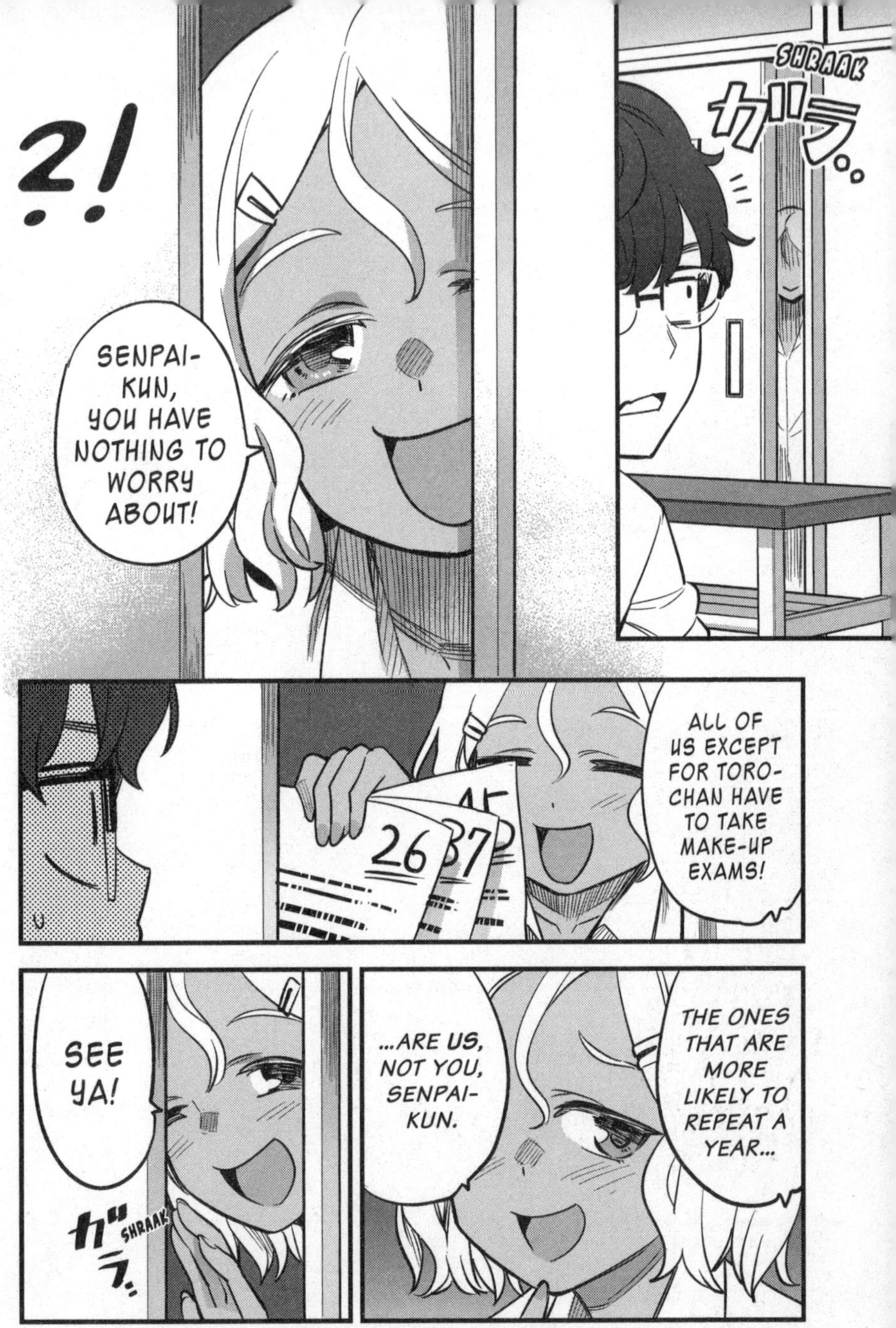
SHRAAK
ガラ
?!
SENPAI-KUN, YOU HAVE NOTHING TO WORRY ABOUT!
ALL OF US EXCEPT FOR TORO-CHAN HAVE TO TAKE MAKE-UP EXAMS!
THE ONES THAT ARE MORE LIKELY TO REPEAT A YEAR...
...ARE US, NOT YOU, SENPAI-KUN.
SEE YA!
SHRAAK
ガラ

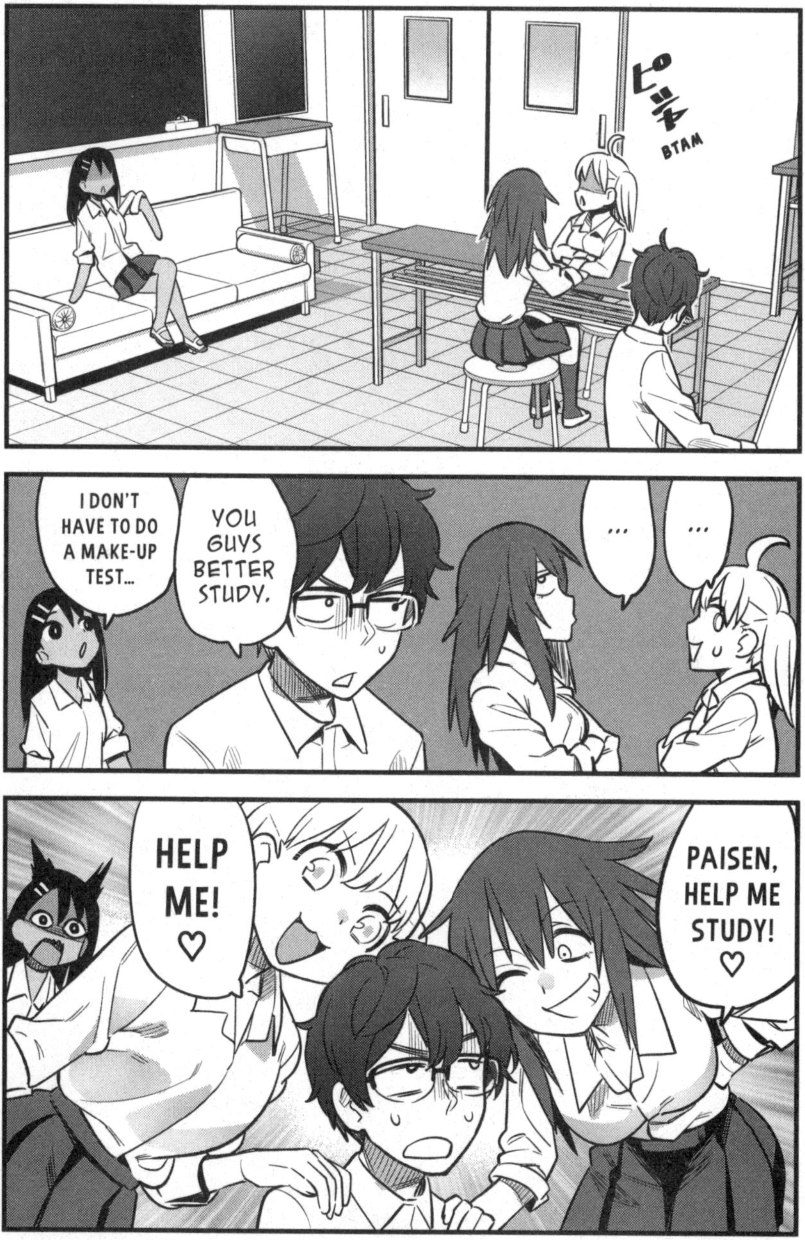
BTAM
...
...
YOU GUYS BETTER STUDY.
I DON'T HAVE TO DO A MAKE-UP TEST...
PAISEN, HELP ME STUDY! ♡
HELP ME! ♡

END

HELP
ME!

CHAPTER 36: SENPAI, YOU MADE ME DO THIS...

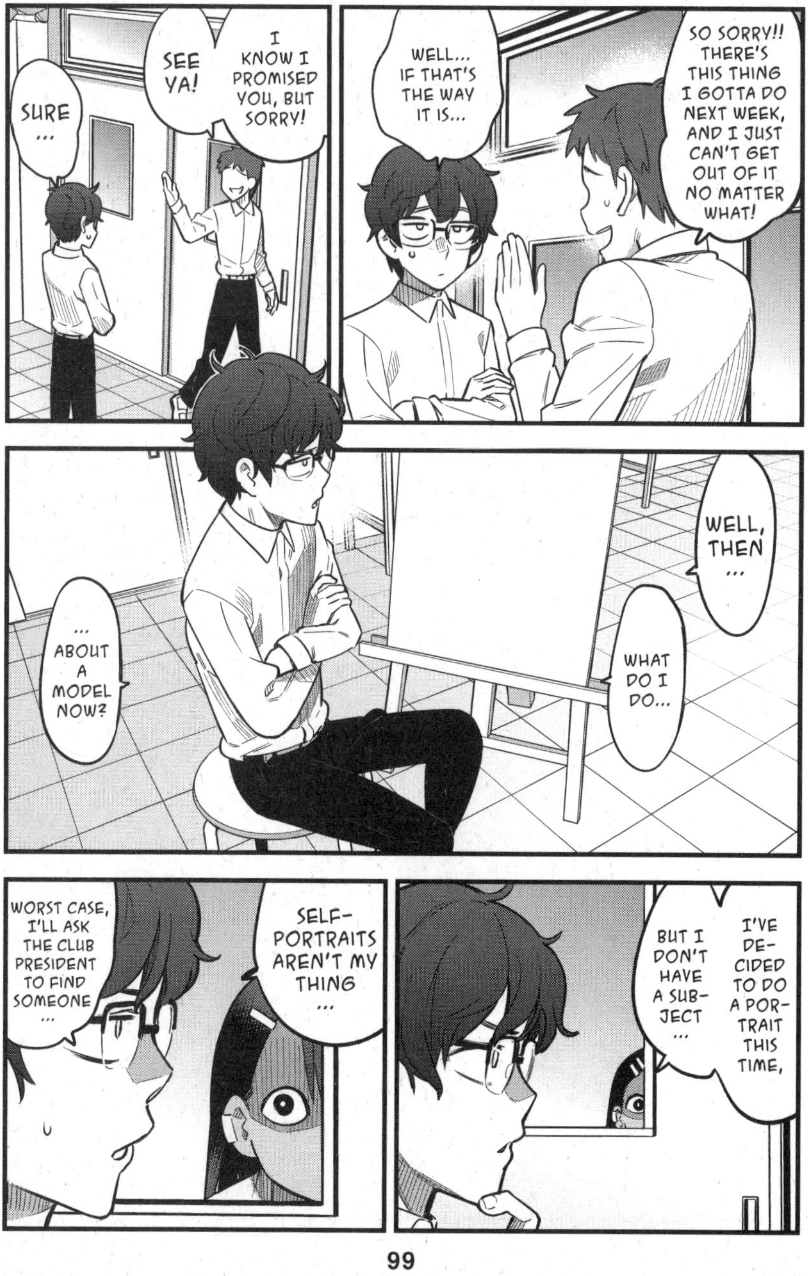
SO SORRY!! THERE'S THIS THING I GOTTA DO NEXT WEEK, AND I JUST CAN'T GET OUT OF IT NO MATTER WHAT!
WELL... IF THAT'S THE WAY IT IS...
I KNOW I PROMISED YOU, BUT SORRY!
SEE YA!
SURE...
WELL, THEN...
WHAT DO I DO...
...ABOUT A MODEL NOW?
I'VE DE-CIDED TO DO A POR-TRAIT THIS TIME,
BUT I DON'T HAVE A SUB-JECT...
SELF-PORTRAITS AREN'T MY THING...
WORST CASE, I'LL ASK THE CLUB PRESIDENT TO FIND SOMEONE...

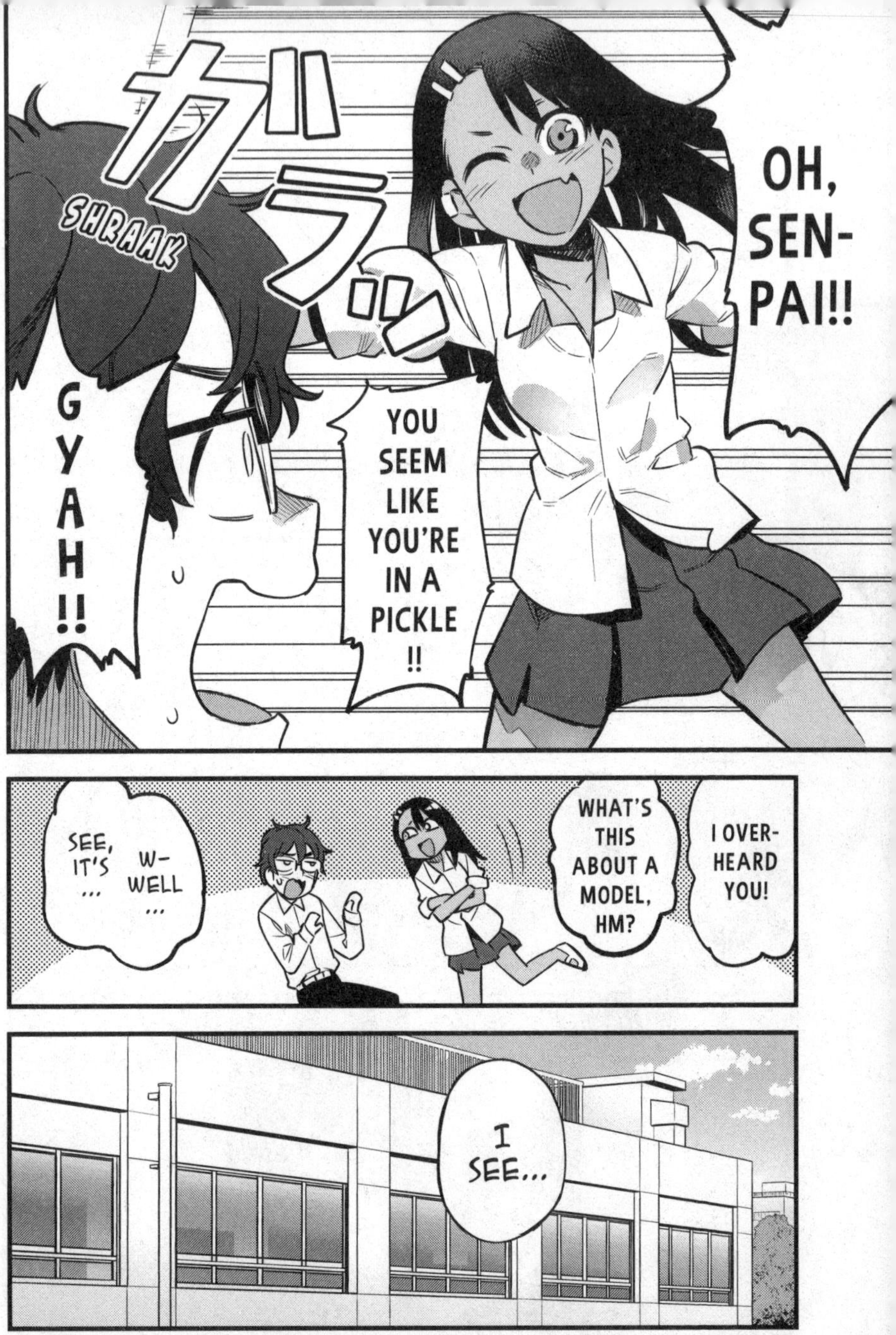
OH, SEN-PAI!!
YOU SEEM LIKE YOU'RE IN A PICKLE!!
ガラッ
SHRAAK
GYAH!!
I OVER-HEARD YOU!
WHAT'S THIS ABOUT A MODEL, HM?
W-WELL...
SEE, IT'S...
I SEE...

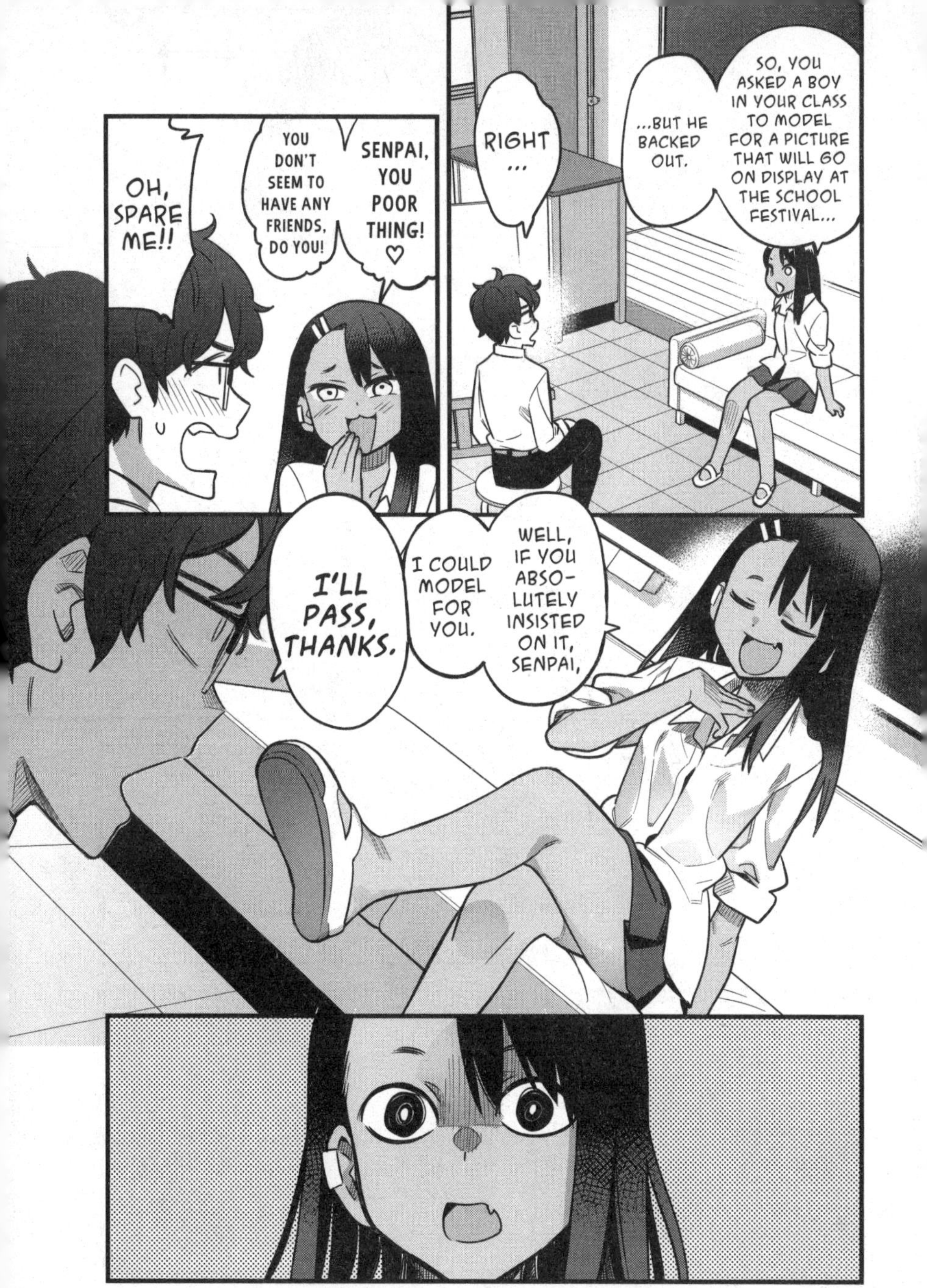
SO, YOU ASKED A BOY IN YOUR CLASS TO MODEL FOR A PICTURE THAT WILL GO ON DISPLAY AT THE SCHOOL FESTIVAL...
...BUT HE BACKED OUT.
RIGHT...
SENPAI, YOU POOR THING! ♡
YOU DON'T SEEM TO HAVE ANY FRIENDS, DO YOU!
OH, SPARE ME!!
WELL, IF YOU ABSO-LUTELY INSISTED ON IT, SENPAI,
I COULD MODEL FOR YOU.
I'LL PASS, THANKS.

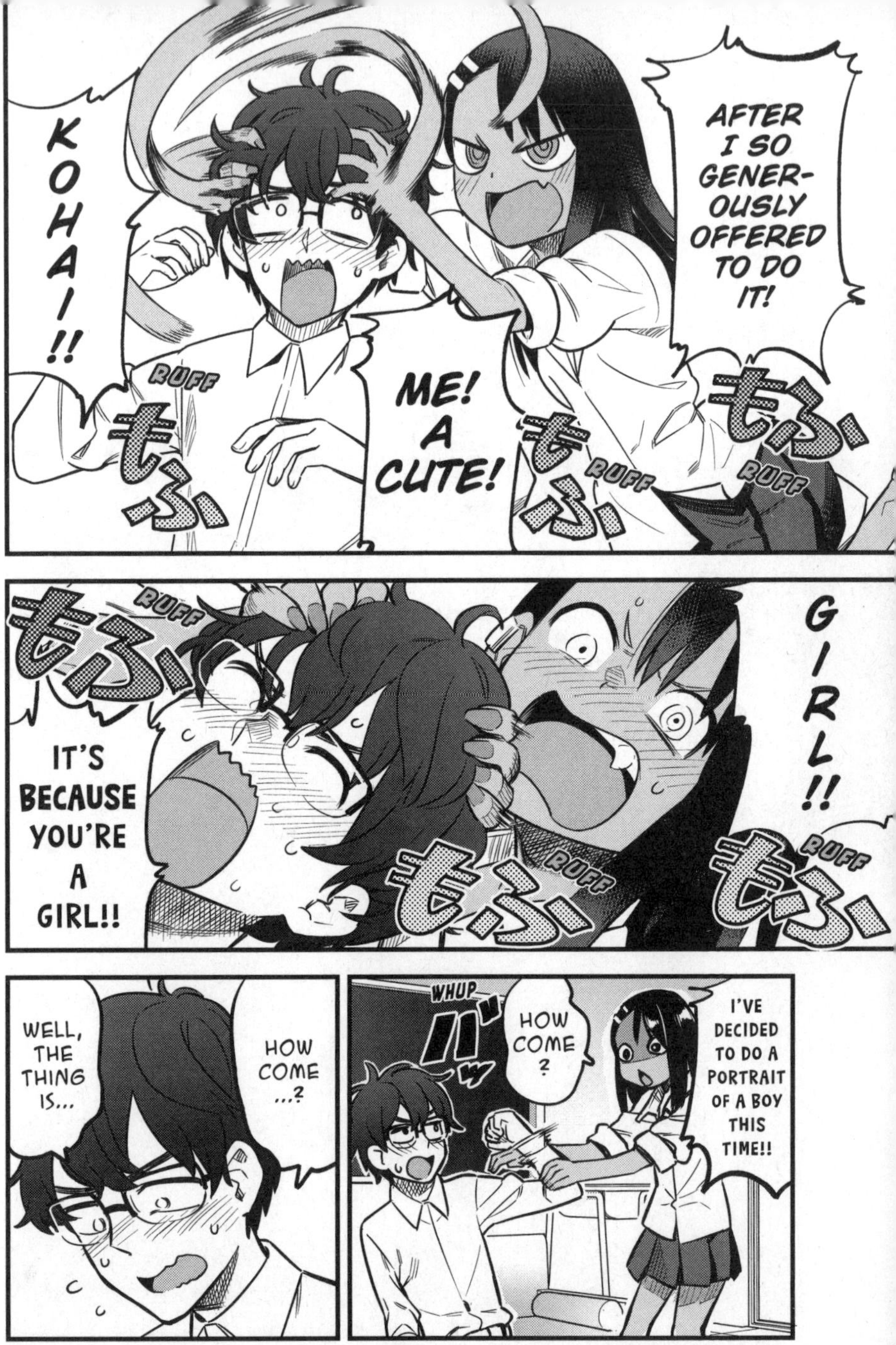
AFTER I SO GENER-OUSLY OFFERED TO DO IT!
RUFF
もふ
ME! A CUTE!
RUFF
もふ
KOHAI!!
RUFF
もふ
GIRL!!
RUFF
もふ
RUFF
もふ
IT'S BECAUSE YOU'RE A GIRL!!
RUFF
もふ
I'VE DECIDED TO DO A PORTRAIT OF A BOY THIS TIME!!
HOW COME?
WHUP
バッ
HOW COME...?
WELL, THE THING IS...

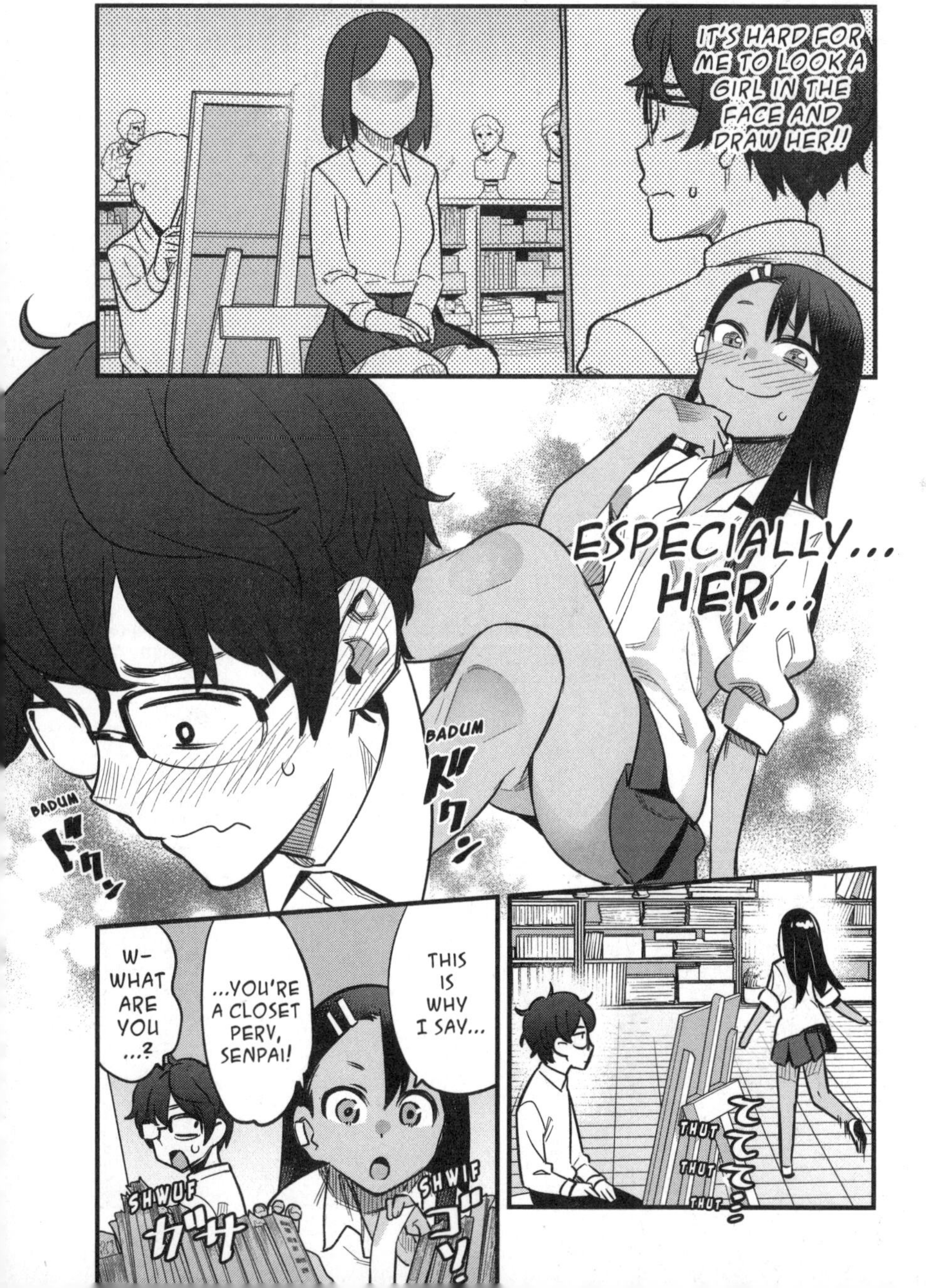
IT'S HARD FOR ME TO LOOK A GIRL IN THE FACE AND DRAW HER!!
ESPECIALLY... HER...!
BADUM
ドクン
BADUM
ドクン
THUT
THUT
THUT
THIS IS WHY I SAY...
...YOU'RE A CLOSET PERV, SENPAI!
W-WHAT ARE YOU ...?
SHWIF
SHWUF

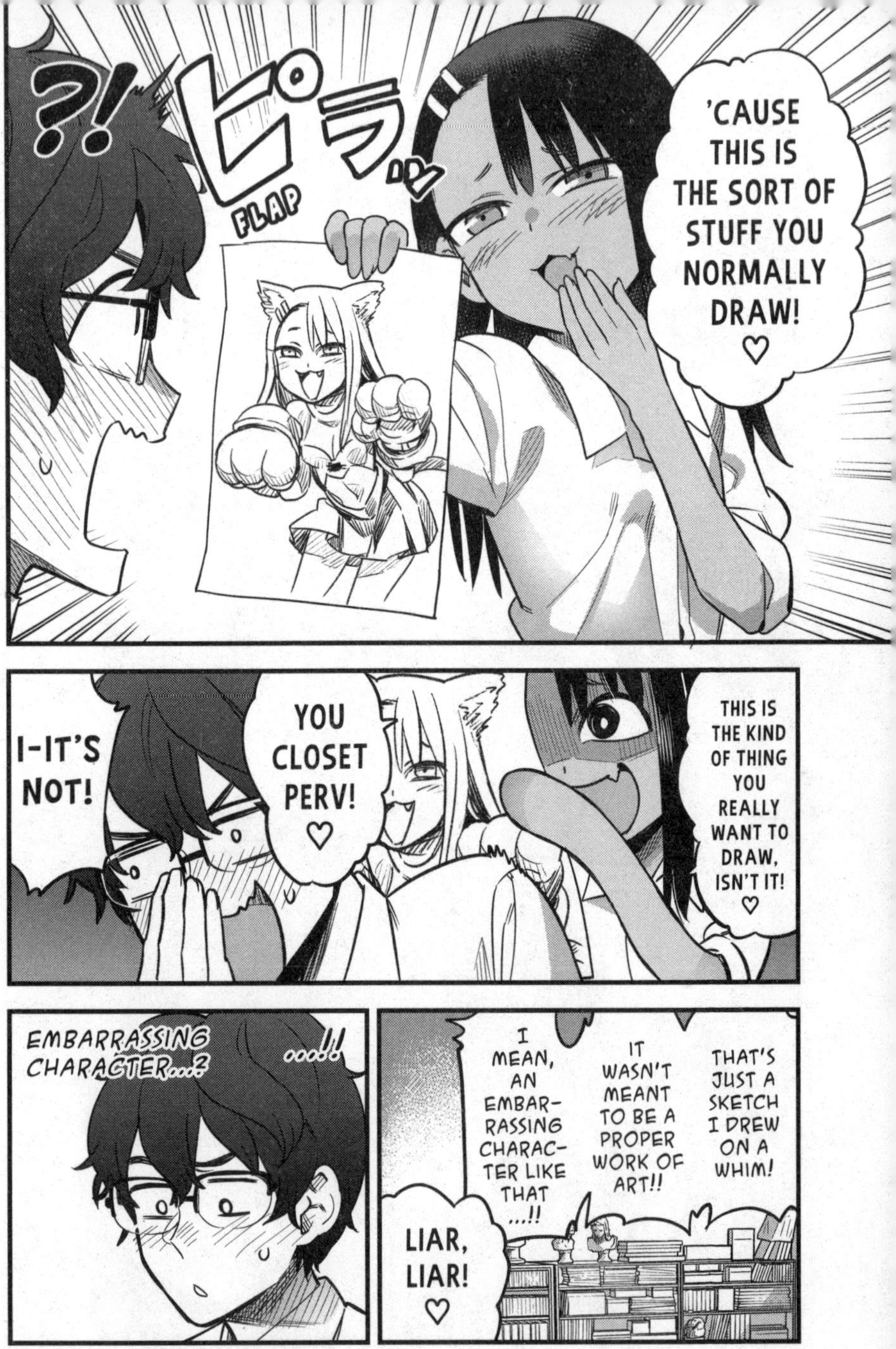
'CAUSE THIS IS THE SORT OF STUFF YOU NORMALLY DRAW! ♡
ピラ
FLAP
?!
THIS IS THE KIND OF THING YOU REALLY WANT TO DRAW, ISN'T IT! ♡
YOU CLOSET PERV! ♡
I-IT'S NOT!
THAT'S JUST A SKETCH I DREW ON A WHIM!
IT WASN'T MEANT TO BE A PROPER WORK OF ART!!
I MEAN, AN EMBAR-RASSING CHARAC-TER LIKE THAT ...!!
LIAR, LIAR! ♡
...!!
EMBARRASSING CHARACTER...?

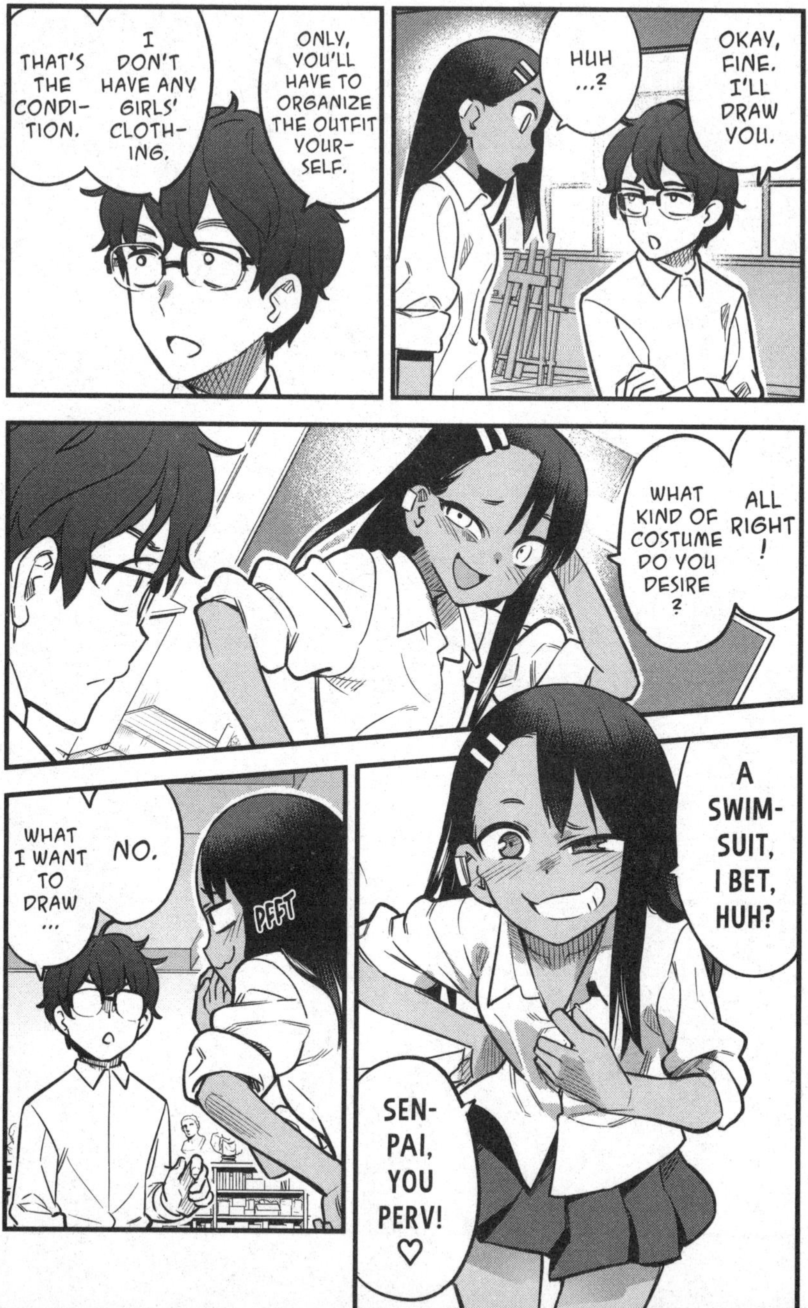
OKAY, FINE. I'LL DRAW YOU.
HUH ...?
ONLY, YOU'LL HAVE TO ORGANIZE THE OUTFIT YOUR-SELF.
I DON'T HAVE ANY GIRLS' CLOTH-ING.
THAT'S THE CONDI-TION.
ALL RIGHT!
WHAT KIND OF COSTUME DO YOU DESIRE?
A SWIM-SUIT, I BET, HUH?
SEN-PAI, YOU PERV! ♡
PFFT
NO.
WHAT I WANT TO DRAW ...

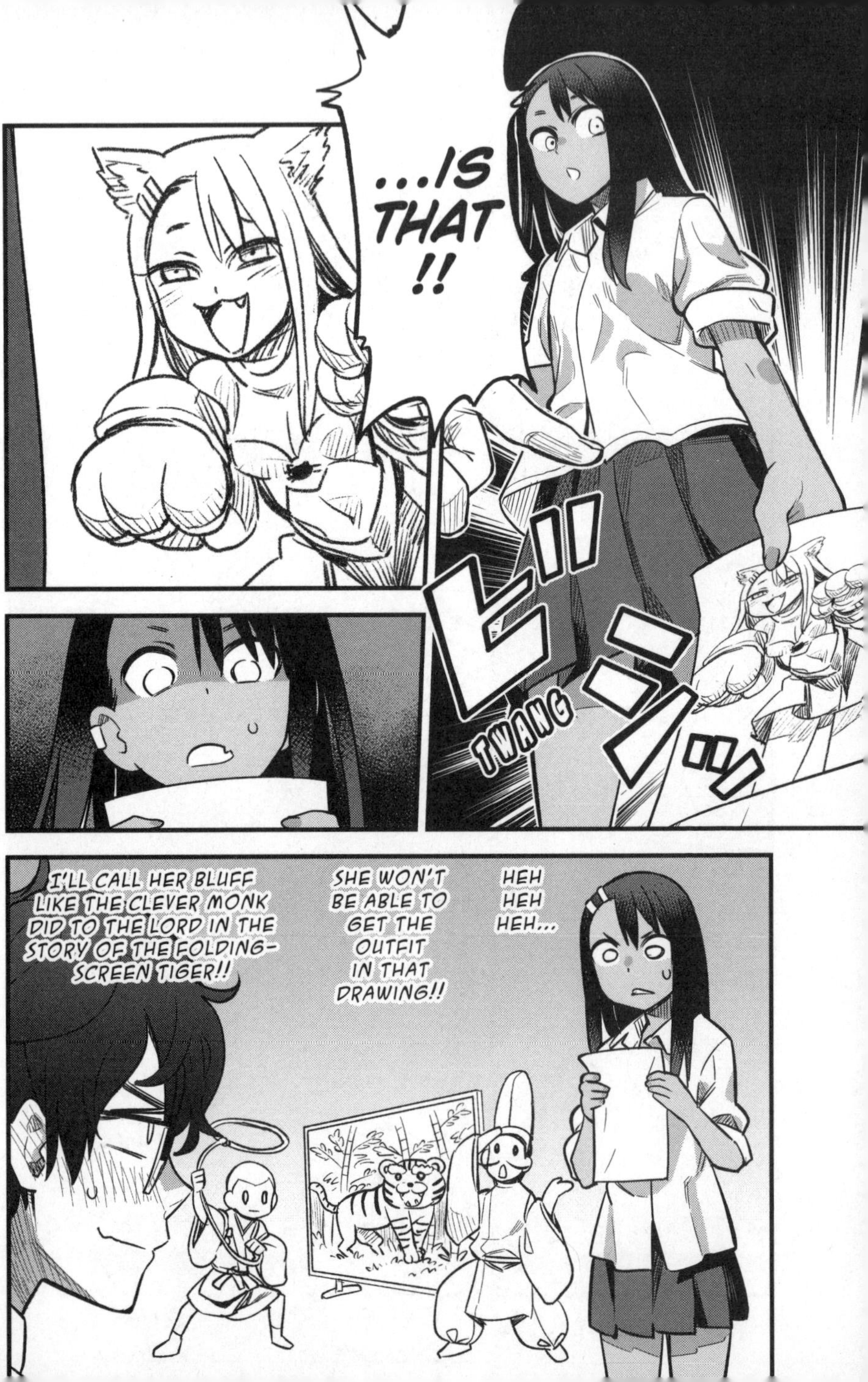
...IS THAT!!
TWANG
HEH HEH HEH...
SHE WON'T BE ABLE TO GET THE OUTFIT IN THAT DRAWING!!
I'LL CALL HER BLUFF LIKE THE CLEVER MONK DID TO THE LORD IN THE STORY OF THE FOLDING-SCREEN TIGER!!

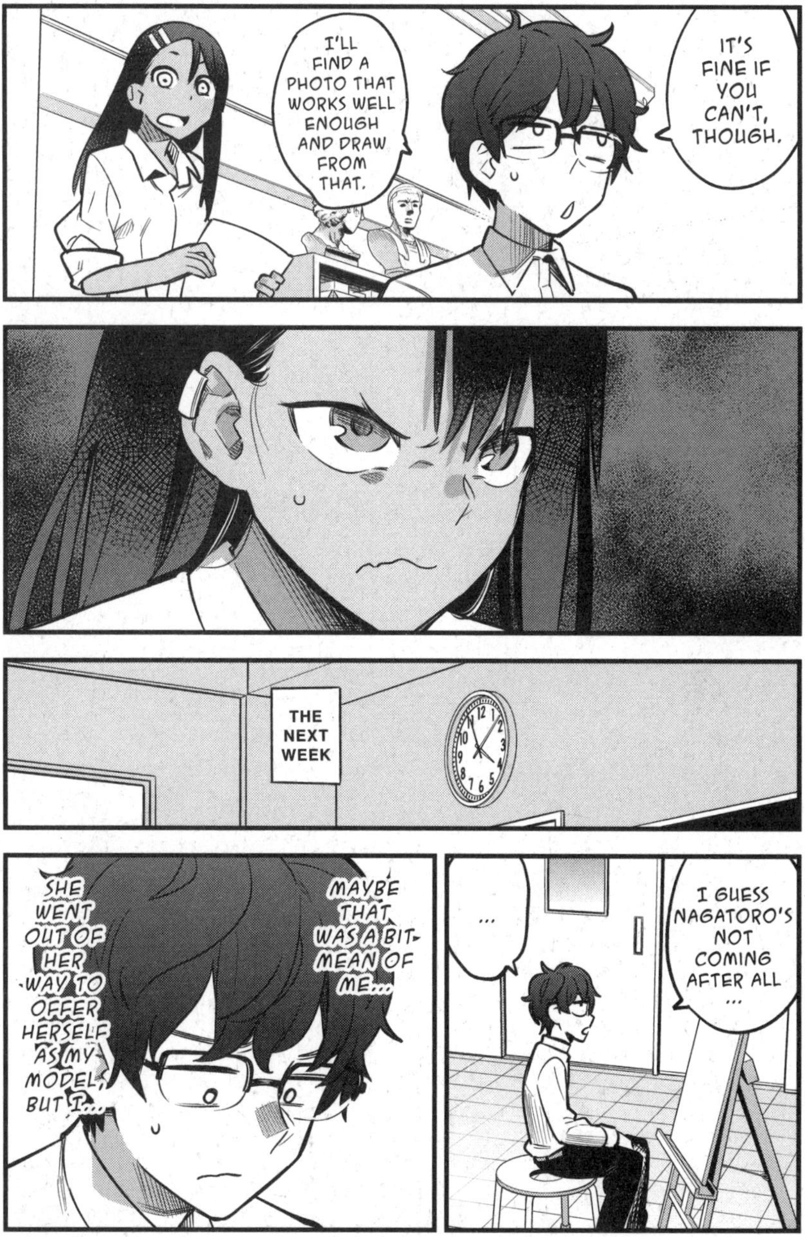
IT'S FINE IF YOU CAN'T, THOUGH.
I'LL FIND A PHOTO THAT WORKS WELL ENOUGH AND DRAW FROM THAT.
THE NEXT WEEK
I GUESS NAGATORO'S NOT COMING AFTER ALL ...
...
MAYBE THAT WAS A BIT MEAN OF ME...
SHE WENT OUT OF HER WAY TO OFFER HERSELF AS MY MODEL, BUT I...

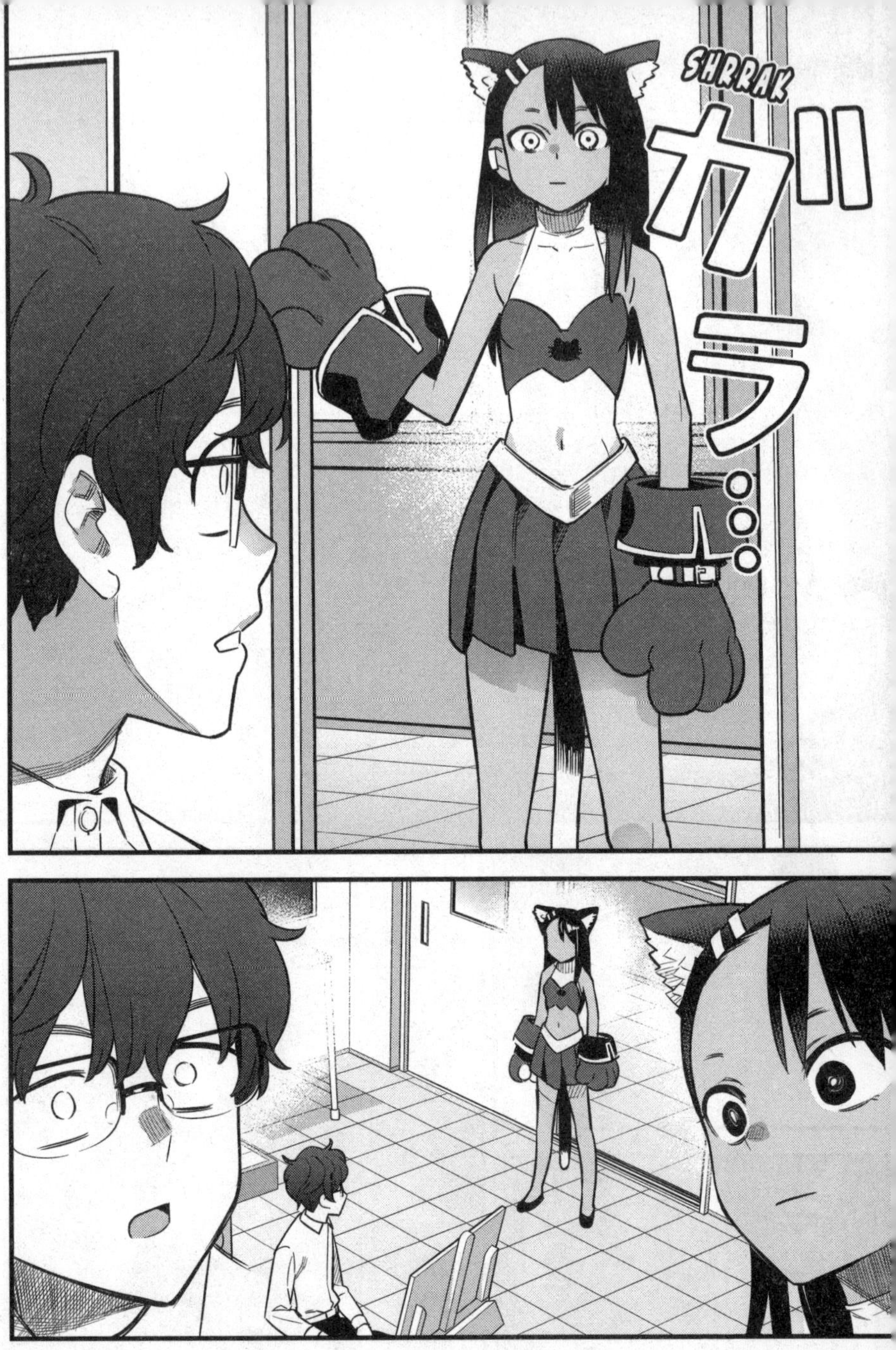
SHRRAK
ガラ…

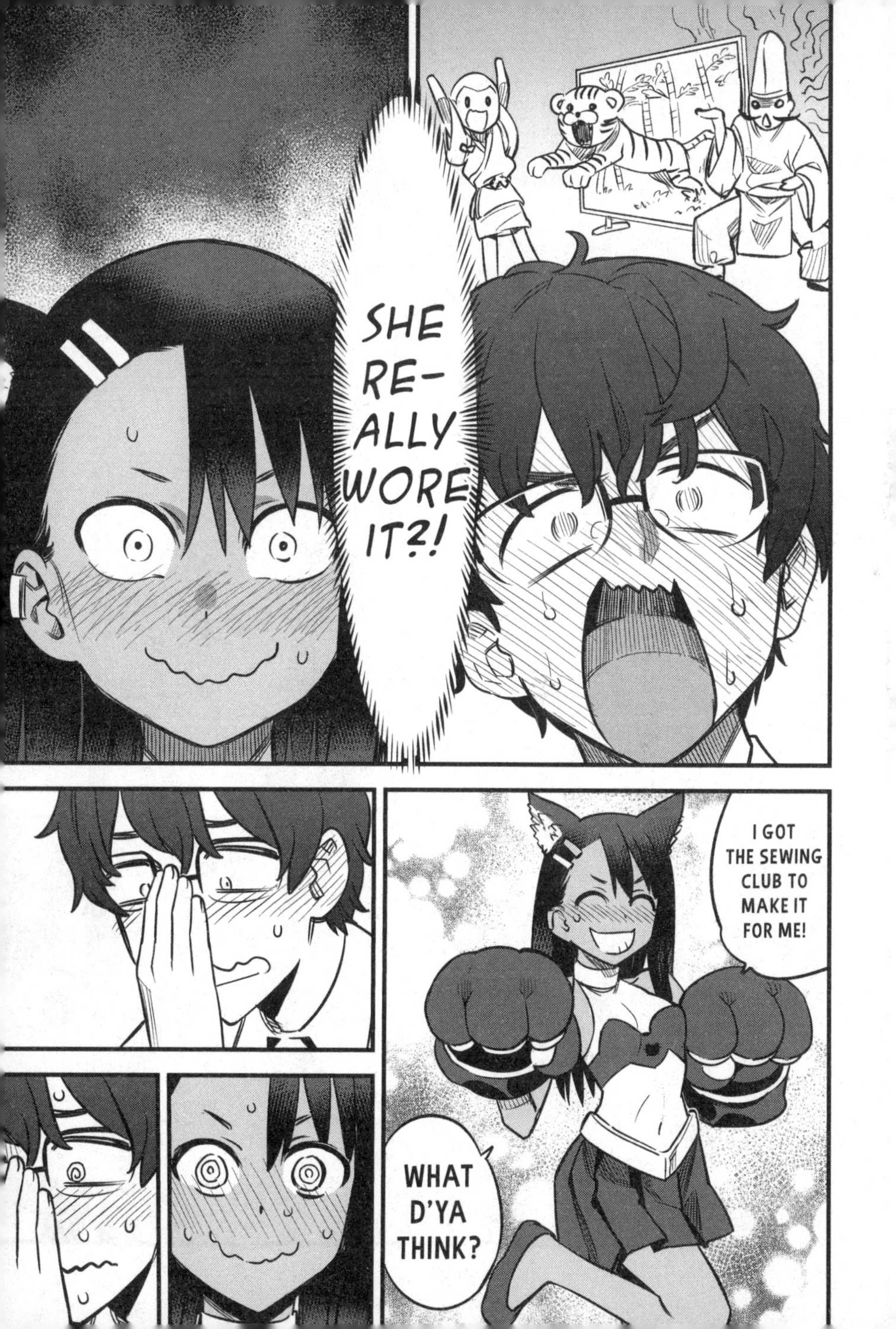
SHE RE-ALLY WORE IT?!
I GOT THE SEWING CLUB TO MAKE IT FOR ME!
WHAT D'YA THINK?

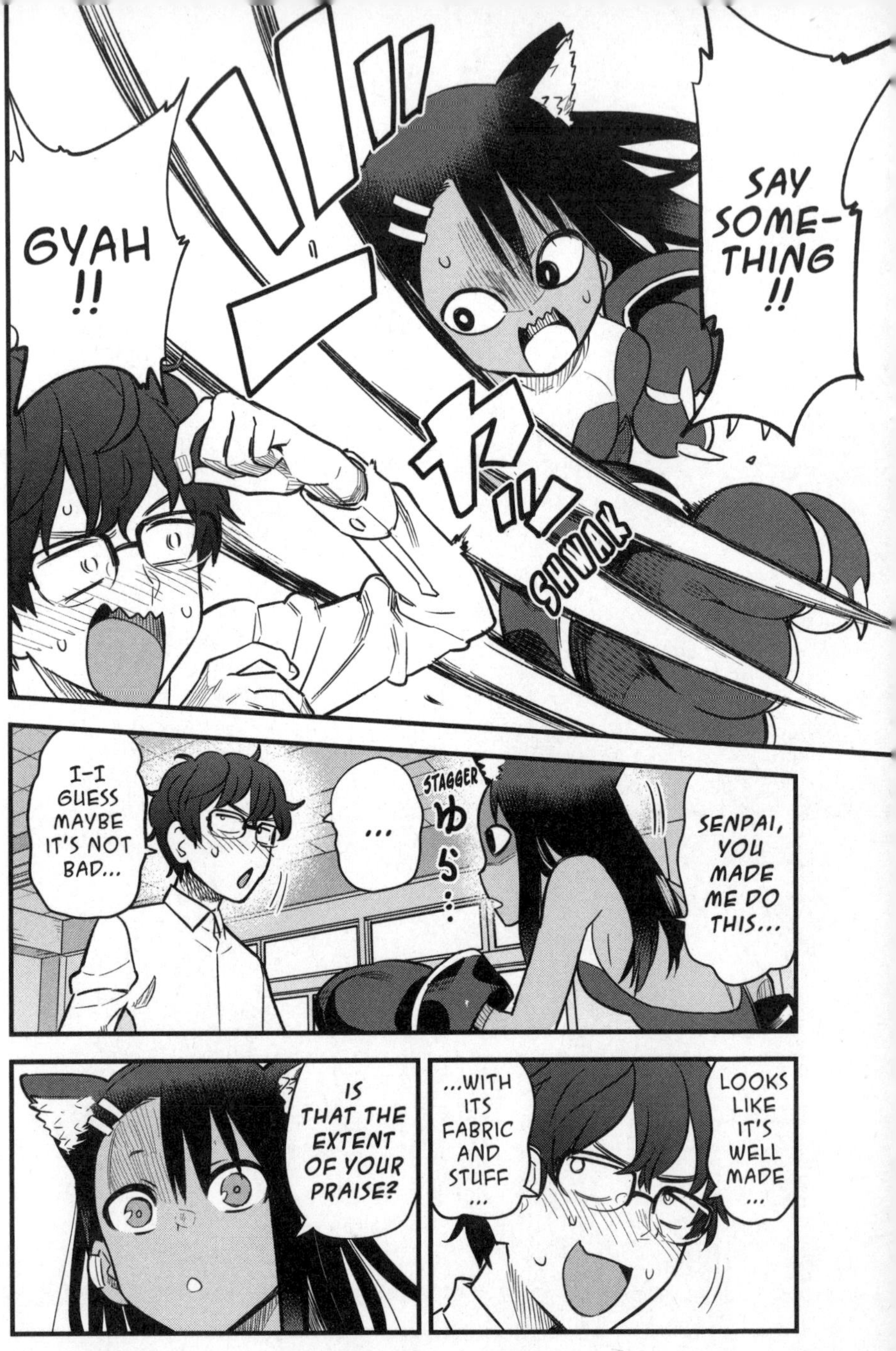
SAY SOMETHING!!
GYAH!!
SHWAK
SENPAI, YOU MADE ME DO THIS...
STAGGER
ゆら…
...
I-I GUESS MAYBE IT'S NOT BAD...
LOOKS LIKE IT'S WELL MADE...
...WITH ITS FABRIC AND STUFF...
IS THAT THE EXTENT OF YOUR PRAISE?

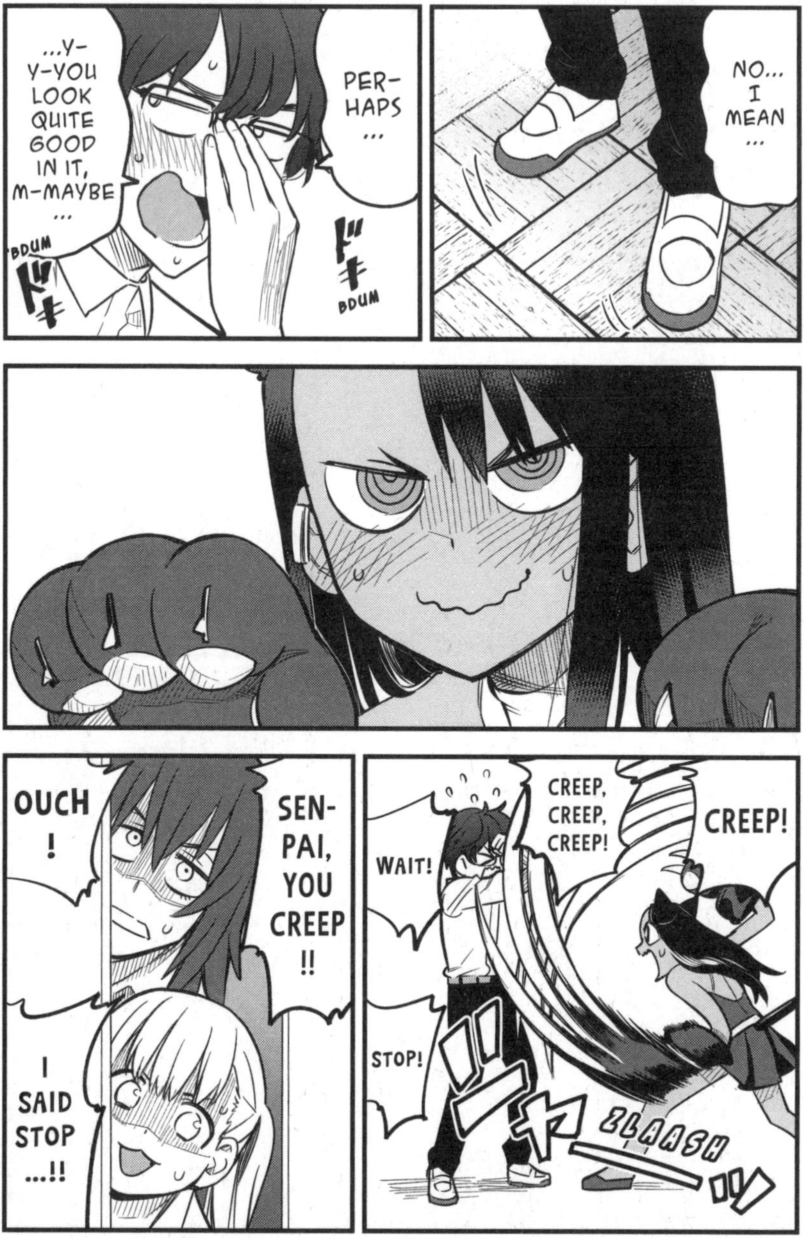
NO... I MEAN ...
PER-HAPS ...
...Y- Y-YOU LOOK QUITE GOOD IN IT, M-MAYBE ...
BDUM
BDUM
CREEP!
CREEP, CREEP, CREEP!
WAIT!
STOP!
ZLAASH
SEN-PAI, YOU CREEP !!
OUCH !
I SAID STOP ...!!

END

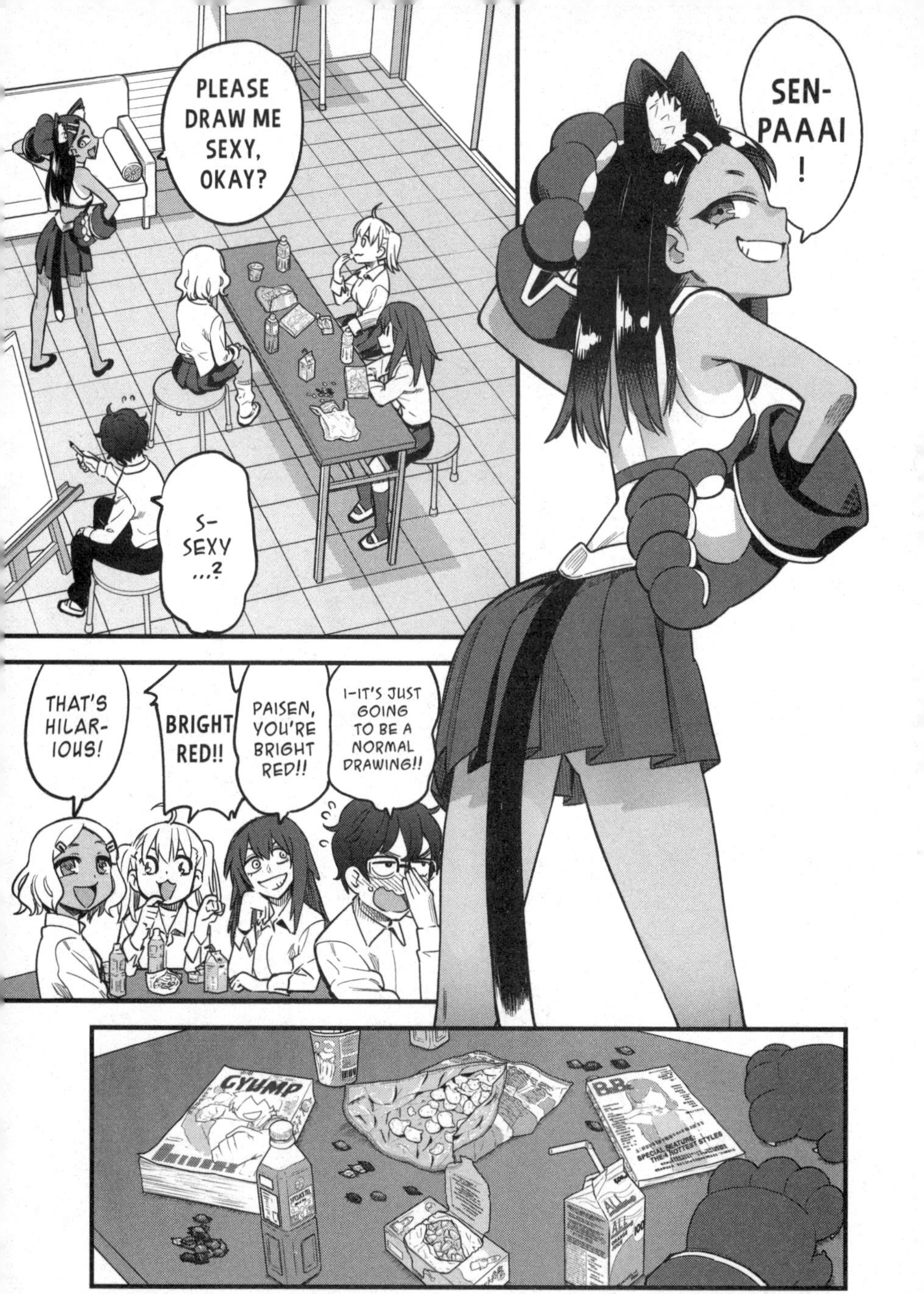
SEN-PAAAI!
PLEASE DRAW ME SEXY, OKAY?
S-SEXY ...?
I-IT'S JUST GOING TO BE A NORMAL DRAWING!!
PAISEN, YOU'RE BRIGHT RED!!
BRIGHT RED!!
THAT'S HILAR-IOUS!

CHAPTER 37: SENPAI, YOU'RE STARING OFF INTO SPACE

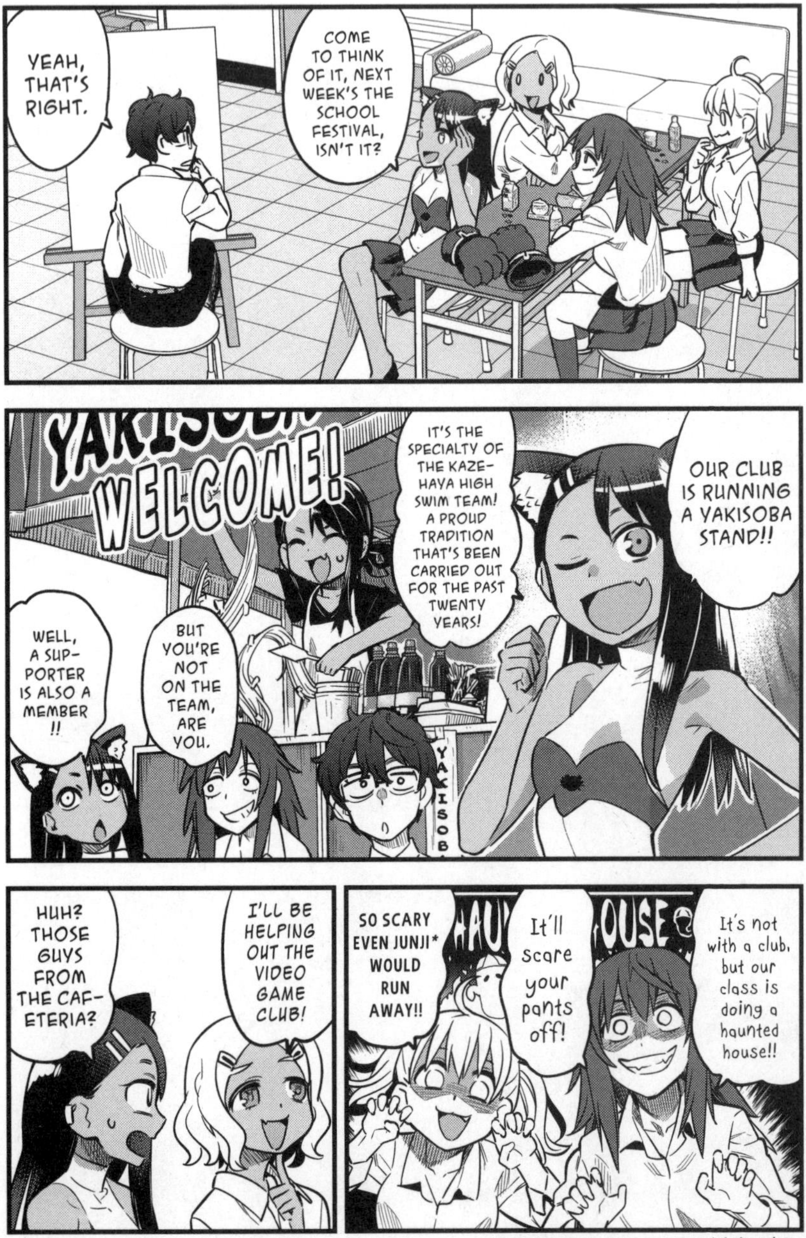
COME TO THINK OF IT, NEXT WEEK'S THE SCHOOL FESTIVAL, ISN'T IT?
YEAH, THAT'S RIGHT.
OUR CLUB IS RUNNING A YAKISOBA STAND!!
IT'S THE SPECIALTY OF THE KAZE-HAYA HIGH SWIM TEAM! A PROUD TRADITION THAT'S BEEN CARRIED OUT FOR THE PAST TWENTY YEARS!
WELCOME!
YAKISOBA
BUT YOU'RE NOT ON THE TEAM, ARE YOU.
WELL, A SUP-PORTER IS ALSO A MEMBER!!
It's not with a club, but our class is doing a haunted house!!
It'll scare your pants off!
SO SCARY EVEN JUNJI* WOULD RUN AWAY!!
I'LL BE HELPING OUT THE VIDEO GAME CLUB!
HUH? THOSE GUYS FROM THE CAF-ETERIA?

*Junji Inagawa: A Japanese celebrity who is famous for his scary-story performances. Similar to Vincent Price for Americans.

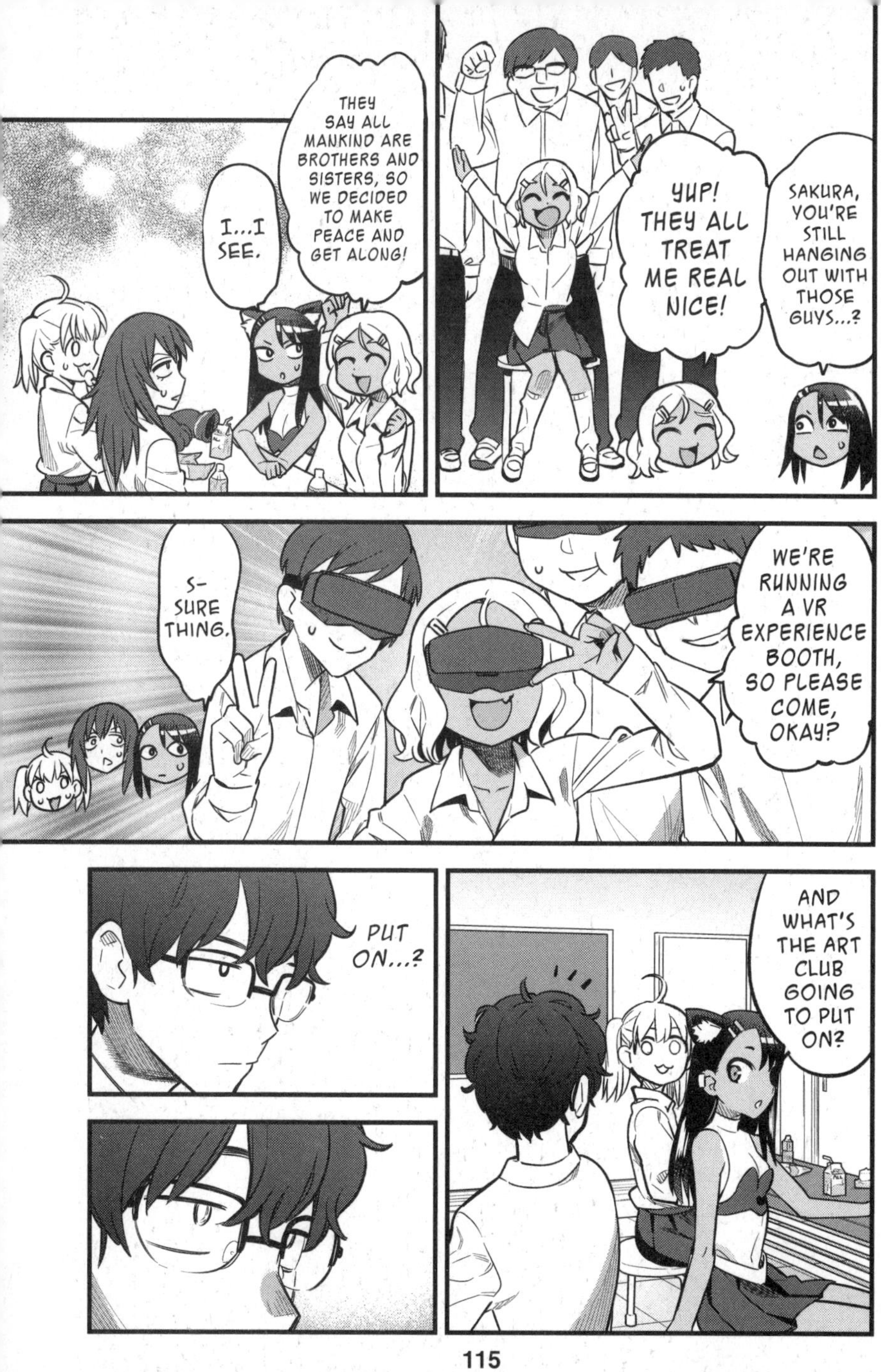
SAKURA, YOU'RE STILL HANGING OUT WITH THOSE GUYS...?
YUP! THEY ALL TREAT ME REAL NICE!
THEY SAY ALL MANKIND ARE BROTHERS AND SISTERS, SO WE DECIDED TO MAKE PEACE AND GET ALONG!
I...I SEE.
WE'RE RUNNING A VR EXPERIENCE BOOTH, SO PLEASE COME, OKAY?
S-SURE THING.
AND WHAT'S THE ART CLUB GOING TO PUT ON?
PUT ON...?

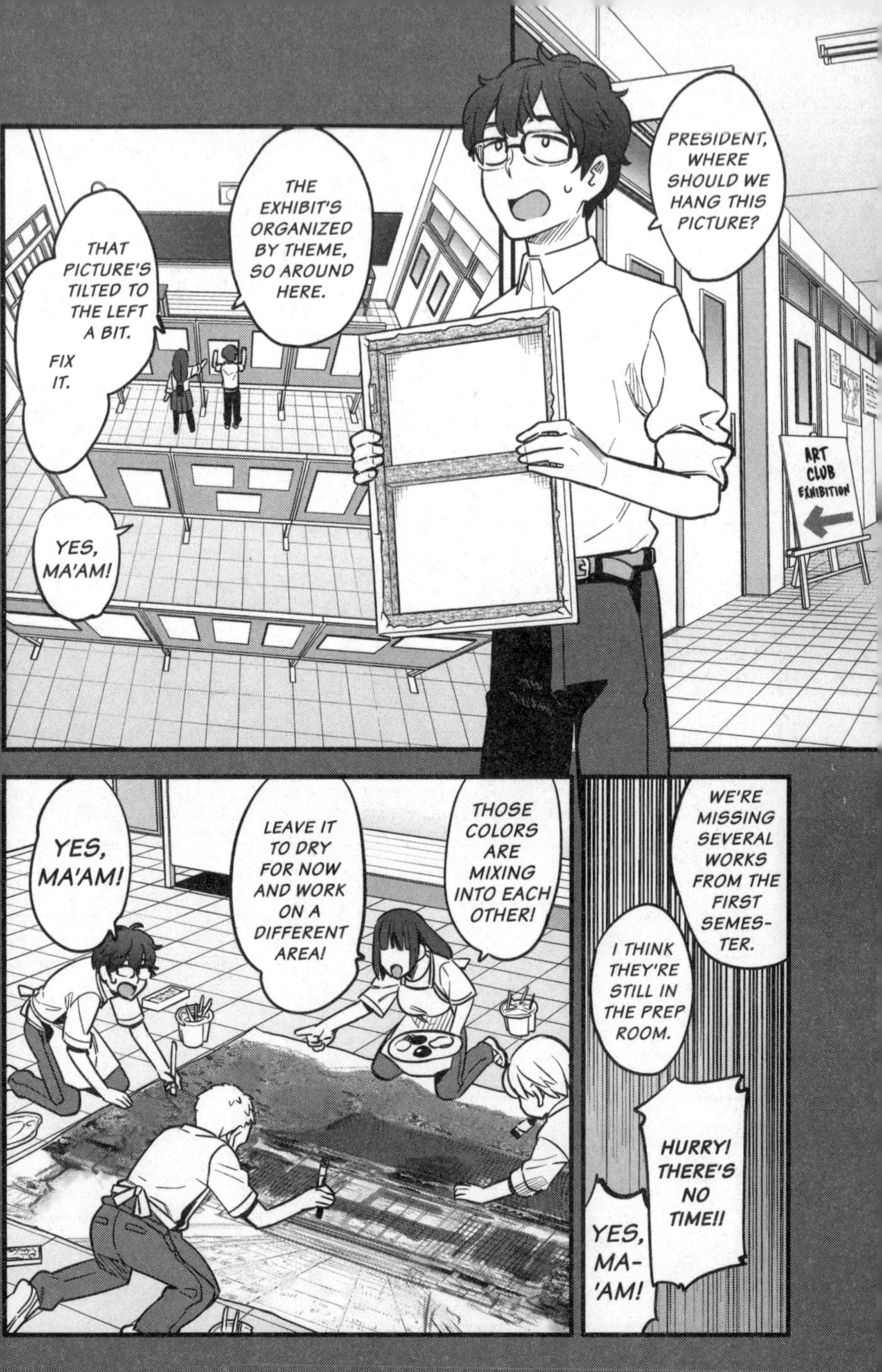
PRESIDENT, WHERE SHOULD WE HANG THIS PICTURE?
ART CLUB EXHIBITION
THE EXHIBIT'S ORGANIZED BY THEME, SO AROUND HERE.
THAT PICTURE'S TILTED TO THE LEFT A BIT.
FIX IT.
YES, MA'AM!
WE'RE MISSING SEVERAL WORKS FROM THE FIRST SEMES-TER.
I THINK THEY'RE STILL IN THE PREP ROOM.
HURRY! THERE'S NO TIME!!
YES, MA-'AM!
THOSE COLORS ARE MIXING INTO EACH OTHER!
LEAVE IT TO DRY FOR NOW AND WORK ON A DIFFERENT AREA!
YES, MA'AM!

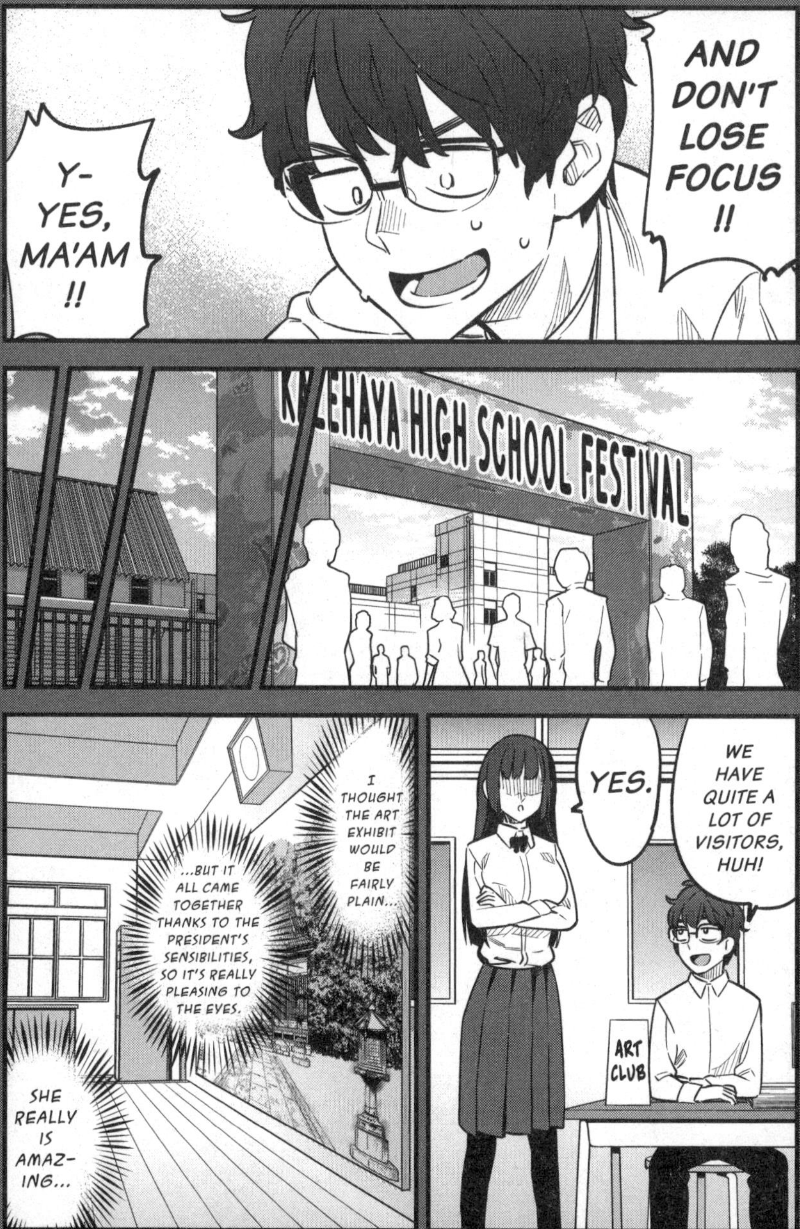
AND DON'T LOSE FOCUS !!
Y-YES, MA'AM !!
HIGH SCHOOL FESTIVAL
WE HAVE QUITE A LOT OF VISITORS, HUH!
YES.
ART CLUB
I THOUGHT THE ART EXHIBIT WOULD BE FAIRLY PLAIN...
...BUT IT ALL CAME TOGETHER THANKS TO THE PRESIDENT'S SENSIBILITIES, SO IT'S REALLY PLEASING TO THE EYES.
SHE REALLY IS AMAZ-ING...

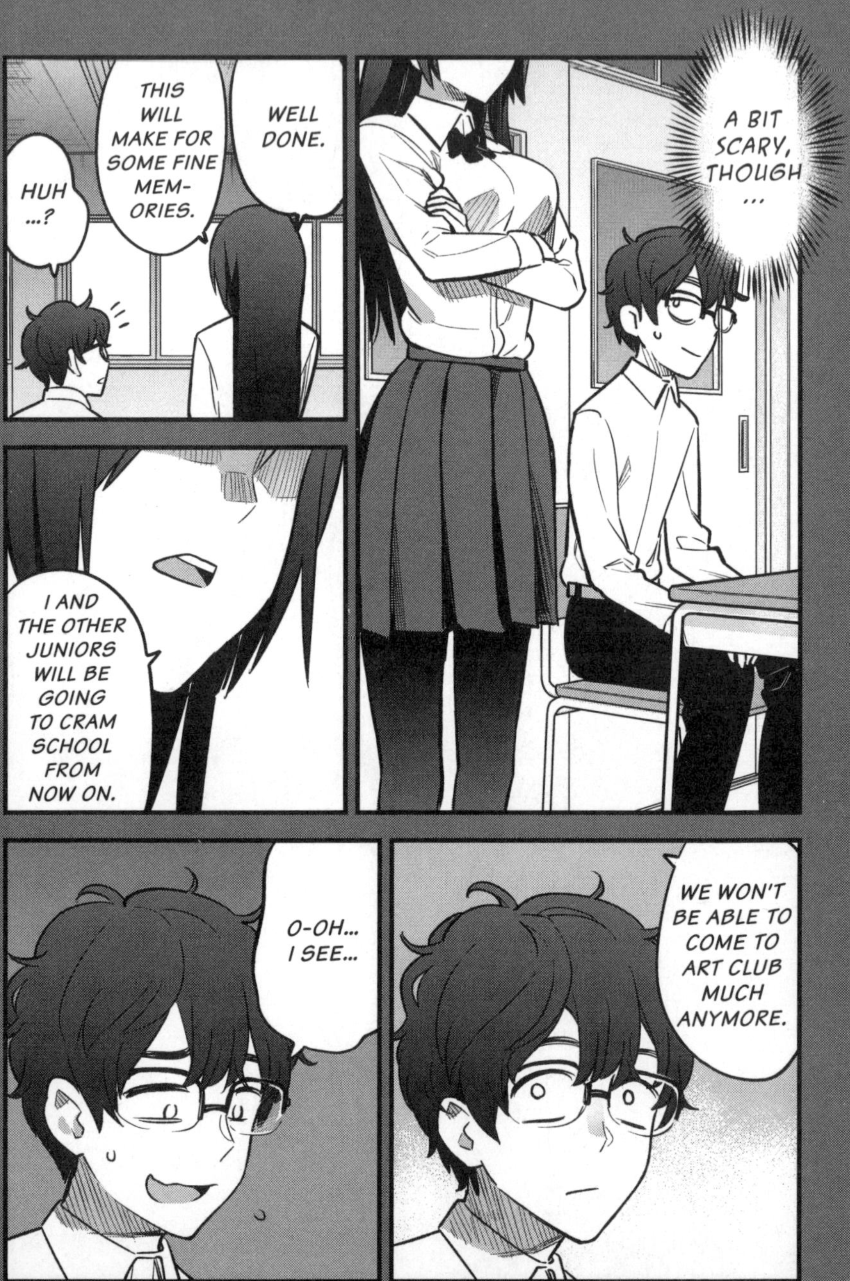
A BIT SCARY, THOUGH ...
WELL DONE.
THIS WILL MAKE FOR SOME FINE MEM- ORIES.
HUH ...?
I AND THE OTHER JUNIORS WILL BE GOING TO CRAM SCHOOL FROM NOW ON.
WE WON'T BE ABLE TO COME TO ART CLUB MUCH ANYMORE.
O-OH... I SEE...

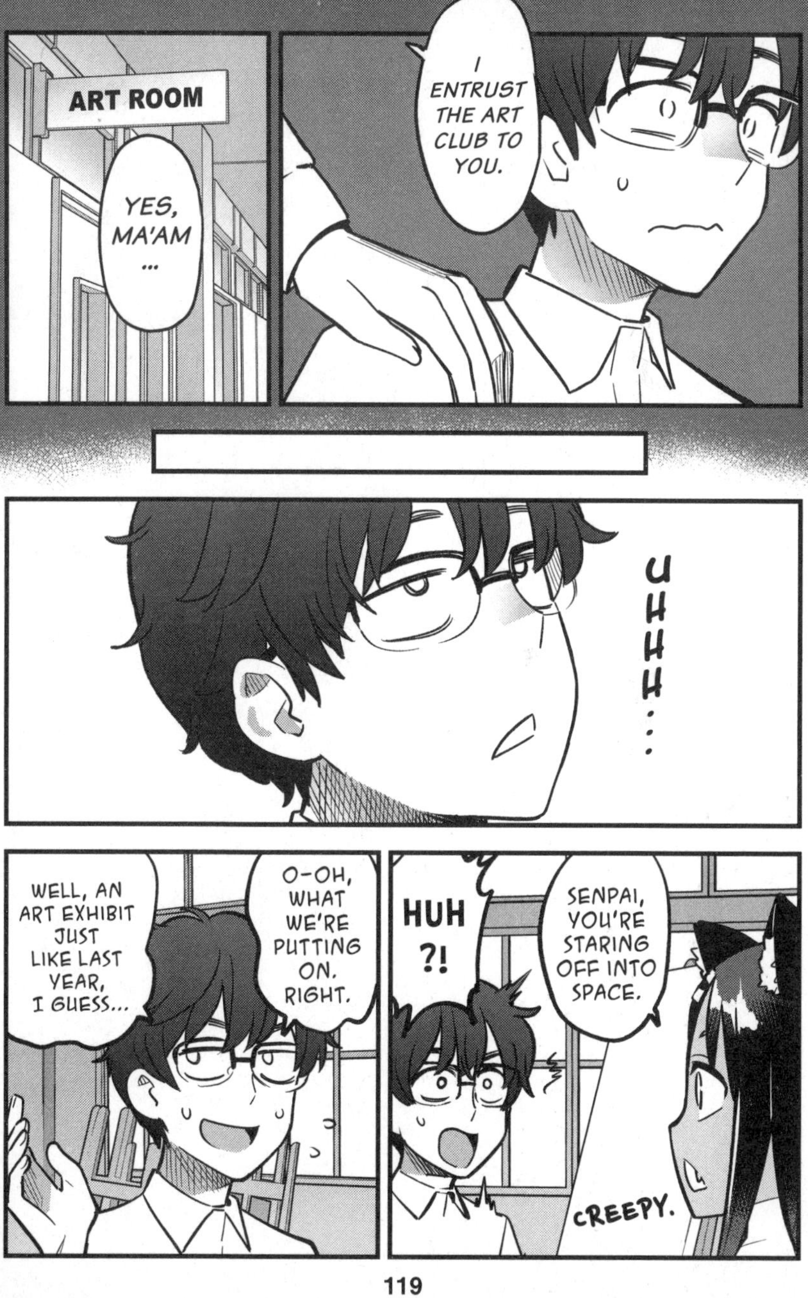
I ENTRUST THE ART CLUB TO YOU.
ART ROOM
YES, MA'AM ...
UHHH...
SENPAI, YOU'RE STARING OFF INTO SPACE.
HUH ?!
CREEPY.
O-OH, WHAT WE'RE PUTTING ON. RIGHT.
WELL, AN ART EXHIBIT JUST LIKE LAST YEAR, I GUESS...

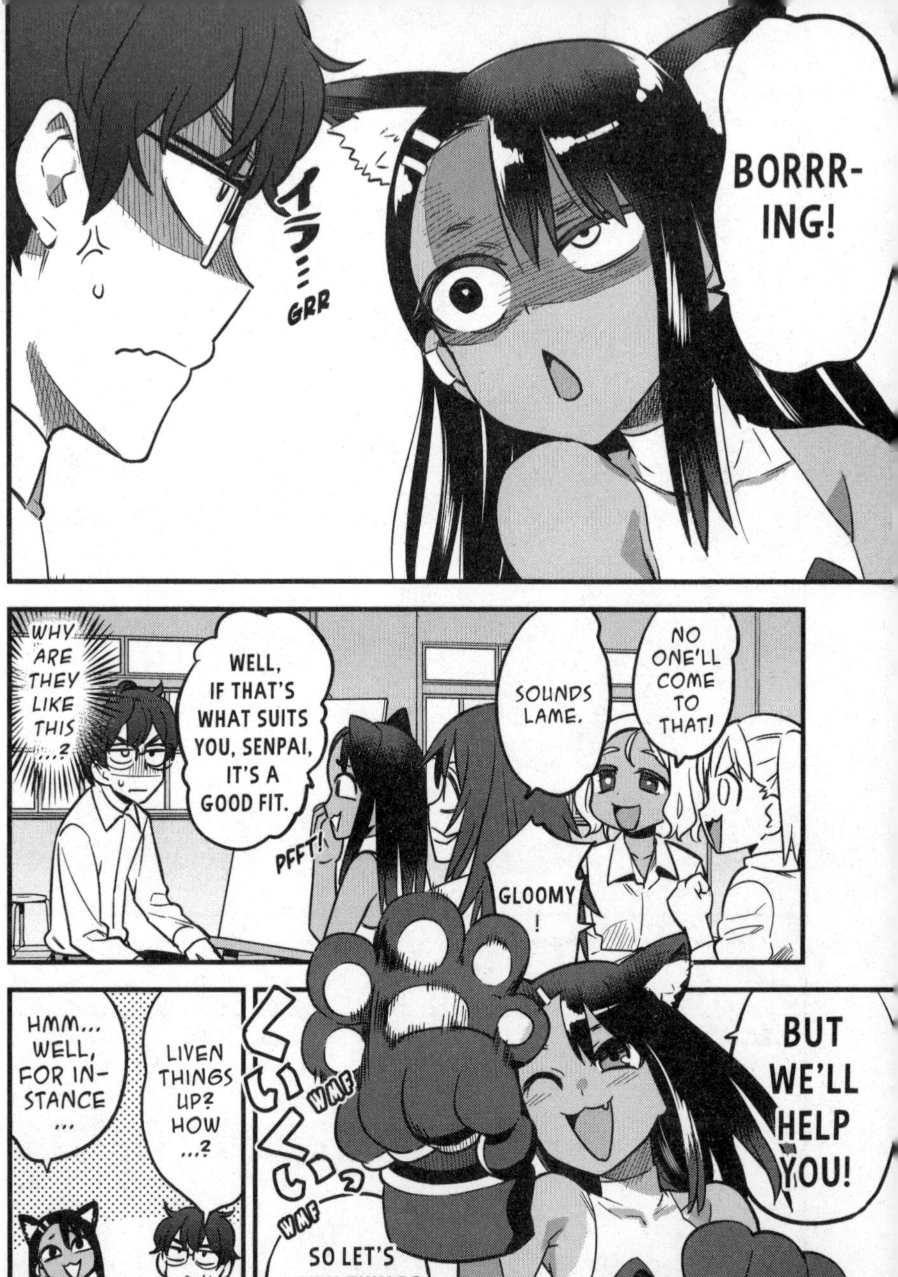
BORRR-ING!
イラ…
GRR
NO ONE'LL COME TO THAT!
SOUNDS LAME.
GLOOMY!
WELL, IF THAT'S WHAT SUITS YOU, SENPAI, IT'S A GOOD FIT.
PFFT!
WHY ARE THEY LIKE THIS …?
BUT WE'LL HELP YOU!
WMF
WMF
SO LET'S LIVEN THINGS UP! GIVE IT SOME PUNCH!
LIVEN THINGS UP? HOW …?
HMM… WELL, FOR IN-STANCE …

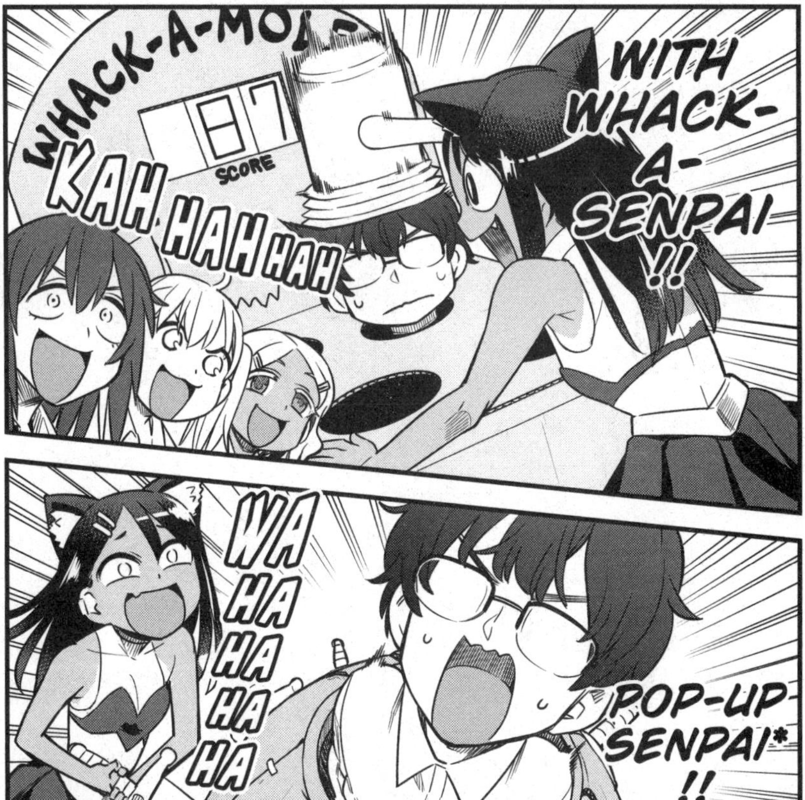
WITH WHACK-A-SENPAI!!
WHACK-A-MOL
SCORE
KAH HAH HAH HAH
POP-UP SENPAI* !!
WA HA HA HA HA HA

*Based on the Pop-up Pirate game by Tomy—a game of luck similar to Crocodile Dentist but with a pirate in a barrel full of swords.

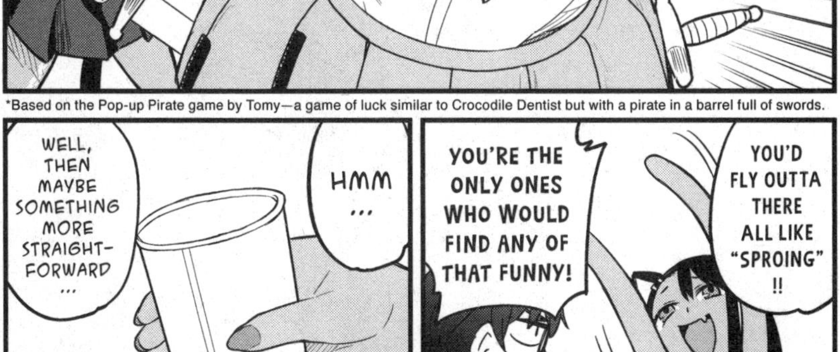
YOU'D FLY OUTTA THERE ALL LIKE "SPROING" !!
YOU'RE THE ONLY ONES WHO WOULD FIND ANY OF THAT FUNNY!
HMM ...
WELL, THEN MAYBE SOMETHING MORE STRAIGHT-FORWARD ...

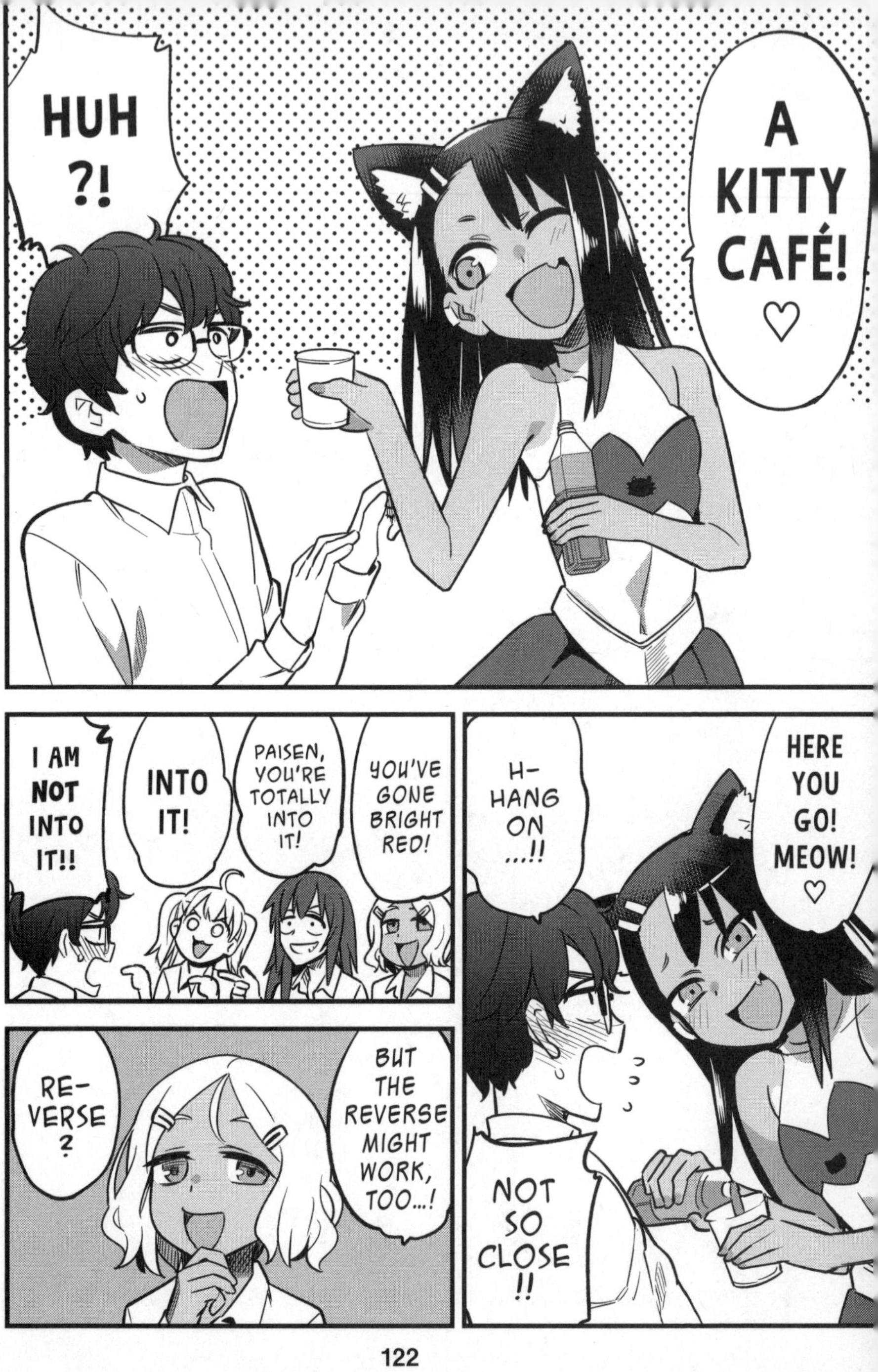
A KITTY CAFÉ! ♡
HUH ?!
HERE YOU GO! MEOW! ♡
H-HANG ON ...!!
NOT SO CLOSE !!
YOU'VE GONE BRIGHT RED!
PAISEN, YOU'RE TOTALLY INTO IT!
INTO IT!
I AM NOT INTO IT!!
BUT THE REVERSE MIGHT WORK, TOO...!
RE-VERSE ?

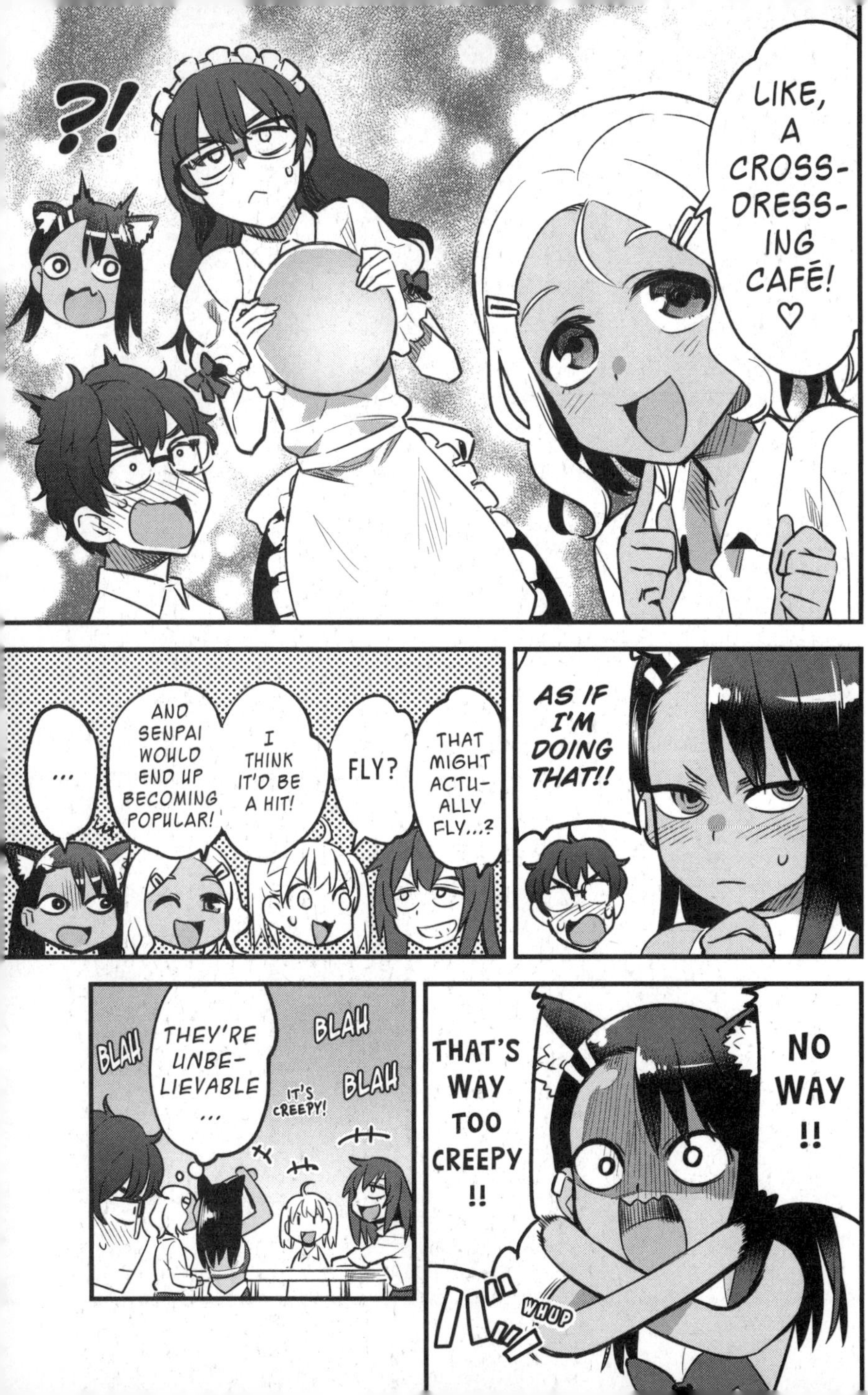
LIKE, A CROSS-DRESSING CAFÉ! ♡
?!
AS IF I'M DOING THAT!!
THAT MIGHT ACTUALLY FLY...?
FLY?
I THINK IT'D BE A HIT!
AND SENPAI WOULD END UP BECOMING POPULAR!
...
NO WAY!!
THAT'S WAY TOO CREEPY!!
WHUP
BLAH
BLAH
IT'S CREEPY!
THEY'RE UNBELIEVABLE...
BLAH

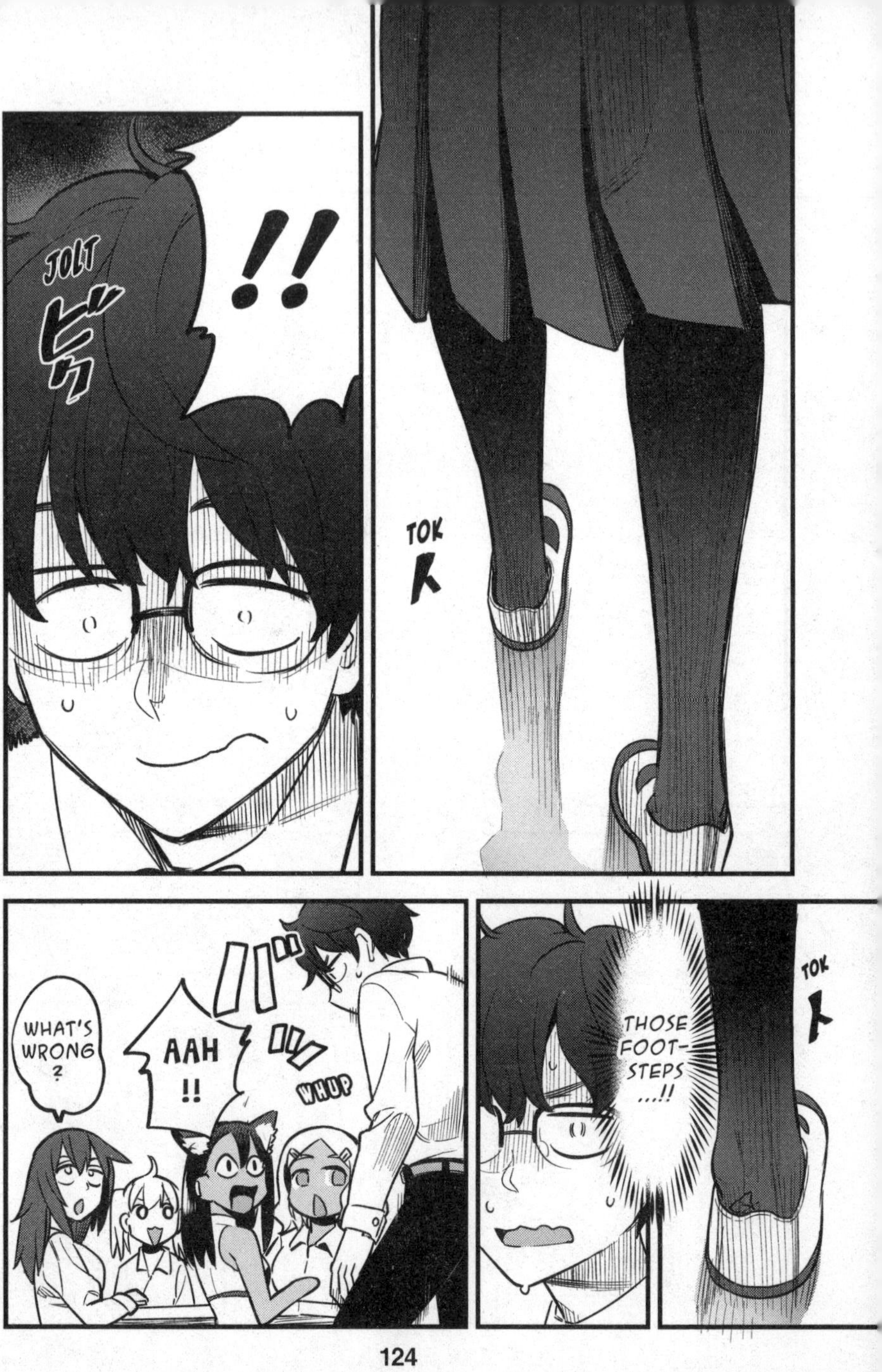
TOK
ト
JOLT
ビク
!!
TOK
ト
THOSE FOOT-STEPS ...!!
WHUP
AAH !!
WHAT'S WRONG?

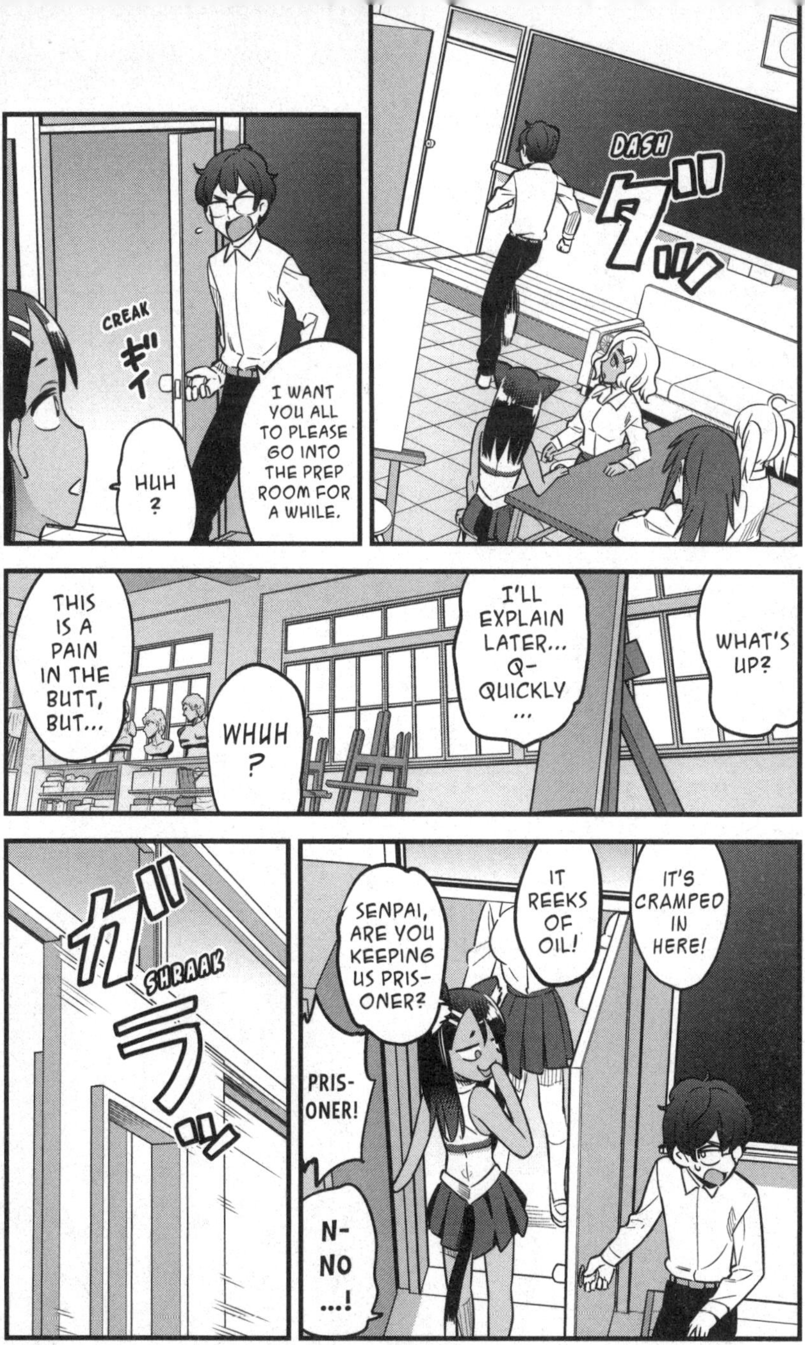
DASH
ダッ
CREAK
ギィ
I WANT YOU ALL TO PLEASE GO INTO THE PREP ROOM FOR A WHILE.
HUH?
WHAT'S UP?
I'LL EXPLAIN LATER... Q-QUICKLY...
WHUH?
THIS IS A PAIN IN THE BUTT, BUT...
IT'S CRAMPED IN HERE!
IT REEKS OF OIL!
SENPAI, ARE YOU KEEPING US PRIS-ONER?
PRIS-ONER!
N-NO...!
ガラッ
SHRAAK

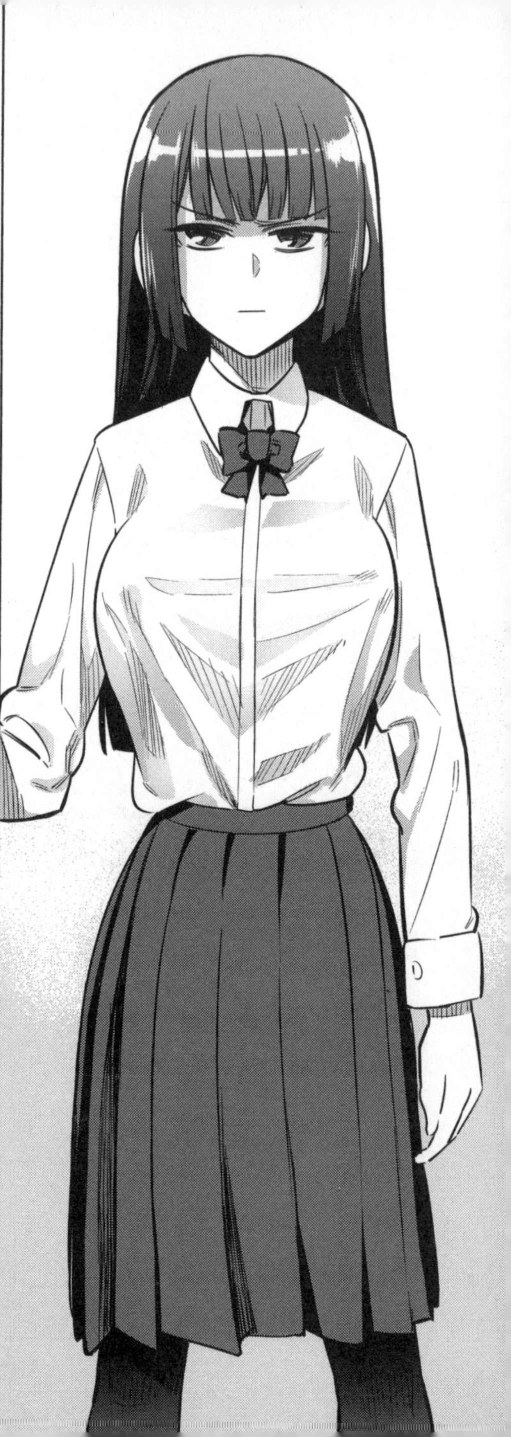

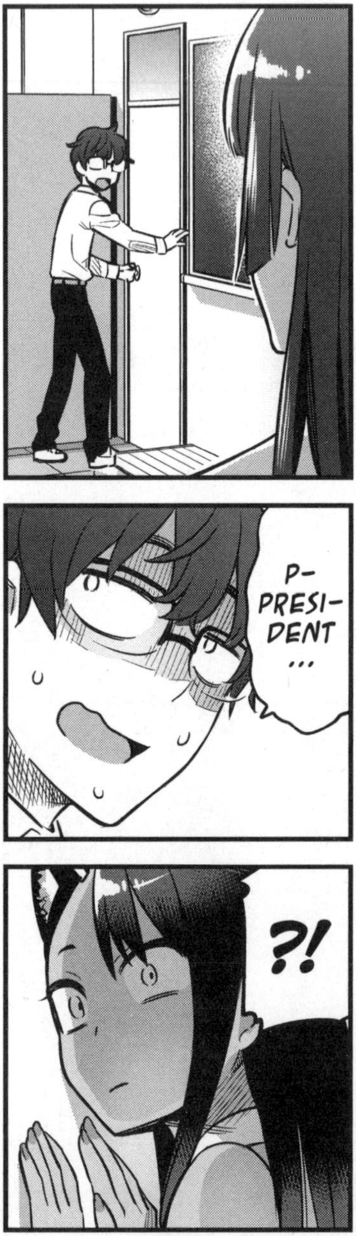
P-PRESIDENT...
?!

END

DON'T TOY WITH ME,
MISS NAGATORO

CHAPTER 38: LET'S GO FOR IT, SENPAI!!

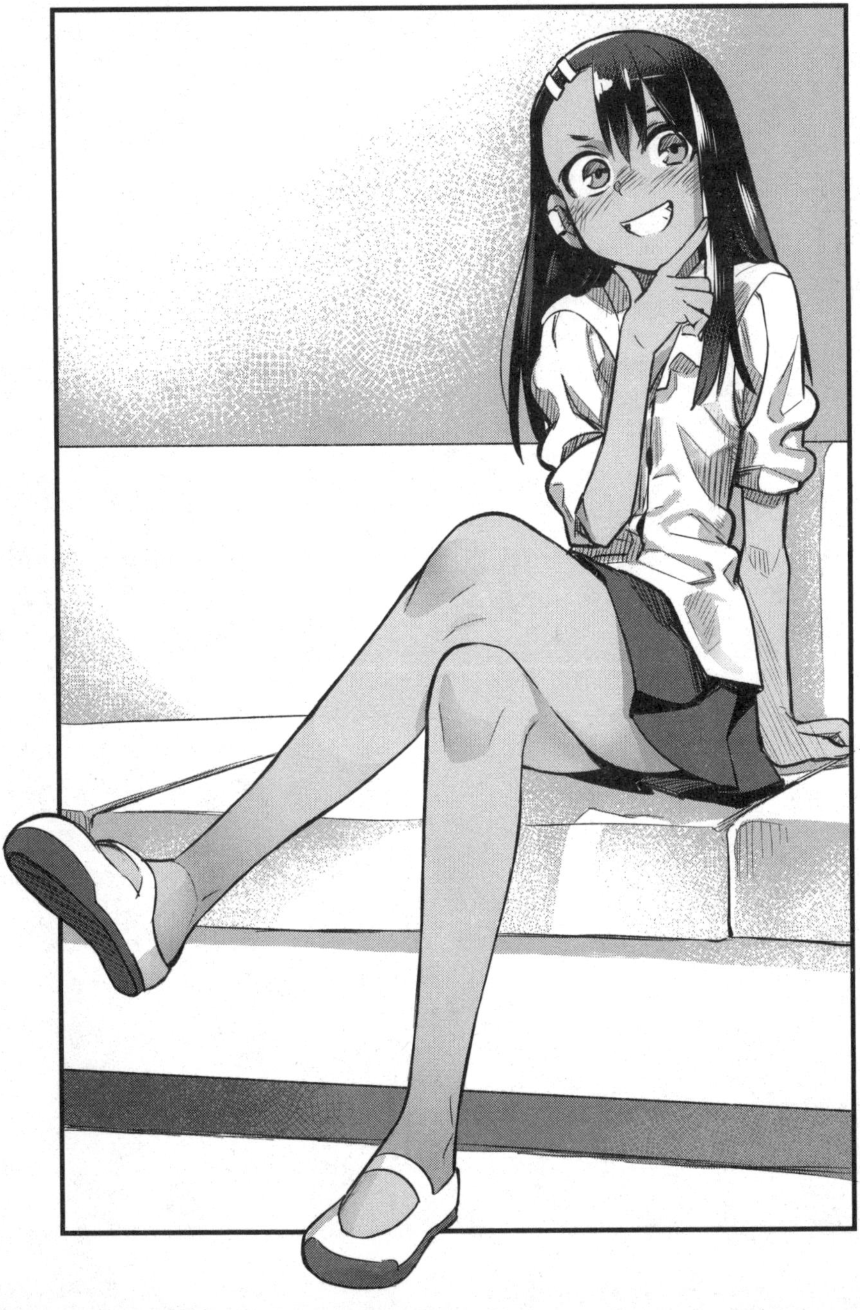

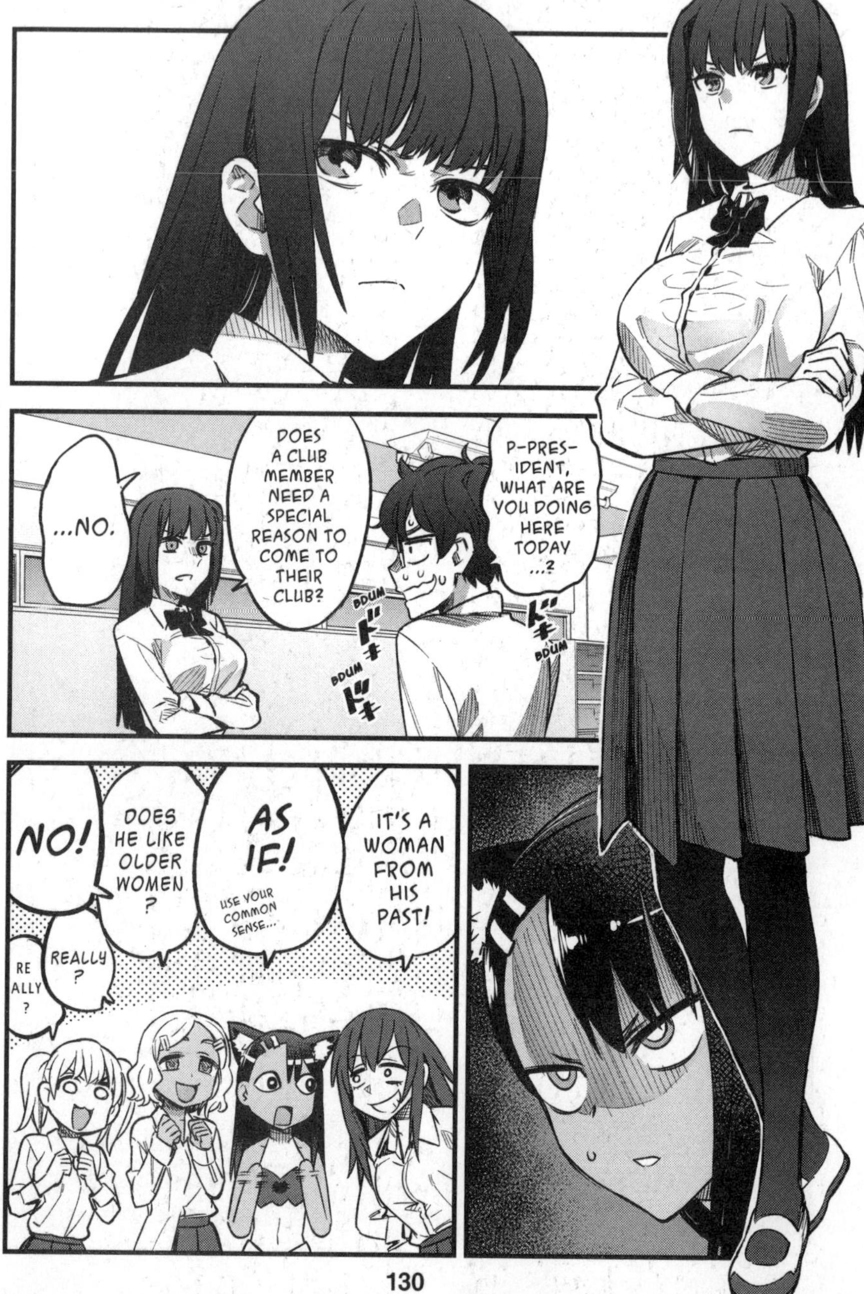
P-PRESIDENT, WHAT ARE YOU DOING HERE TODAY...?
BDUM
BDUM
DOES A CLUB MEMBER NEED A SPECIAL REASON TO COME TO THEIR CLUB?
BDUM
...NO.
IT'S A WOMAN FROM HIS PAST!
AS IF!
USE YOUR COMMON SENSE...
DOES HE LIKE OLDER WOMEN?
NO!
REALLY?
RE ALLY?

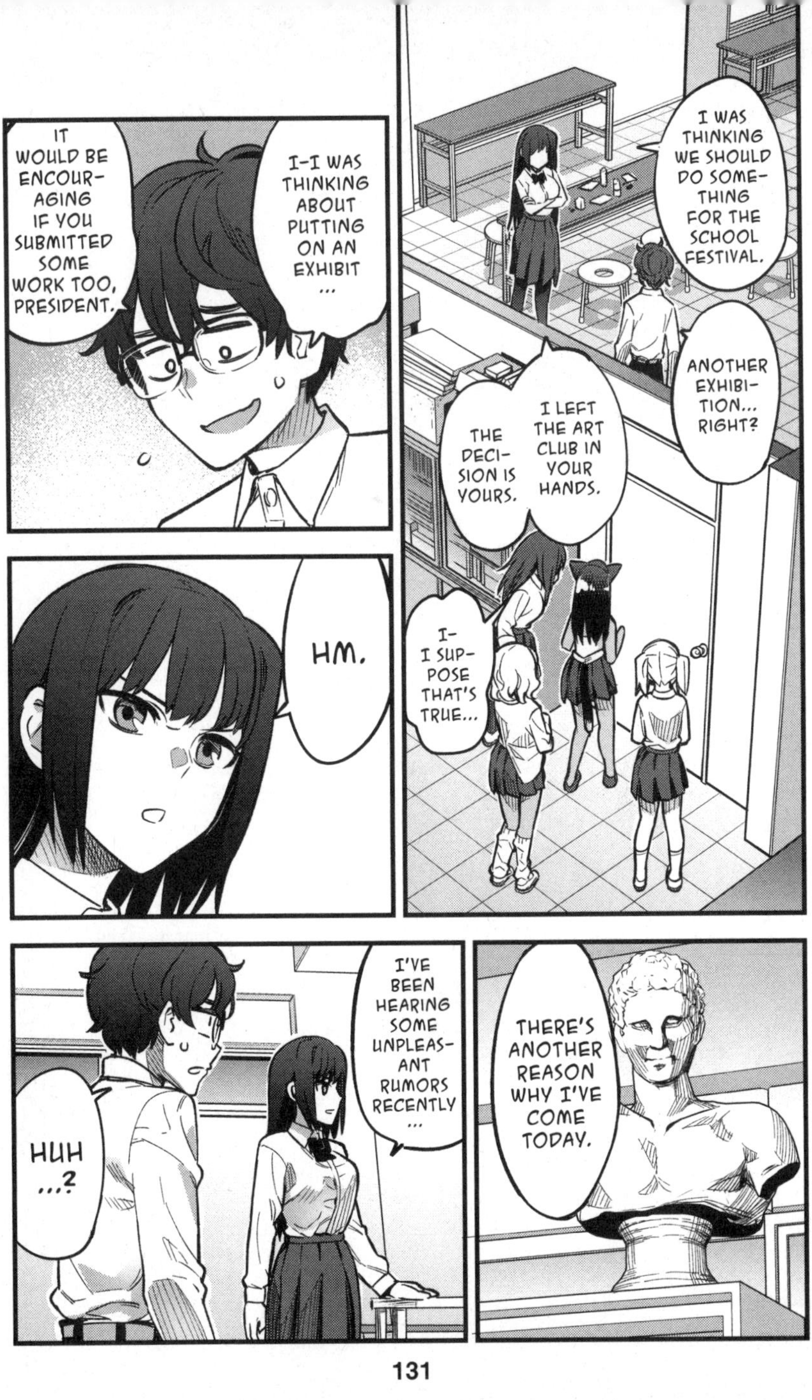
I WAS THINKING WE SHOULD DO SOMETHING FOR THE SCHOOL FESTIVAL.
ANOTHER EXHIBITION... RIGHT?
I LEFT THE ART CLUB IN YOUR HANDS.
THE DECISION IS YOURS.
I- I SUPPOSE THAT'S TRUE...
I-I WAS THINKING ABOUT PUTTING ON AN EXHIBIT...
IT WOULD BE ENCOURAGING IF YOU SUBMITTED SOME WORK TOO, PRESIDENT.
HM.
THERE'S ANOTHER REASON WHY I'VE COME TODAY.
I'VE BEEN HEARING SOME UNPLEASANT RUMORS RECENTLY...
HUH...?

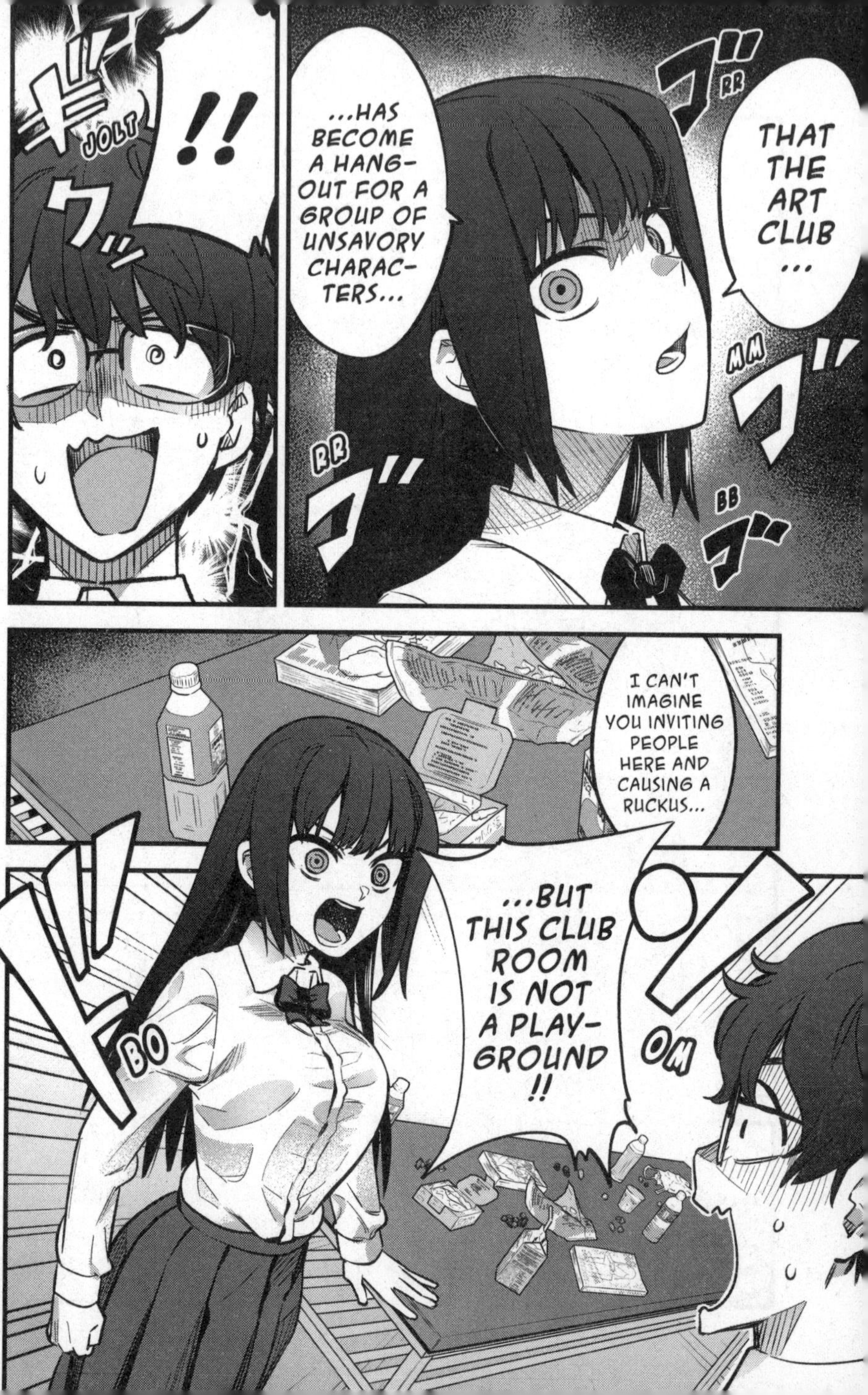
RR
THAT THE ART CLUB ...
...HAS BECOME A HANG-OUT FOR A GROUP OF UNSAVORY CHARAC-TERS...
MM
BB
RR
!!
JOLT
I CAN'T IMAGINE YOU INVITING PEOPLE HERE AND CAUSING A RUCKUS...
...BUT THIS CLUB ROOM IS NOT A PLAY-GROUND !!
OM
BO

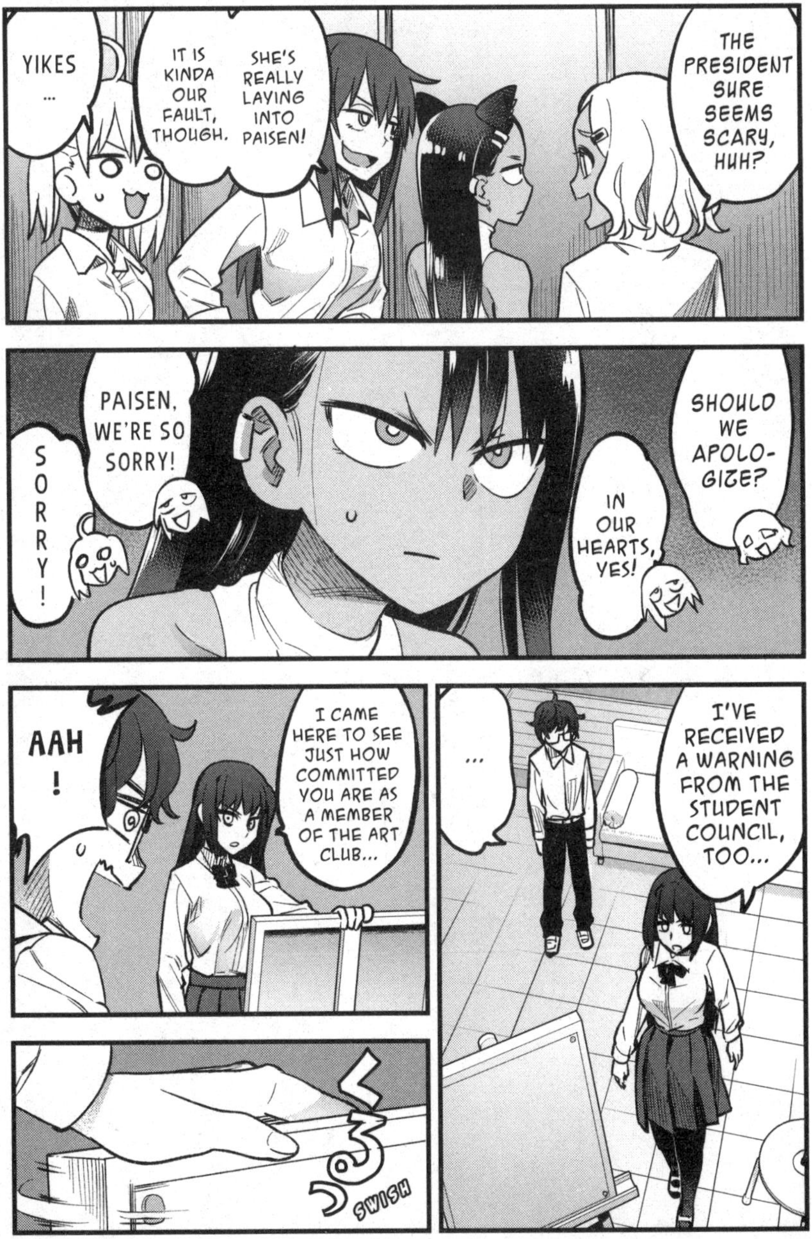
THE PRESIDENT SURE SEEMS SCARY, HUH?
SHE'S REALLY LAYING INTO PAISEN!
IT IS KINDA OUR FAULT, THOUGH.
YIKES ...
SHOULD WE APOLOGIZE?
IN OUR HEARTS, YES!
PAISEN, WE'RE SO SORRY!
SORRY!
I'VE RECEIVED A WARNING FROM THE STUDENT COUNCIL, TOO...
...
I CAME HERE TO SEE JUST HOW COMMITTED YOU ARE AS A MEMBER OF THE ART CLUB...
AAH!
SWISH

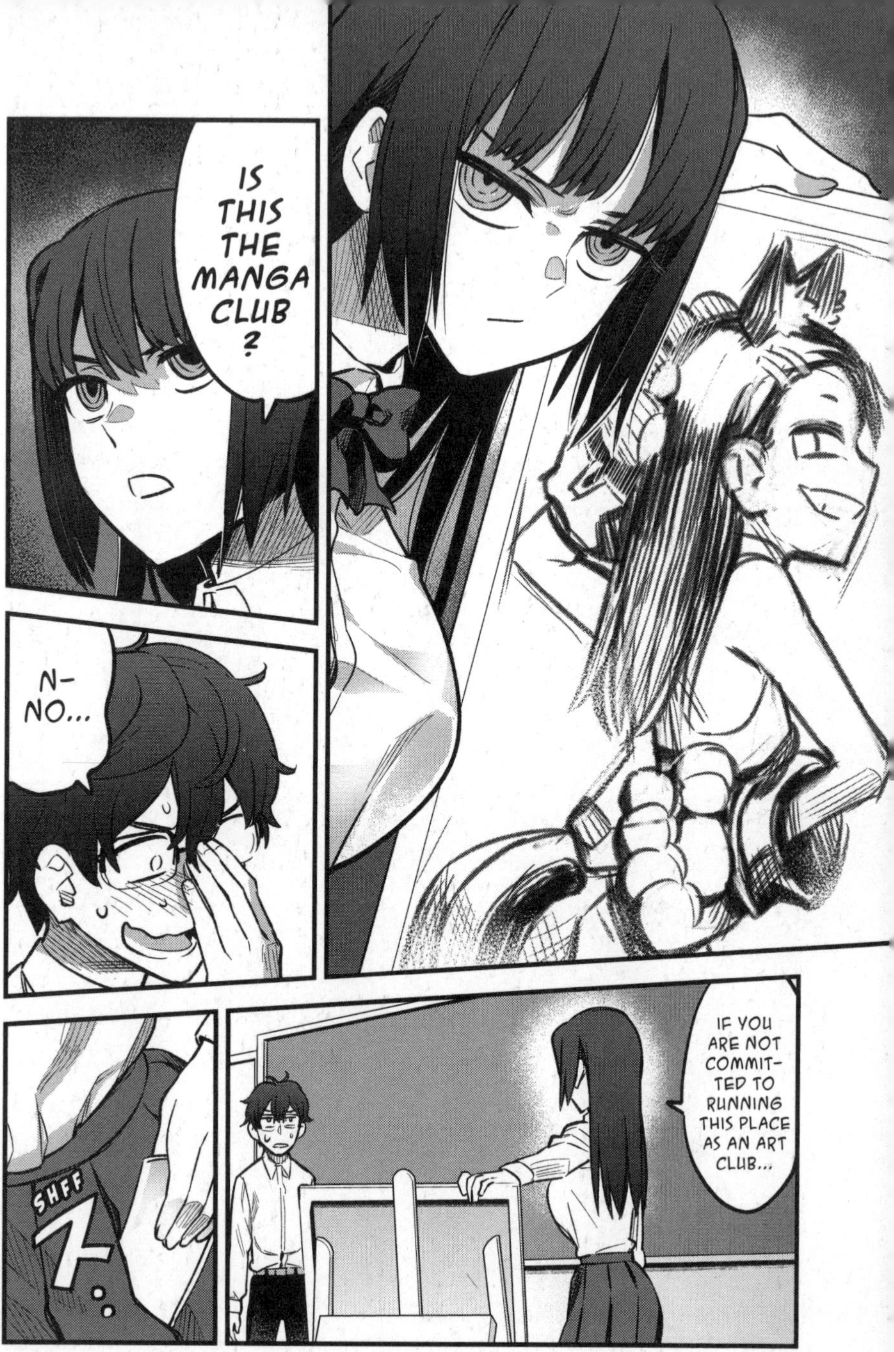
IS THIS THE MANGA CLUB?
N-NO...
IF YOU ARE NOT COMMITTED TO RUNNING THIS PLACE AS AN ART CLUB...
SHFF

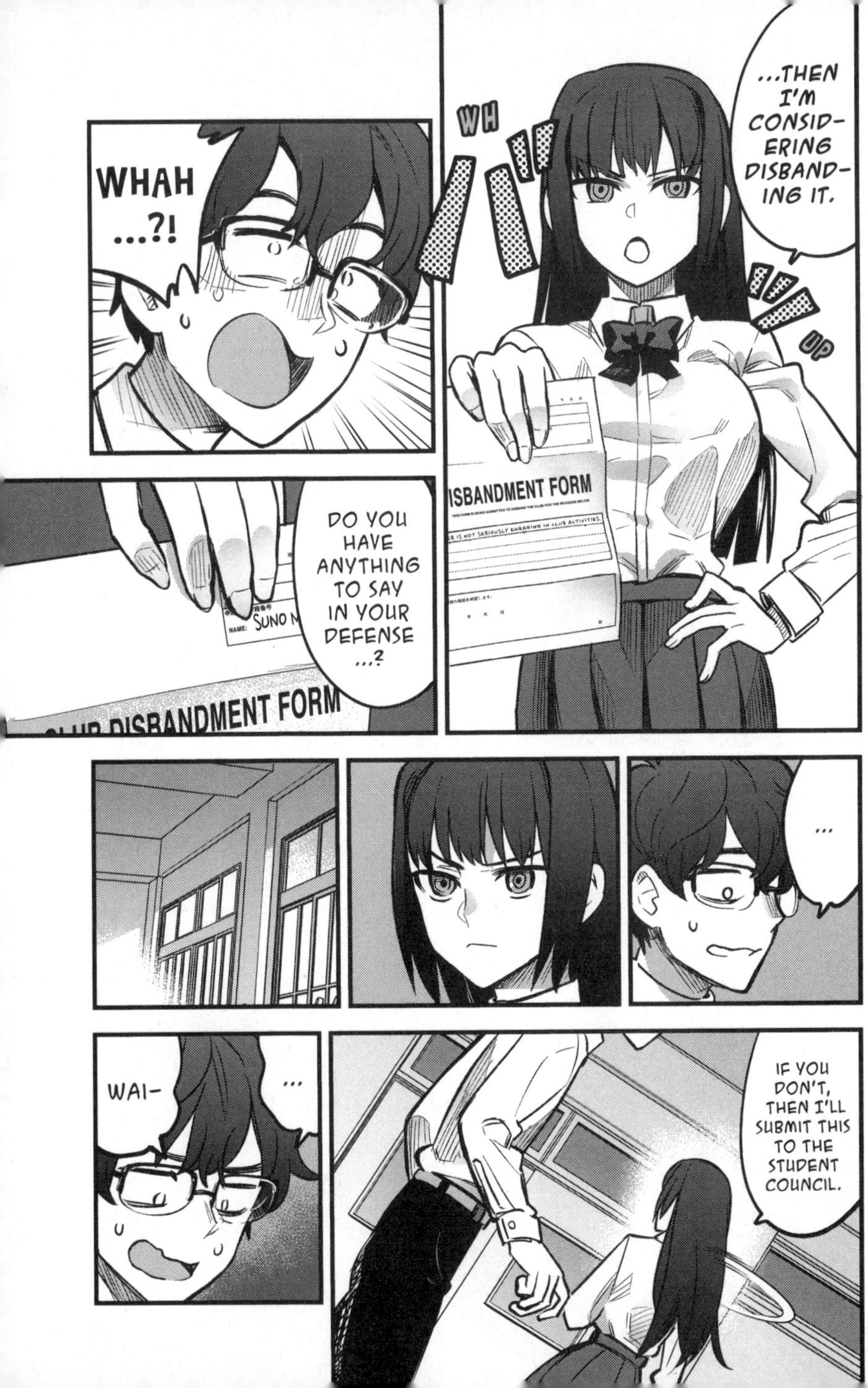
WH
UP
...THEN I'M CONSIDERING DISBANDING IT.
ISBANDMENT FORM
THIS FORM IS BEING SUBMITTED TO DISBAND THE CLUB FOR THE REASONS BELOW.
ER IS NOT SERIOUSLY ENGAGING IN CLUB ACTIVITIES.
WHAH ...?!
NAME: SUNO M
CLUB DISBANDMENT FORM
DO YOU HAVE ANYTHING TO SAY IN YOUR DEFENSE ...?
...
IF YOU DON'T, THEN I'LL SUBMIT THIS TO THE STUDENT COUNCIL.
WAI-
...

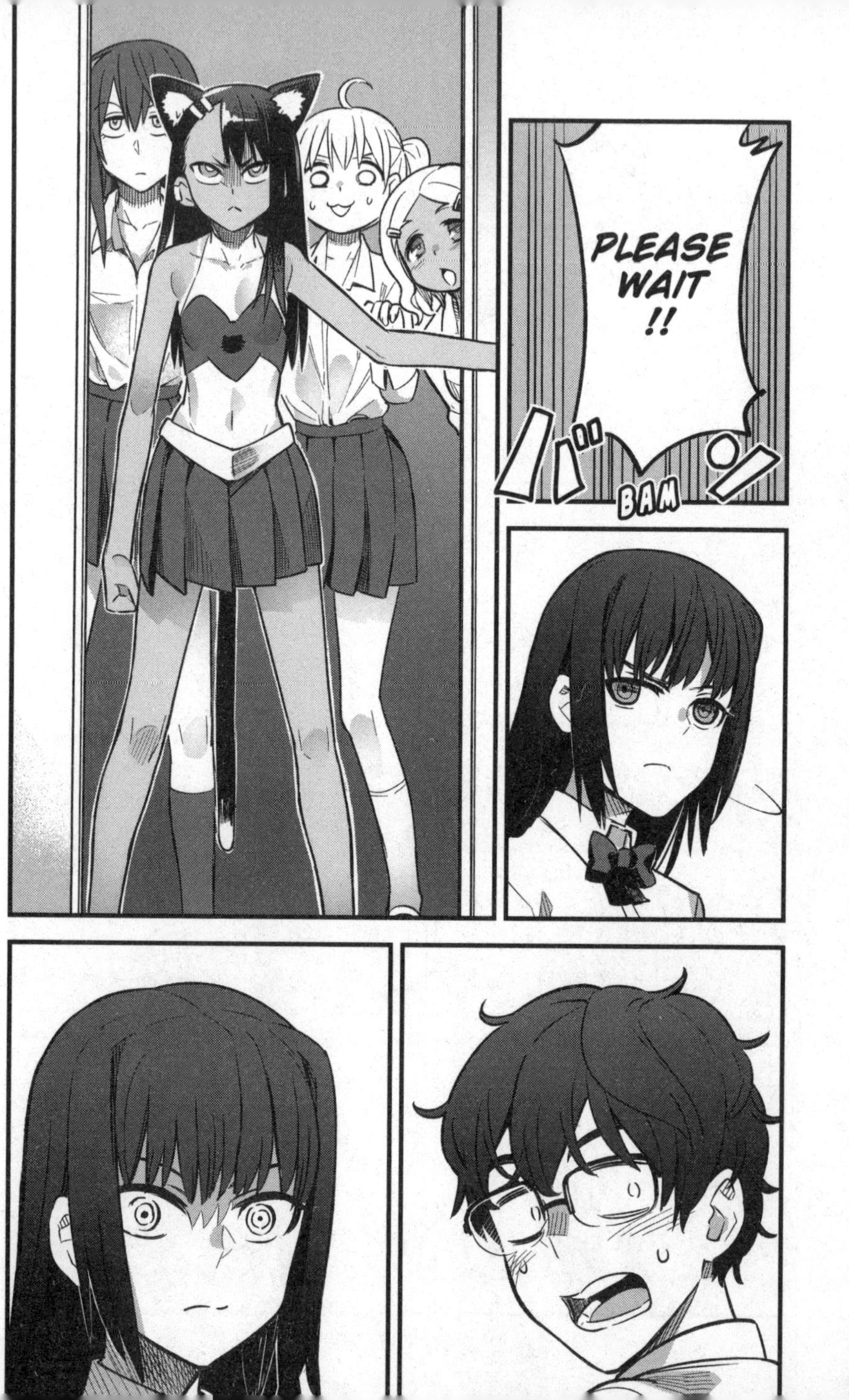
PLEASE WAIT !!
BAM

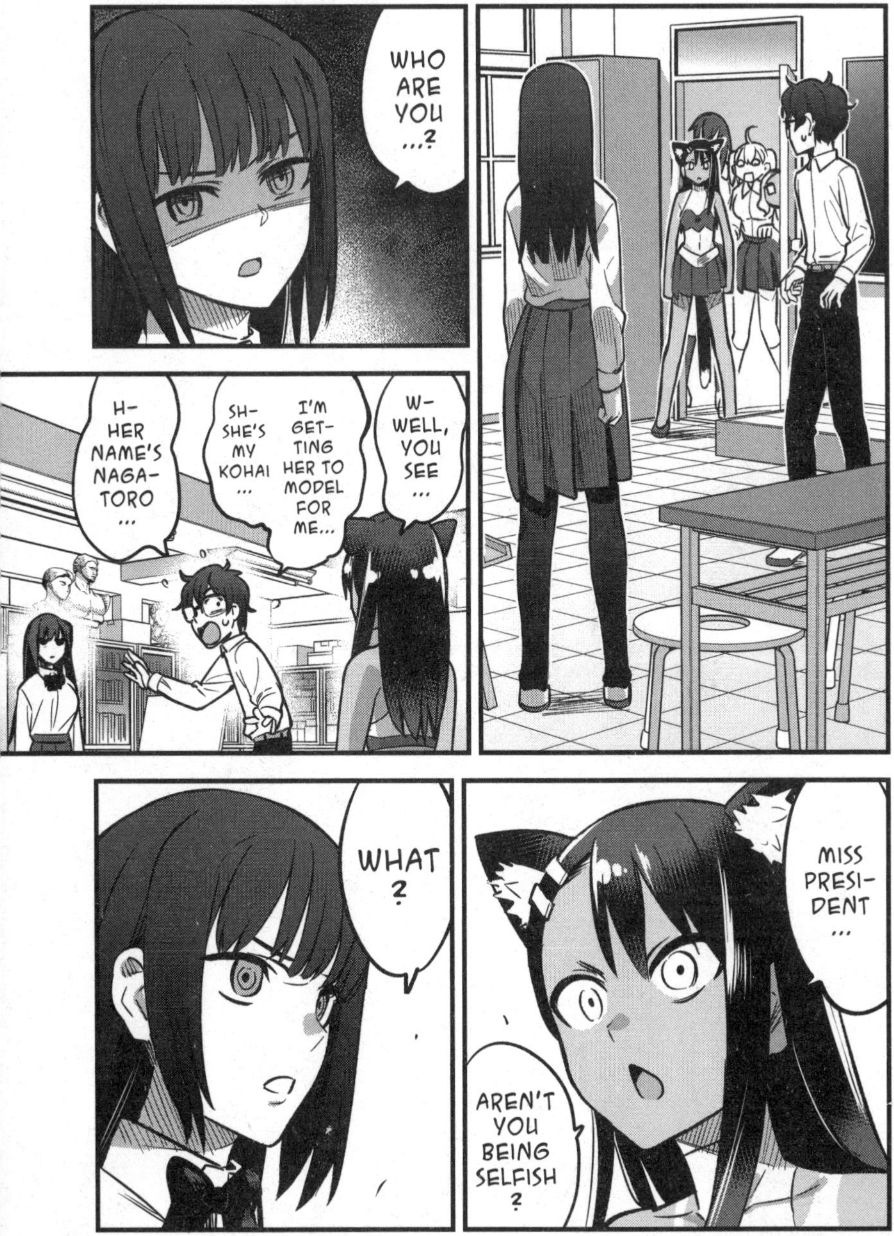
WHO ARE YOU ...?
W-WELL, YOU SEE ...
I'M GETTING HER TO MODEL FOR ME...
SH-SHE'S MY KOHAI ...
H-HER NAME'S NAGATORO ...
MISS PRESIDENT ...
AREN'T YOU BEING SELFISH?
WHAT?

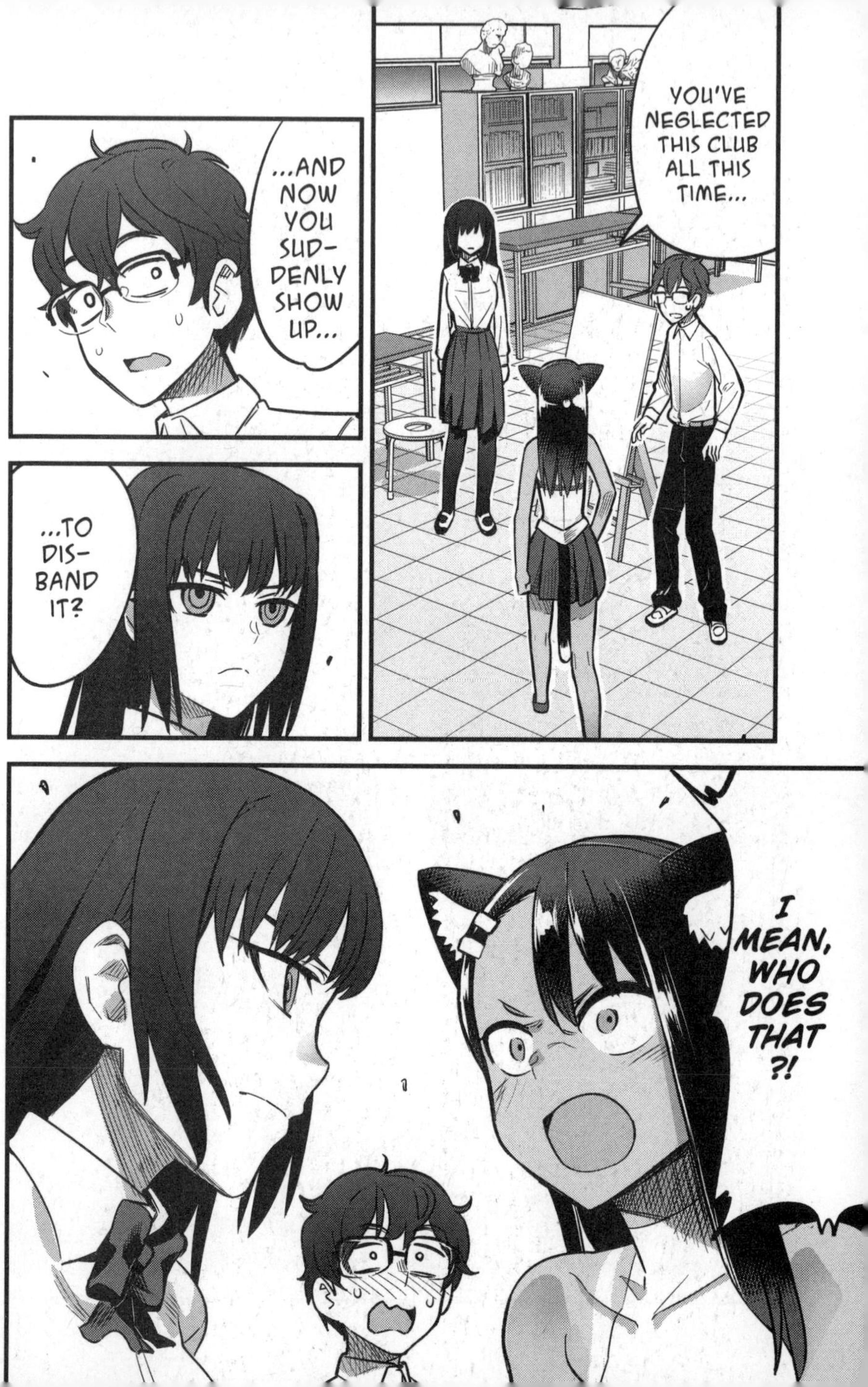
YOU'VE NEGLECTED THIS CLUB ALL THIS TIME...
...AND NOW YOU SUDDENLY SHOW UP...
...TO DISBAND IT?
I MEAN, WHO DOES THAT?!

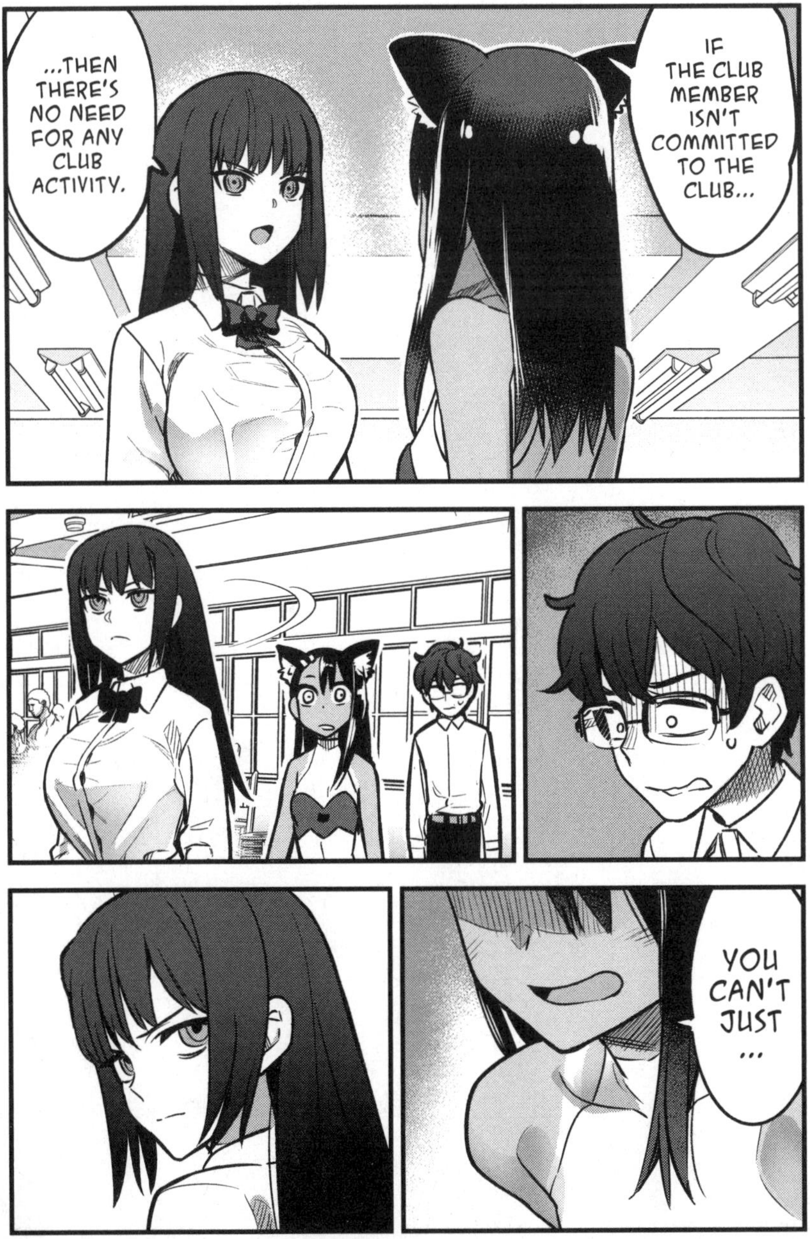
IF THE CLUB MEMBER ISN'T COMMITTED TO THE CLUB...
...THEN THERE'S NO NEED FOR ANY CLUB ACTIVITY.
YOU CAN'T JUST ...

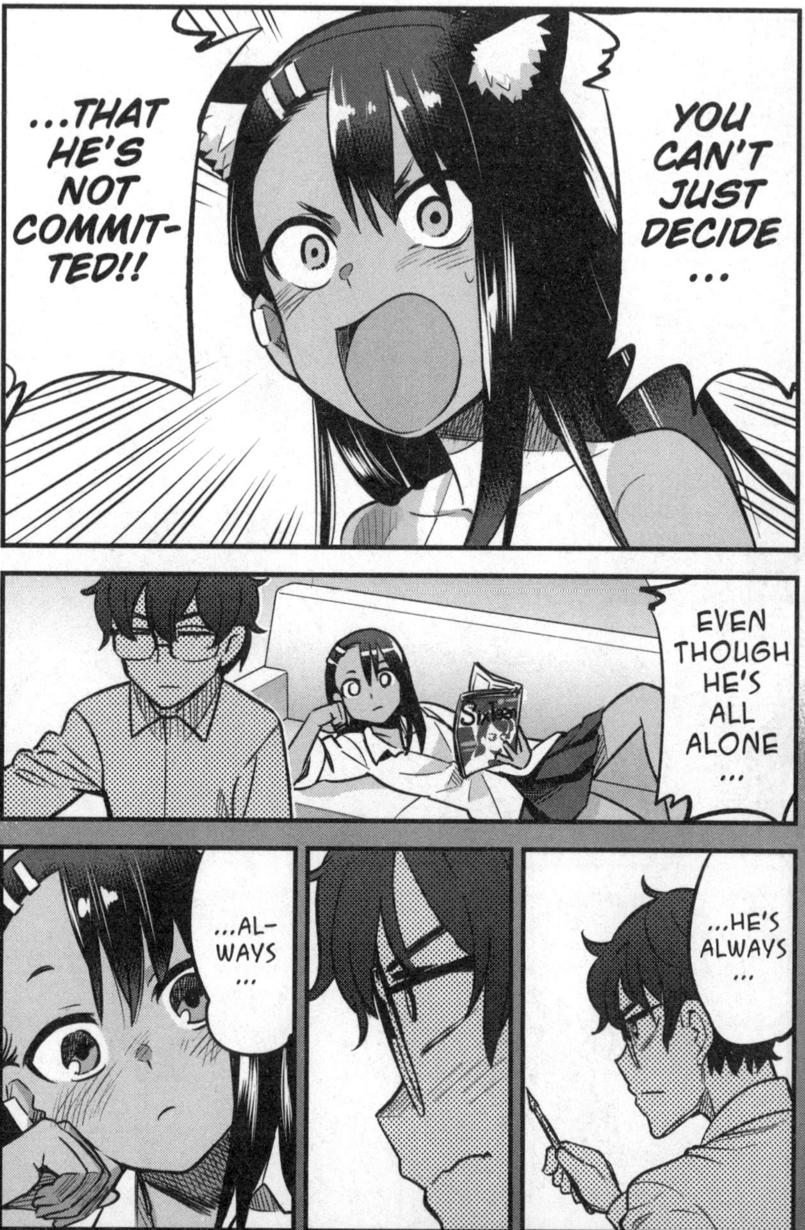
YOU CAN'T JUST DECIDE ...
...THAT HE'S NOT COMMIT-TED!!
EVEN THOUGH HE'S ALL ALONE ...
...HE'S ALWAYS ...
...AL-WAYS ...

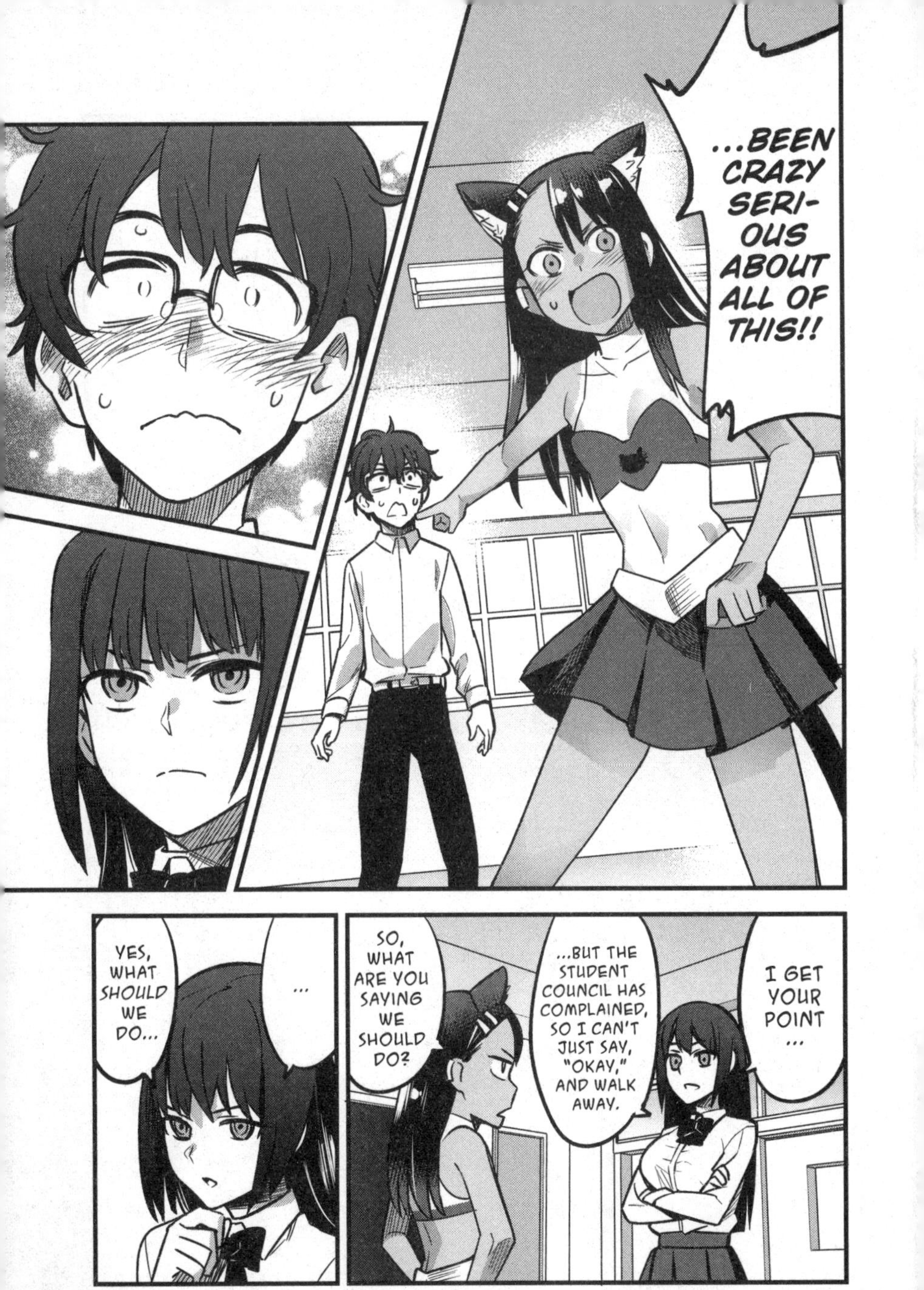
...BEEN CRAZY SERI- OUS ABOUT ALL OF THIS!!
I GET YOUR POINT ...
...BUT THE STUDENT COUNCIL HAS COMPLAINED, SO I CAN'T JUST SAY, "OKAY," AND WALK AWAY.
SO, WHAT ARE YOU SAYING WE SHOULD DO?
...
YES, WHAT SHOULD WE DO...

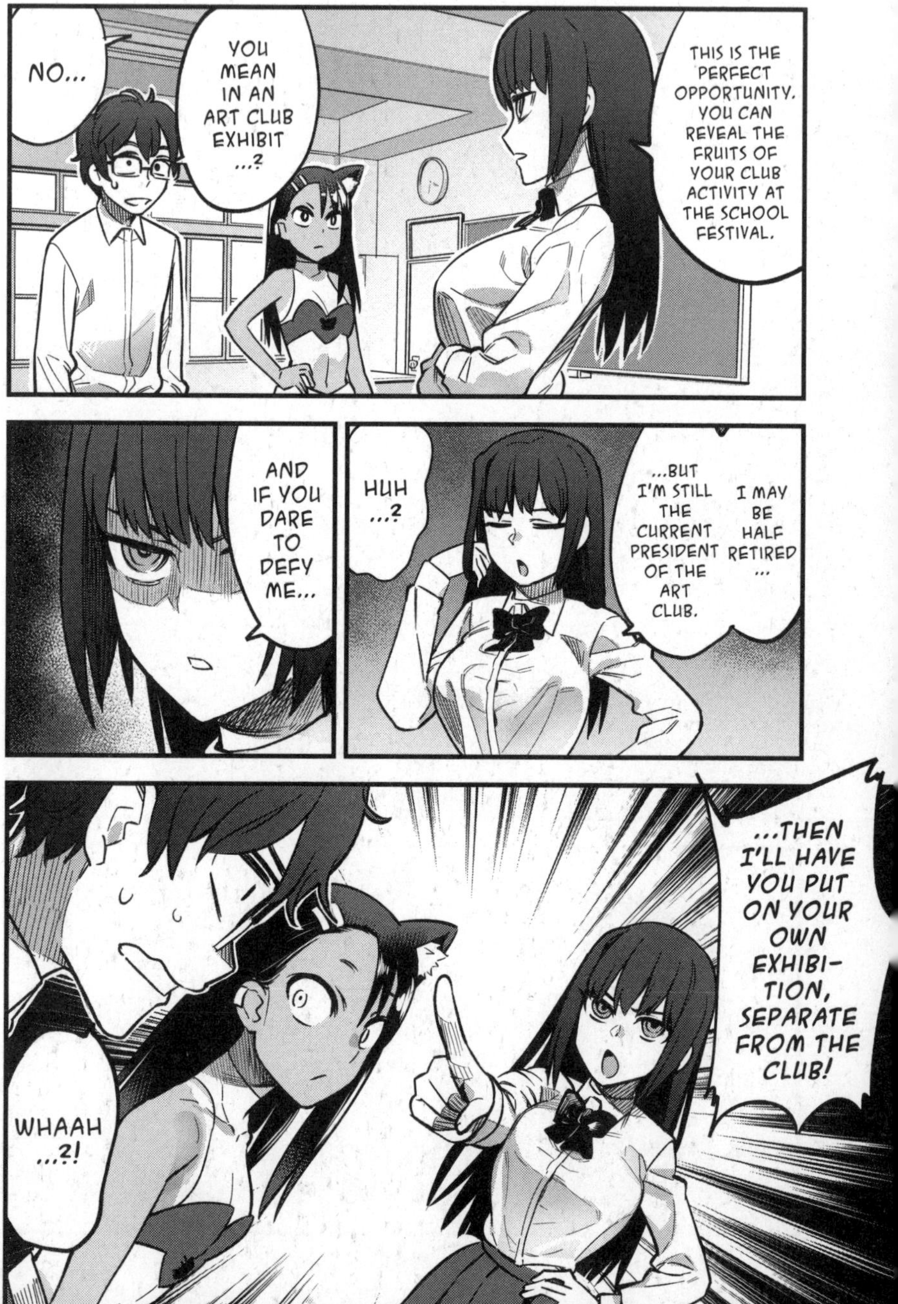
THIS IS THE PERFECT OPPORTUNITY. YOU CAN REVEAL THE FRUITS OF YOUR CLUB ACTIVITY AT THE SCHOOL FESTIVAL.
YOU MEAN IN AN ART CLUB EXHIBIT ...?
NO...
I MAY BE HALF RETIRED ...
...BUT I'M STILL THE CURRENT PRESIDENT OF THE ART CLUB.
HUH ...?
AND IF YOU DARE TO DEFY ME...
...THEN I'LL HAVE YOU PUT ON YOUR OWN EXHIBI-TION, SEPARATE FROM THE CLUB!
WHAAH ...?!

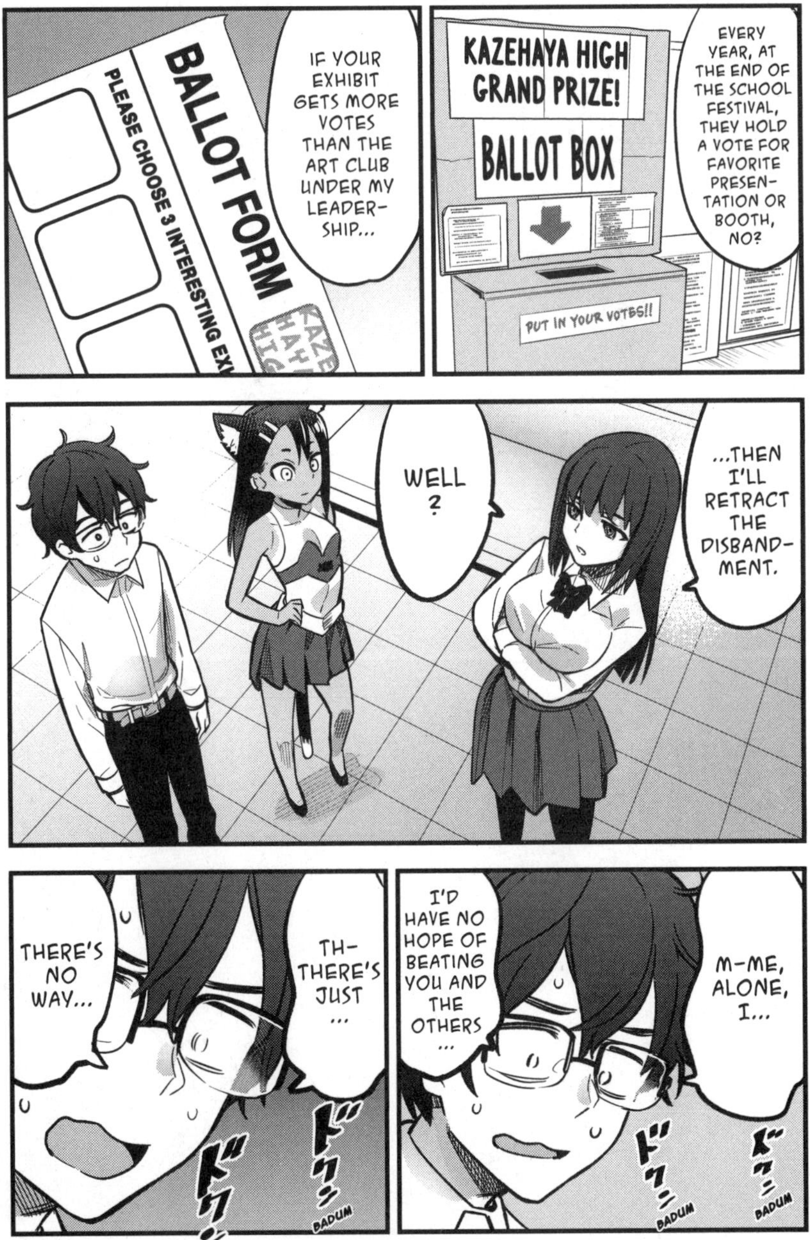
KAZEHAYA HIGH GRAND PRIZE!
BALLOT BOX
PUT IN YOUR VOTES!!
EVERY YEAR, AT THE END OF THE SCHOOL FESTIVAL, THEY HOLD A VOTE FOR FAVORITE PRESENTATION OR BOOTH, NO?
BALLOT FORM
IF YOUR EXHIBIT GETS MORE VOTES THAN THE ART CLUB UNDER MY LEADERSHIP...
...THEN I'LL RETRACT THE DISBANDMENT.
WELL?
M-ME, ALONE, I...
I'D HAVE NO HOPE OF BEATING YOU AND THE OTHERS ...
BADUM
BADUM
TH-THERE'S JUST ...
THERE'S NO WAY...
BADUM
BADUM

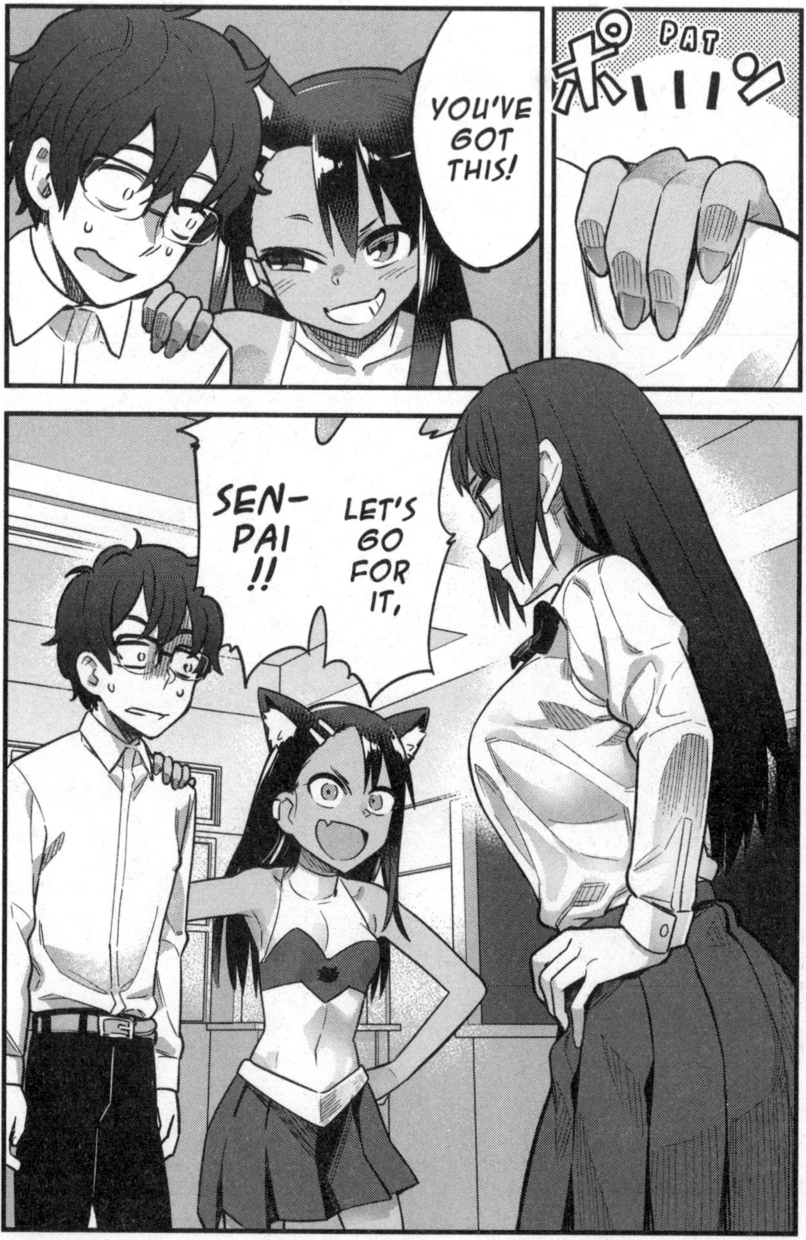
PAT
YOU'VE GOT THIS!
LET'S GO FOR IT, SEN-PAI!!

END

DON'T TOY WITH ME, MISS NAGATORO

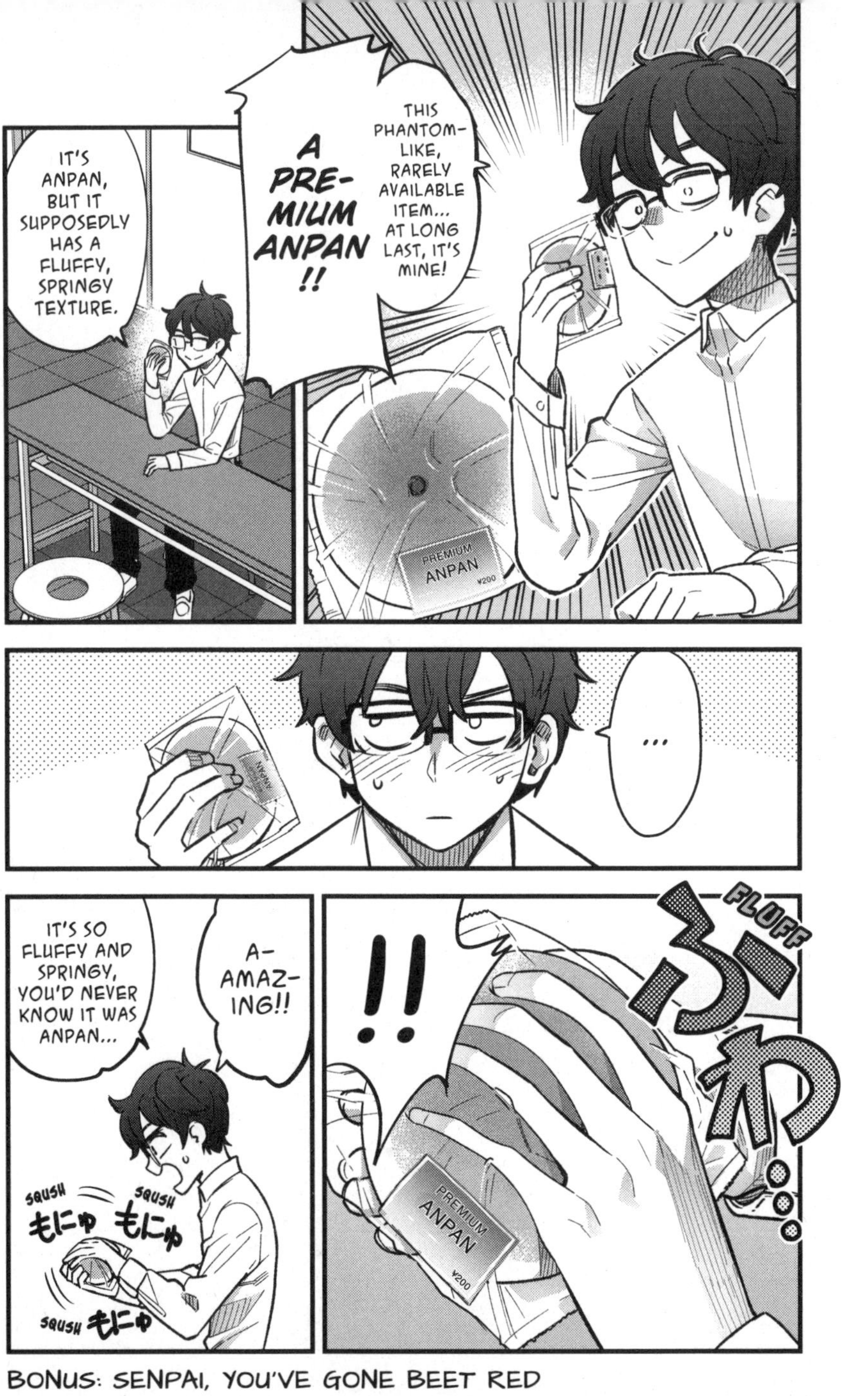
THIS PHANTOM-LIKE, RARELY AVAILABLE ITEM... AT LONG LAST, IT'S MINE!
A PRE-MIUM ANPAN!!
PREMIUM ANPAN ¥200
IT'S ANPAN, BUT IT SUPPOSEDLY HAS A FLUFFY, SPRINGY TEXTURE.
...
FLUFF
ふわ…
!!
PREMIUM ANPAN ¥200
A-AMAZ-ING!!
IT'S SO FLUFFY AND SPRINGY, YOU'D NEVER KNOW IT WAS ANPAN...
SQUSH もにゅ
SQUSH もにゅ
SQUSH もにゅ

BONUS: SENPAI, YOU'VE GONE BEET RED

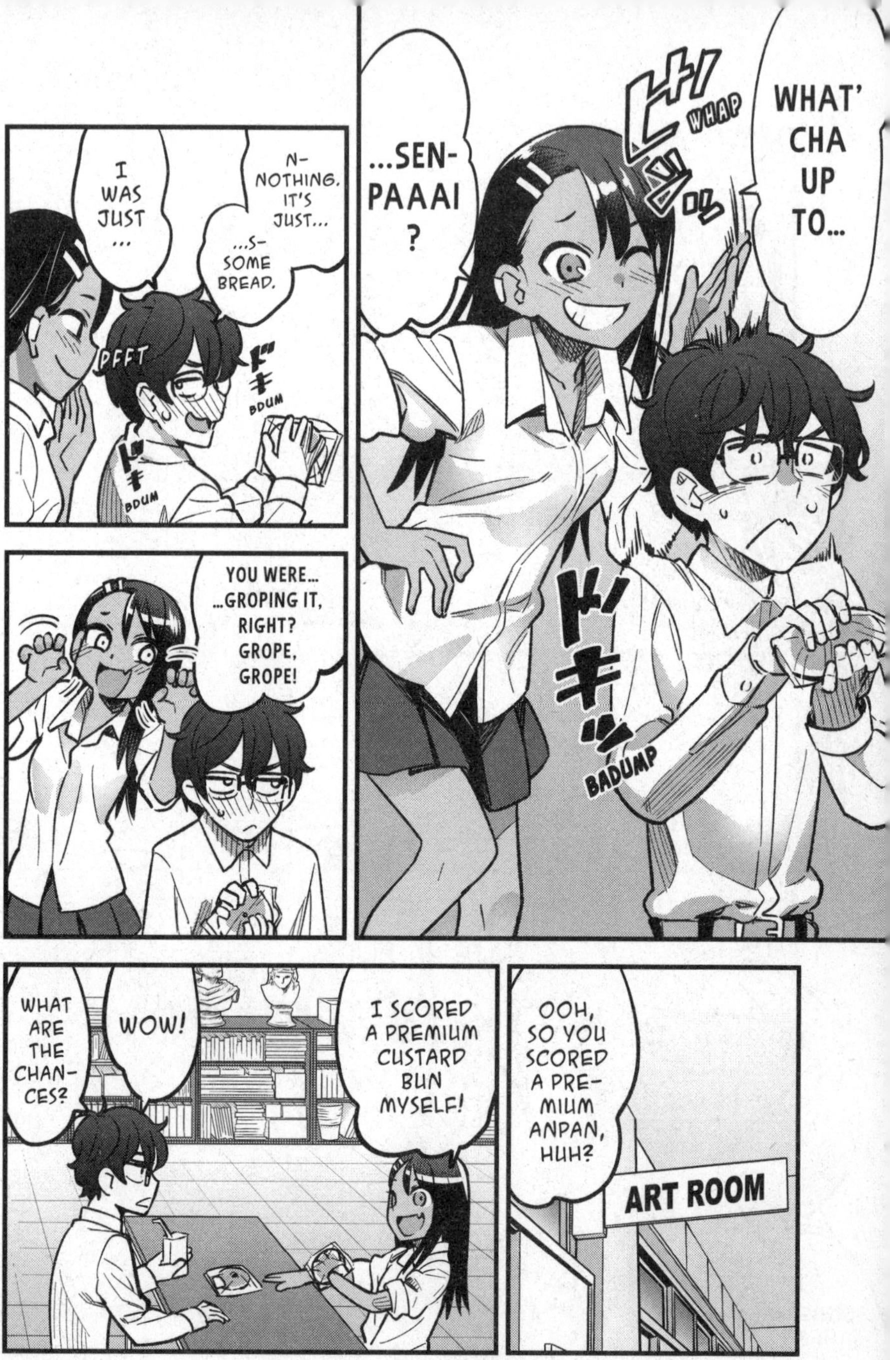
WHAT'CHA UP TO...
WHAP
...SEN-PAAAI?
BADUMP
N-NOTHING. IT'S JUST...
...S-SOME BREAD.
I WAS JUST ...
PFFT
BDUM
BDUM
YOU WERE... ...GROPING IT, RIGHT? GROPE, GROPE!
OOH, SO YOU SCORED A PREMIUM ANPAN, HUH?
ART ROOM
I SCORED A PREMIUM CUSTARD BUN MYSELF!
WOW!
WHAT ARE THE CHANCES?

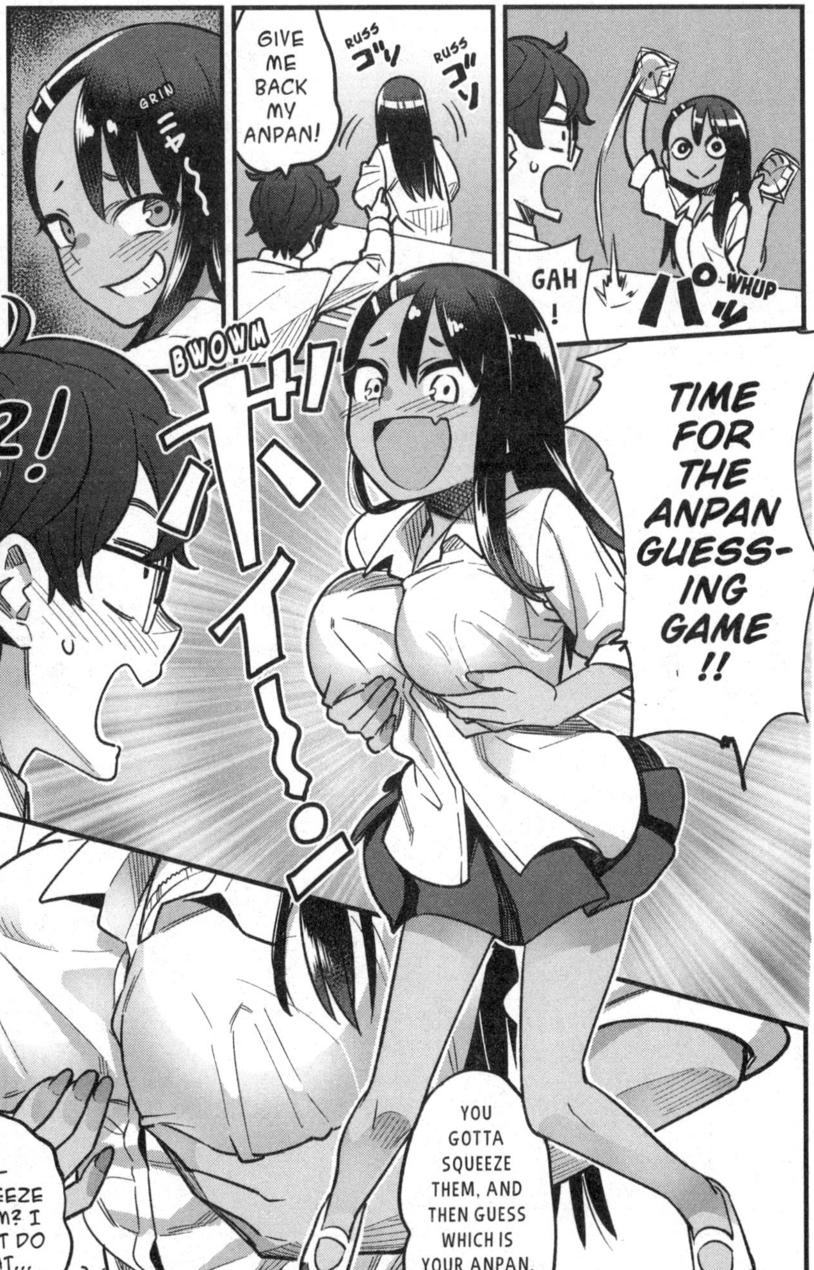
GAH!
WHUP
RUSS
RUSS
GIVE ME BACK MY ANPAN!
GRIN
TIME FOR THE ANPAN GUESSING GAME!!
BWOWM
?!
YOU GOTTA SQUEEZE THEM, AND THEN GUESS WHICH IS YOUR ANPAN, SENPAI!
S-SQUEEZE THEM? I CAN'T DO THAT...

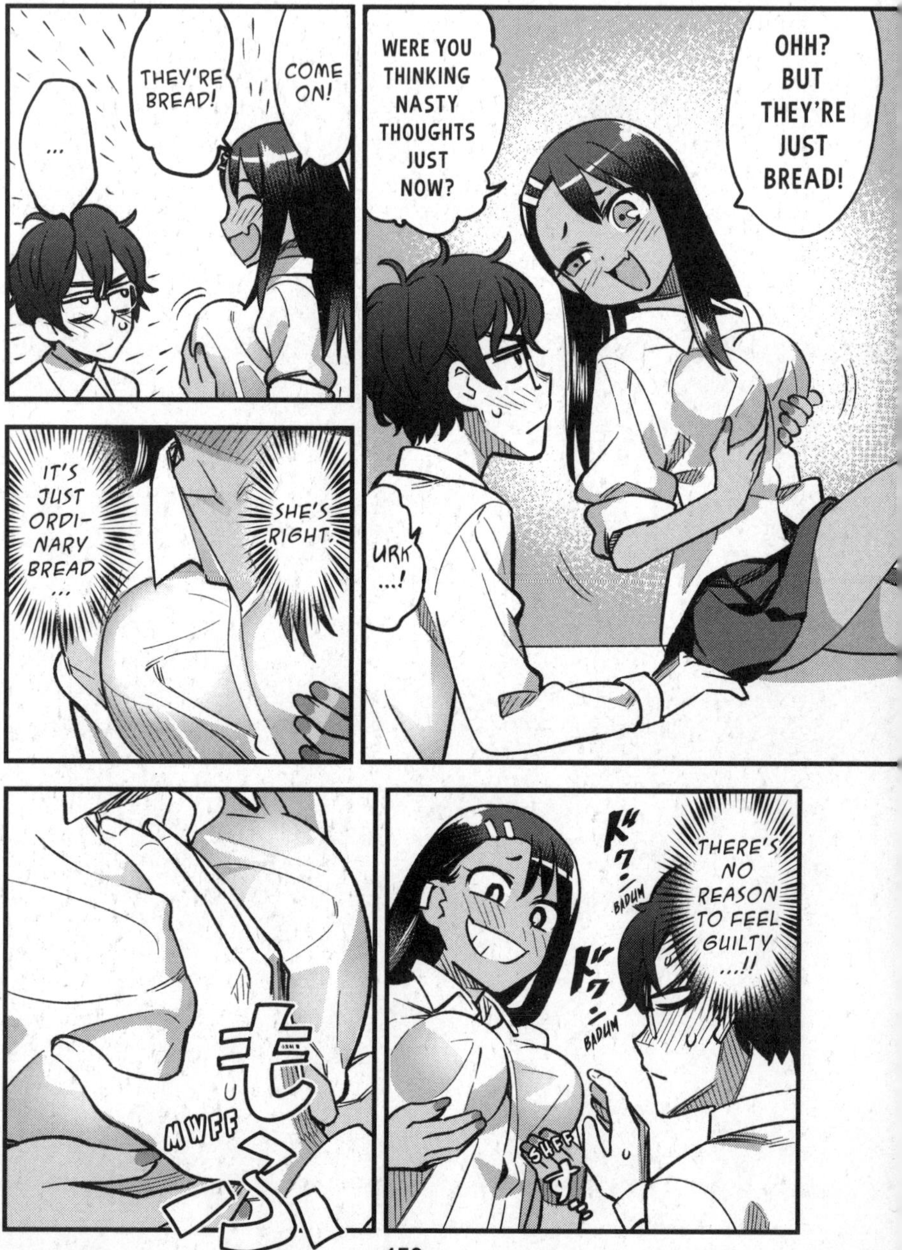
OHH? BUT THEY'RE JUST BREAD!
WERE YOU THINKING NASTY THOUGHTS JUST NOW?
URK ....!
COME ON!
THEY'RE BREAD!
...
SHE'S RIGHT.
IT'S JUST ORDINARY BREAD ...
THERE'S NO REASON TO FEEL GUILTY ....!!
BADUM
BADUM
SHFF
MWFF

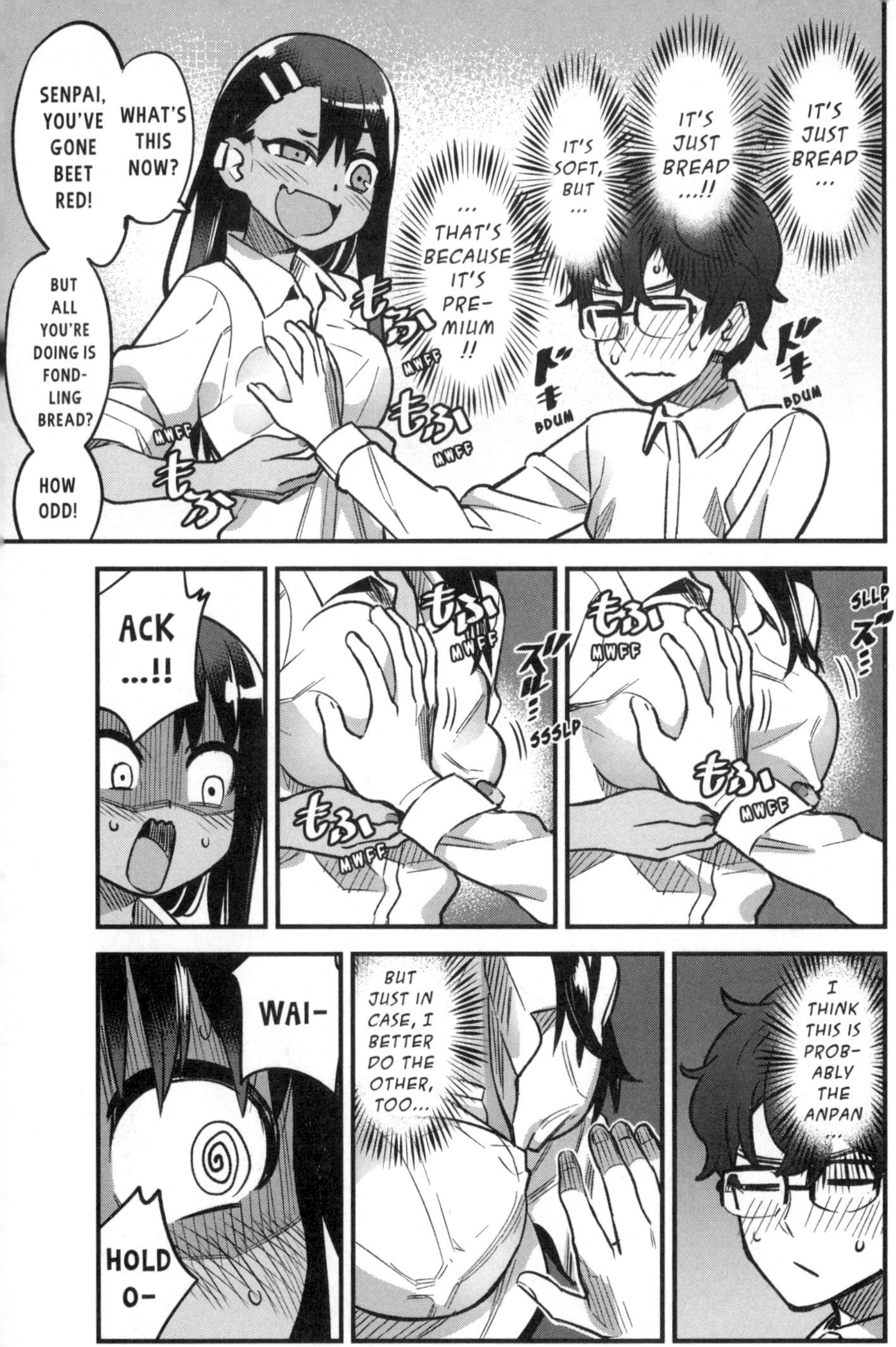
IT'S JUST BREAD...
IT'S JUST BREAD...!!
IT'S SOFT, BUT...
...THAT'S BECAUSE IT'S PREMIUM!!
BDUM
BDUM
MWFF
MWFF
WHAT'S THIS NOW?
SENPAI, YOU'VE GONE BEET RED!
BUT ALL YOU'RE DOING IS FONDLING BREAD?
MWFF
HOW ODD!
SLLP
MWFF
MWFF
MWFF
SSSLP
MWFF
ACK...!!
I THINK THIS IS PROBABLY THE ANPAN...
BUT JUST IN CASE, I BETTER DO THE OTHER, TOO...
WAI-
HOLD O-

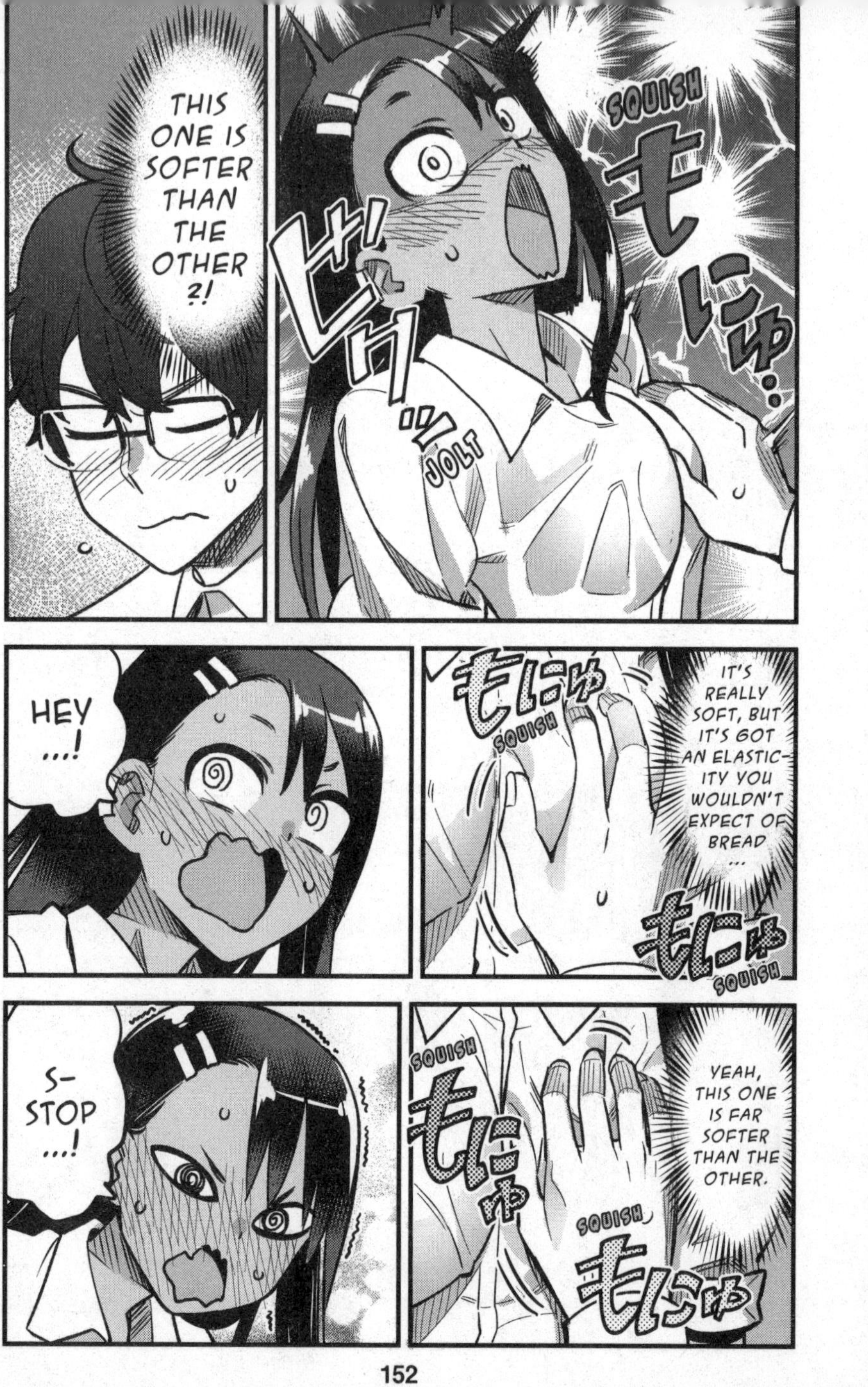
SQUISH
もにゅ…
JOLT
THIS ONE IS SOFTER THAN THE OTHER?!
もにゅ
SQUISH
IT'S REALLY SOFT, BUT IT'S GOT AN ELASTIC-ITY YOU WOULDN'T EXPECT OF BREAD...
もにゅ
SQUISH
HEY...!
SQUISH
もにゅ
YEAH, THIS ONE IS FAR SOFTER THAN THE OTHER.
SQUISH
もにゅ
S-STOP...!

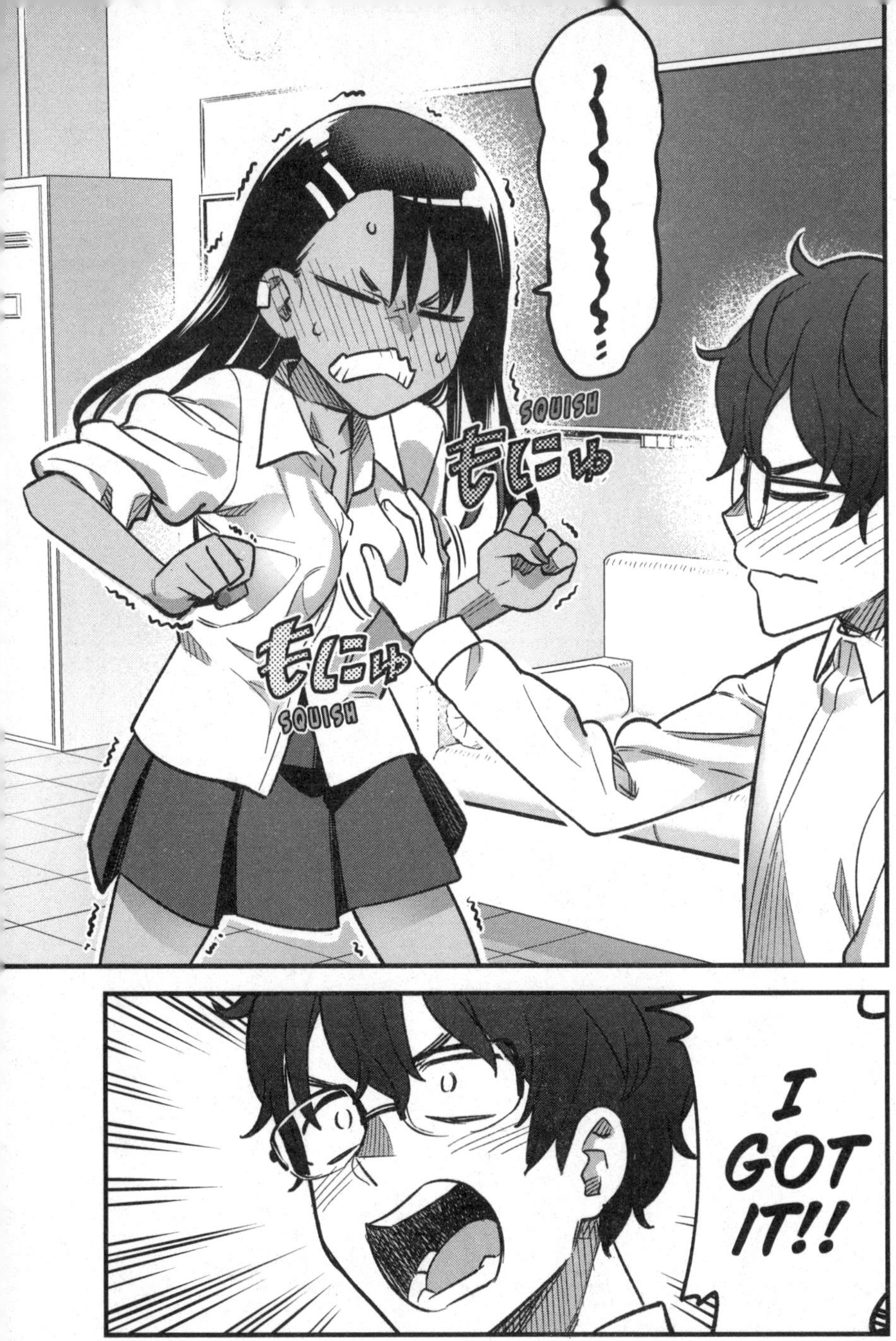
SQUISH
もにゅ
もにゅ
SQUISH
I GOT IT!!

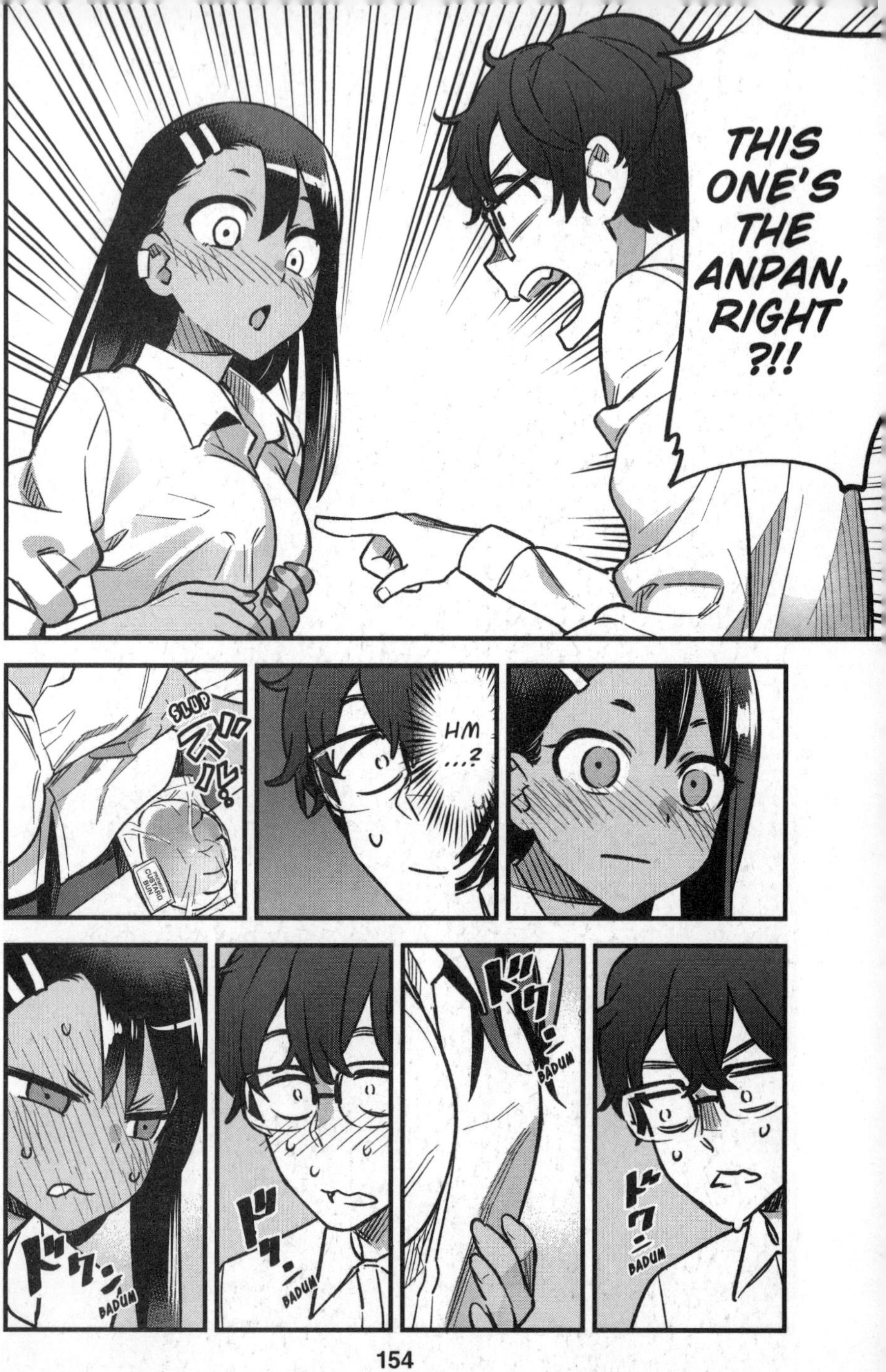
THIS ONE'S THE ANPAN, RIGHT ?!!
HM ...?
SLUP
CUSTARD BUN
BADUM
BADUM
BADUM
BADUM

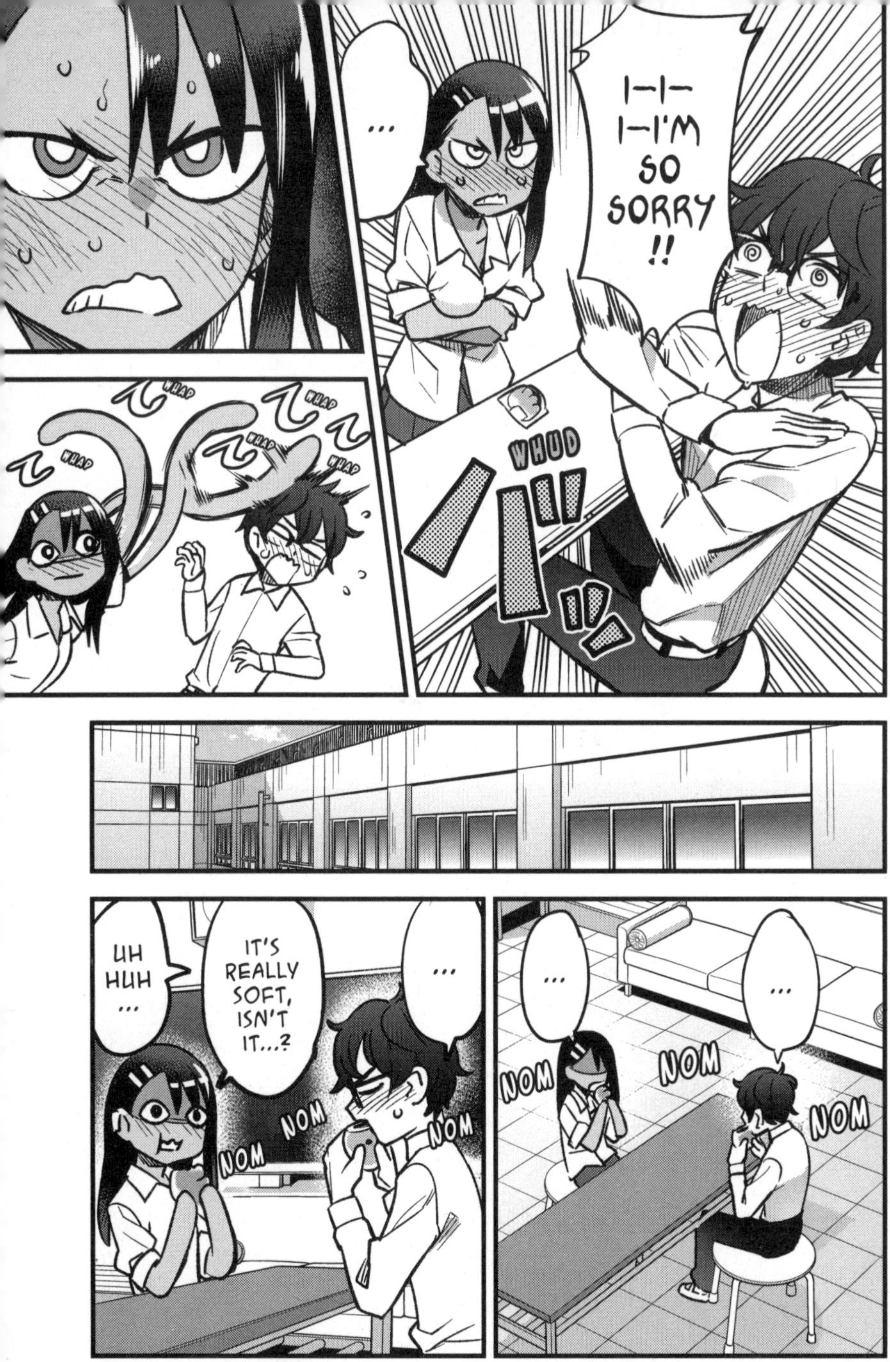
I-I-I-I'M SO SORRY!!
...
WHUD
WHAP
WHAP
WHAP
WHAP
...
...
NOM
NOM
NOM
...
IT'S REALLY SOFT, ISN'T IT...?
UH HUH ...
NOM
NOM
NOM

END

DON'T TOY WITH ME,
MISS NAGATORO

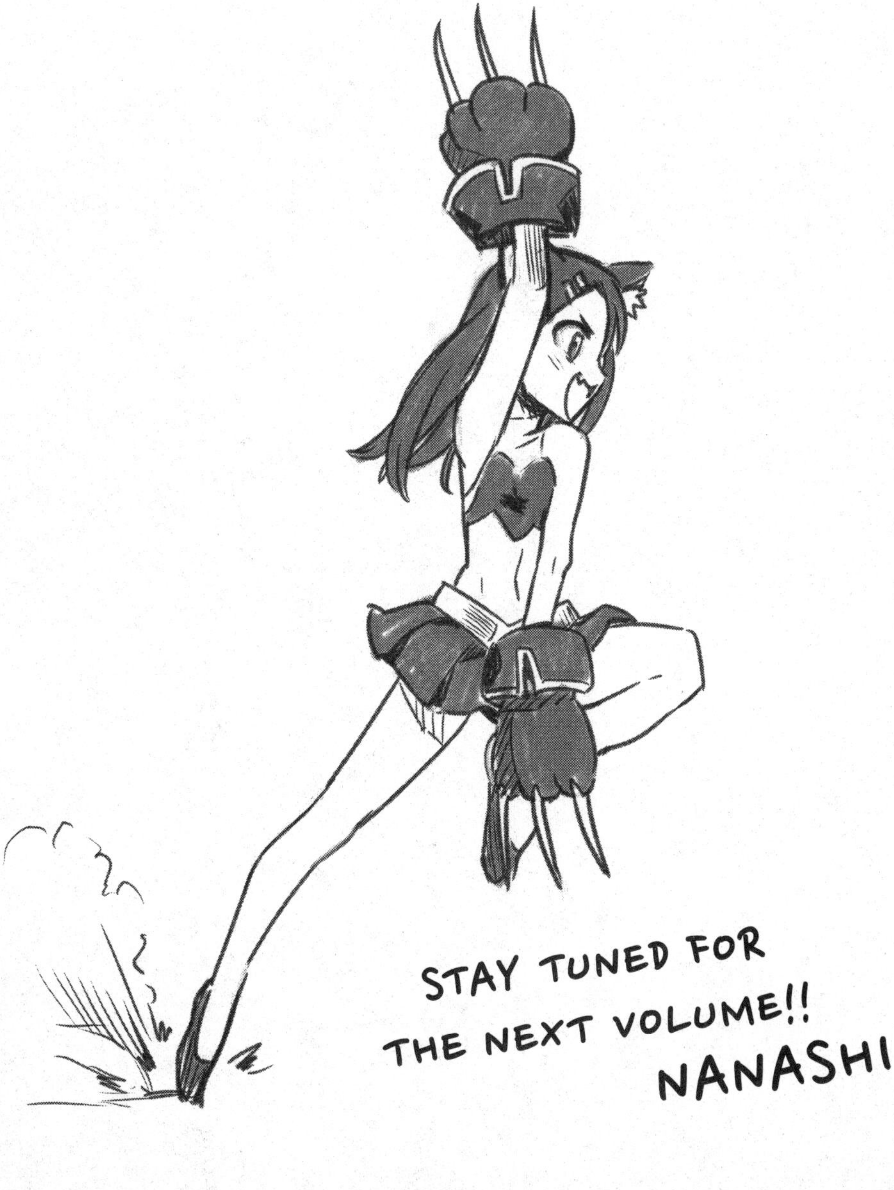
STAY TUNED FOR
THE NEXT VOLUME!!
NANASHI

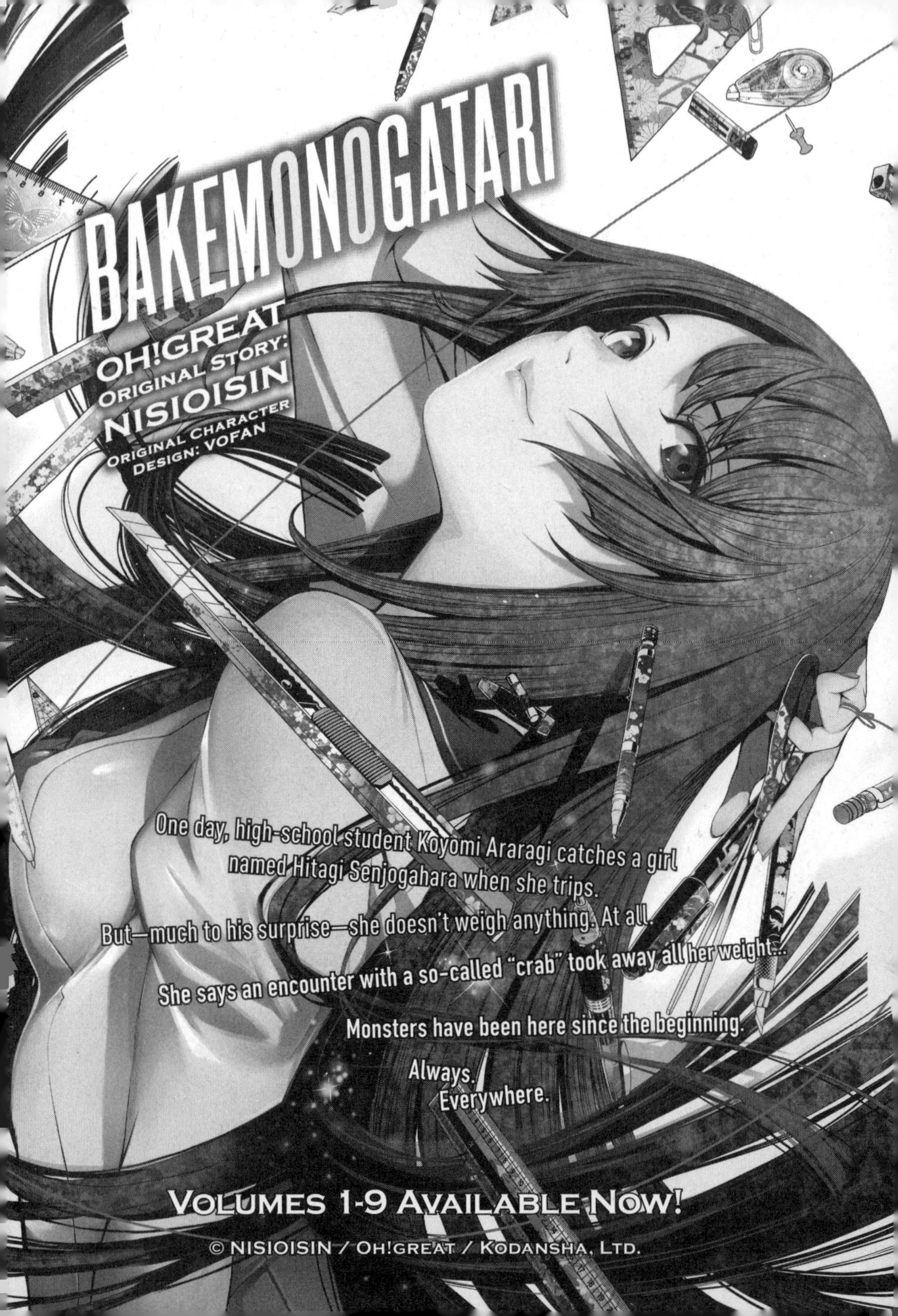
BAKEMONOGATARI
OH!GREAT
ORIGINAL STORY: NISIOISIN
ORIGINAL CHARACTER DESIGN: VOFAN
One day, high-school student Koyomi Araragi catches a girl named Hitagi Senjogahara when she trips.
But—much to his surprise—she doesn't weigh anything. At all.
She says an encounter with a so-called "crab" took away all her weight...
Monsters have been here since the beginning.
Always.
Everywhere.
VOLUMES 1-9 AVAILABLE NOW!
© NISIOISIN / OH!GREAT / KODANSHA, LTD.

A School Frozen in Time

Art by Naoshi Arakawa
Story by Mizuki Tsujimura

On a snowy school day like any other, classmates and childhood friends Hiroshi and Mizuki arrive at school to find the campus eerily empty. Before long, they find themselves trapped inside with six other friends, and even stranger, all the clocks have stopped at a very specific moment—the exact time when a former classmate jumped off the school roof to their death three months earlier. It turns out that this departed friend is their way out of their current predicament and may even be among their group...but no one can remember who it was that took their life on that sad day. The students must face themselves and their past memories to piece together the identity of this suicide victim or risk a similar fate—with their lives lost and forgotten inside these frigid school walls.

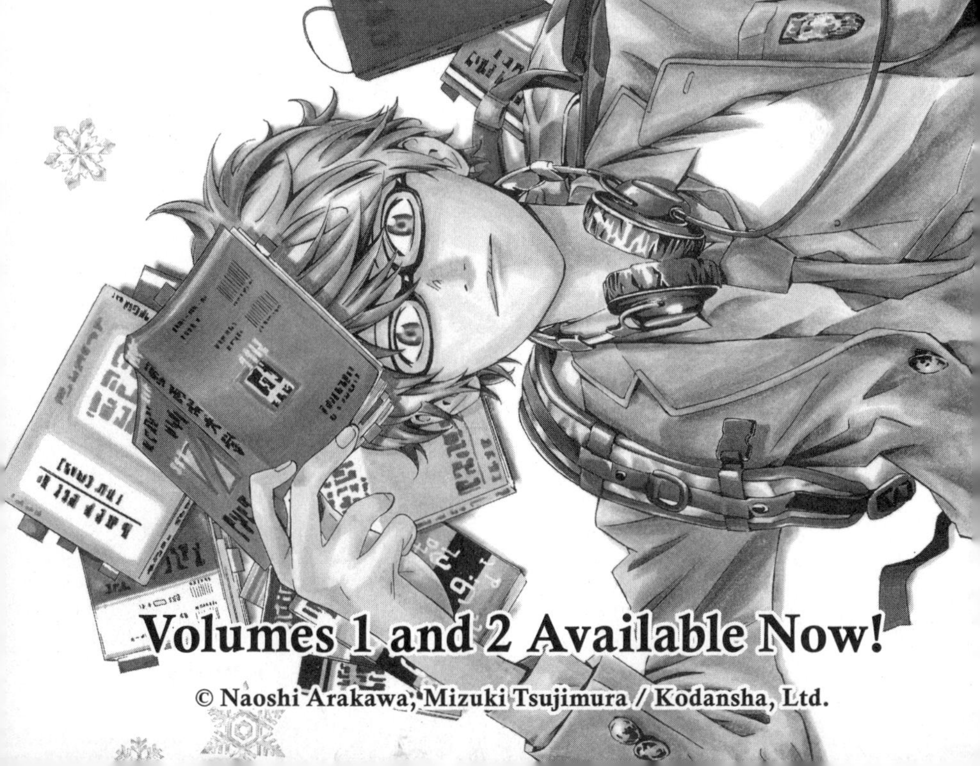

Volumes 1 and 2 Available Now!

Don't Toy With Me, Miss Nagatoro 5

A Vertical Comics Edition

Editing: Ajani Oloye
Translation: Kumar Sivasubramanian
Production: Risa Cho
Eve Grandt

First published in Japan in 2019 by Kodansha, Ltd., Tokyo
Publication rights for this English edition arranged through Kodansha, Ltd., Tokyo
English language version produced by Vertical Comics, an imprint of
Kodansha USA Publishing, LLC

Translation provided by Vertical Comics, 2020
Published by Kodansha USA Publishing, LLC, New York

Originally published in Japanese as *Ijiranaide, Nagatorosan 5* by Kodansha, Ltd., 2019
Ijiranaide, Nagatorosan first serialized in *Magazine Poketto*, Kodansha, Ltd., 2017-

ISBN: 978-1-949980-85-1

Manufactured in the United States of America

First Edition

Fourth Printing

Kodansha USA Publishing, LLC
451 Park Avenue South
7th Floor
New York, NY 10016
www.kodansha.us

Vertical books are distributed through Penguin-Random House Publish

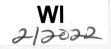